'Written in an accessible and engaging way that will appeal to trainee and experienced therapists alike, *Humour and Healing in the Person-centred Therapy Room* provides a wide-ranging examination of the place and practice of humour in psychotherapeutic encounters and training. Kentish offers an interesting historical exploration of therapeutic engagement with humour, advocating for levity to be seriously considered in person-centred therapy in myriad ways. With "pause for thought", "reflection" boxes, and comic illustrations throughout, this book offers important food for thought for counsellors and education providers on the role of humour and laughter to support personal and professional growth and healing'.

—**Elizabeth Peel**, *Professor of Communication and Social Interaction at Loughborough University and person-centred therapist*

Humour and Healing in the Person-centred Therapy Room

Mainstream therapeutic modalities have very little to say about humour in therapy, but every therapist will tell you that it is impossible to banish it from the therapy room. This book begins with a historical exploration of humour's function in society and in relationships and considers how humour came to be something of a taboo in psychotherapy. It offers insights from psychological, sociological and neuroscientific research into what humour reveals about a person's character and emotional state, and how that enables the counsellor to connect and empathise with the client. The second half of the book is devoted to how humour can enhance the therapeutic alliance, drawing on the research literature and first-hand experience. Taking the principles of person-centred counselling as its foundation, the book describes how humour materialises in practice and how it can be embraced to the benefit of the client and practitioner alike.

Providing practical advice on how to work with humour as and when it arises, this is an essential tool for students, and novice and experienced practitioners alike.

Micheal Kentish is a person-centred counsellor and a lecturer in person-centred and humanistic counselling at the University of Keele.

Humour and Healing in the Person-centred Therapy Room

Micheal Kentish

Routledge
Taylor & Francis Group
LONDON AND NEW YORK

First published 2027
by Routledge
4 Park Square, Milton Park, Abingdon, Oxon OX14 4RN

and by Routledge
605 Third Avenue, New York, NY 10158

Routledge is an imprint of the Taylor & Francis Group, an informa business

British Library Cataloguing-in-Publication Data
A catalogue record for this book is available from the British Library

ISBN: 978-1-041-07093-1 (hbk)
ISBN: 978-1-041-07089-4 (pbk)
ISBN: 978-1-003-63877-3 (ebk)

DOI: 10.4324/9781003638773

Typeset in Times New Roman
by SPi Technologies India Pvt Ltd (Straive)

Contents

Acknowledgements

My thinking about humour in my life and in the therapy space has been profoundly influenced by my good fortune as a postgraduate student at Keele University. There I found encouragement from my tutors, especially Lois de Cruz and Sally Chisholm, also my lovely peers, colleagues, students and even clients who laugh with me (mostly), and not forgetting the life-savers Cheryl Backham and Mani Alexander. I am indebted to Chris Brown and Keith Christie for their enthusiasm and inspiration and to many others in the community of person-centred counsellors for their generosity and engagement.

My special thanks to the very talented Sophie Hopson for her amazing artwork and illustrations, and to my editors Alice Maher and Grace McDonnell and all at Routledge for their support and patience.

Finally, my amazing wife Tracy, from whom I have learned so much about love, to whom this book is dedicated and in whose favour I will hopefully remain as I fulfil the promise to share her favourite joke:

What have Henry VIII and Kermit the Frog in common?
The same middle name.

Introduction

Why this book is needed

Why?

This book started life as a personal quest: simply put, is there a place for humour in the person-centred therapy room? Humour, mirth and laughter are fundamental elements of our everyday lives. First, as babies, we learn to cry. Then, before we can speak or even understand what our caregivers are saying to us, we laugh. It is a pure, trustful, involuntary expression of joy, and so perhaps because of this, we think of humour as obviously healthy. In the therapy room, the humour can come from the client as well as the therapist, yet researchers report that not only is working with humour omitted from the textbooks, it is practically a taboo subject on training courses.

> Humour in therapy?
> You're joking!
> People don't go to therapy for fun!

This is not the first ever book attempting to tackle the subject of therapy and humour; it is the first to focus on person-centred therapy, the modality developed by Carl Rogers in the mid-twentieth century and practised today on all of the planet's continents with the possible exception of Antarctica. A reaction against the expert-driven traditions of psychology dominant at the time, Rogers proposed two main theories:

A *personality theory*: underlined by the premise that people are driven by an innate desire to – at the least – make the best of the circumstances as they perceive them and generally to grow and develop their own authentic selves. Being social in nature, people need the positive regard of others but rarely receive it unconditionally; this absence hampers their ability to grow and leads to emotional distress.

A *theory of therapy*: therapeutic change emerges not from medicalised expert advice or interpretation but from a relationship formed between the therapist and the client (not the "patient") that enables the client to reconnect

DOI: 10.4324/9781003638773-1

with his or her authentic self. The key contributions to the therapeutic alliance from the therapist are genuineness, openness and an empathic understanding of the client's world.

These theories are explored in depth later in the book.

You might well ask, what business did I have in undermining my newly adopted Important And Very Serious Vocation with such trivialities? Indeed, this was the question I posed myself. But, in only my second session of therapy, my own counsellor said to me, "Ah, there goes Micheal's self-deprecating humour again". My initial reaction was to ignore it for, although I didn't know it at the time, I was uncomfortably stuck in what Rogers referred to as a defensive stasis (1959). Nonetheless, her words accompanied me home afterwards, ringing insistently in my ears. I agonised over the significance of both what she had said and how it had made me feel. I had always considered humour – my sense of humour – to be a positive thing. I had said something in that counselling session that was intended to be amusing, and instead of my counsellor responding to it as such, she had calmly and kindly handed it back to me as if it were a snotty hanky I might have dropped. What did all of that say about me?

Growing up, I imagined that I might attract more parental love, affection and/or attention if I could only be as funny as Morecambe and Wise or Tommy Cooper or Terry Wogan (the younger reader might want to Google these names). Naturally, I failed. I'm not that funny. But the introjection joined the rapidly growing congregation of "conditions of worth" (Rogers, 1959). But since then, I've found that humour has evolved for me into a kind of verbal Swiss army knife, with many uses:

- It shields me when I am feeling uncomfortable or exposed, the shield's intensity ranging from a bashful verbal blushing to a deflector shield worthy of the U.S.S. Enterprise;
- It eases the pain, temporarily dissociating;
- Because everyone loves funny people (don't they?);
- Because no one loves scary people;
- Because it kept people awake, as I discovered while lecturing on accountancy in a former life;
- For the truth and wisdom even the most absurd humour can reveal;
- Because I have a very low (physical) pain threshold, it defuses bombs and bullies, though I've never needed to defuse a bomb, so I can't be sure;
- Because I find there are fewer things more alluring than the sound of a woman's laughter. And I haven't got a Maserati;
- Because, I'm ashamed to say, I sometimes find a secret pleasure in an acerbic put-down, even if this isn't really funny; and
- For the hell of it, because you spell onomatopoeia how it sounds, because similes are like metaphors, because Irish people say, "Get yourself outside of this Guinness".

Pause for thought

Throughout this book are invitations to reflect on what you have just read. So now I invite you to take a moment to remind yourself what it is that makes you laugh. It could be gags or jokes (maybe you have a favourite?), comedians, cartoons and/or romcoms. Perhaps it's the absurdities we encounter, such as *Freudian* slips, cute cat videos or presidents pardoning turkeys? And on the other side of the coin, what is it that you find unfunny? And why?

As time passed and my counselling experience – as both counsellor and counsellee – deepened, I came to appreciate that humour wore many guises. I began questioning whether my affinity for humour was a superpower after all. Perhaps it was merely a mask. This uncertainty crept deeper into my work. During a session, a client might say something funny: how should I react? Does how I should react depend on whether the client is consciously being funny or whether I find something innately funny in what the client is saying? In our training, we are taught to be "congruent" but only to the extent that what is coming up for us is relevant to the client. Does that include or exclude humour? And how will the client react if I allow myself to introduce humour? Will it be taken as empathic or as a sign that I am not taking the client's distress seriously enough? That I am mocking my client?

It turned out that my experience was far from unique. So why does the "profession" seem so humourless? The textbooks on students' reading lists are brilliant and profound, and yet they make no mention of humour, mirth or laughter – not even to say that they should be avoided. Is it perhaps because, as Louis Franzini observed, practitioners:

> …not only see their professional work as very important and serious, they see themselves as very important and serious.
>
> (2001)

It might be argued, particularly by counsellors who rely on the healing "power" of their skills and technique, that adding humour to the therapeutic "armamentarium" (Franzini's words) is simply unnecessary. Do person-centred counsellors feel the same way? The six conditions for effective therapeutic change are, after all, described as "sufficient" (though Rogers (1959) also acknowledged that other "elements are often or usually present").

I very much hope that Franzini was wrong when he suggested:

> Most people, including therapists, can tolerate any epithet about themselves except that they are humorless.
>
> (2001)

Of course, being capable of appreciating humour is not the same as being able to initiate it. We might love hearing jokes and also feel terror at the prospect of having just to remember a joke, let alone tell one.

Which brings us to…

This book

This book lays out the discoveries I have made about humour in counselling and psychotherapy. Although my training and practice are grounded in person-centred theory, I propose that those discoveries might also apply to other therapeutic modalities which place the therapist-client relationship at the centre of their approach.

We start with an attempt at demystifying the phenomenon of humour. We ask if humour is universal and eternal by comparing cultural variations and norms. An alternative perspective on humour is applied when considering differing senses of humour, including among the neurodiverse. Part I concludes with an exploration of research into people's differing senses of humour. The aim here is to help therapists better understand their clients' characters and emotions.

Part II examines the connection between humour and therapy. Models attempting the empirical measurement of a person's sense of humour and openness to humour, before, during and after therapeutic treatments, have been developed. A number of therapeutic approaches use humour as the principal therapeutic tool. We explore their premises and claims, the research into their effectiveness and their usage today.

In Part III, we focus on the person-centred approach developed by Rogers, starting with his views and practices. Although his writings do not directly address the subject, I argue that when considering the principles laid out by Rogers and reviewing transcripts and recordings of his practice, we can only conclude that humour properly belongs in the person-centred therapy room.

Part IV consolidates the messages in previous chapters and, drawing on practitioners' experiences, offers concrete guidance on how counsellors can *work with humour* to the benefit of the client. Risks are also considered. It is hoped that trainee and qualified practitioners alike will gain greater confidence and improved competence. Similarly, supervisors and educators will gain insight into how to communicate these skills. Finally, I lay out guidance and suggestions on how practitioners and supervisors can educate themselves in preparation for working with humour in therapy and how the topic can be incorporated into mainstream training programmes.

Is this a manual?

Yes and no. "Yes" because I hope it offers practical guidance that will help enhance the reader's confidence and competence, and "No" because I sometimes fear we can overload ourselves with *skills*. Weighed down with techniques and tips and methods, we run the risk of losing sight of the real benefit we offer clients, which is our presence. If this book succeeds, it is because it gives the practitioner greater confidence to be *real* (in other words, *congruent*) and to offer the client genuine empathy and unconditional positive regard.

What else?

The terms *counselling*, *therapy* and *psychotherapy* are used interchangeably in this book, with apologies for any confusion that might be caused.

When Rogers first started writing, the convention was to use the masculine personal pronoun; in later works, he adopted the rather cumbersome *he or she* construction. At the time of writing, a person is often referred to less cumbersomely as *they* and *them*. In writing this book, I have adopted the usage of Mearns and Thorne (1988) and used more or less randomly allocated pronouns. Thus, clients and therapists alike may be referred to as *he* or *she*. I should also add that in order to preserve confidentiality, the case studies referred to are all anonymised.

As is the case with many therapists, counselling was not my first career choice, though it is definitely the best one. I'm getting on a bit, too. I hope that the professional (as well as the personal) experiences usefully inform my work with clients, with students and with this book. They include being born to parents who didn't finish school and couldn't spell Michael, somehow getting into university, falling into chartered accountancy, ten years living and working overseas, messing up a marriage and learning that my good fortune is largely just that: fortuitous. In writing this book, I have tried to make its essential messages as universal as possible, and I ask the reader to help me bridge my cultural and other shortcomings.

References

Franzini, L. R. (2001). Humor in therapy: The case for training therapists in its uses and risks. *The Journal of General Psychology*, *128*(2), 170–193. https://doi.org/10.1080/00221300109598906

Mearns, D., & Thorne, B. (1988). *Person-centred counselling in action*. SAGE Publications.

Rogers, C. R. (1959). A theory of therapy, personality, and interpersonal relationships, as developed in the client-centered framework. In S. Koch (Ed.), *Psychology: A study of a science, study 1, volume 3: Formulations of the person and the social context* (pp. 184–256). McGraw-Hill.

Part I

Humour defined and theorised

Chapter 1

Definitions and theories

Introduction

What is humour? Google it and a list of quotes much, much longer than the screen on your phone will unfurl, many of which conflate humour with laughter. And since they aren't the same thing, we could also ask: what is laughter? After all, something might amuse us, but not so much or in such a way that we laugh out loud. At other times, we laugh not because we are amused but because we are nervous or afraid. Or we want to punctuate a statement we have just made – a verbal shrug. We might also laugh simply because one or more people in our presence are laughing. Humour pops up in the unlikeliest of places. In eulogies, in Christian, Jewish and Muslim holy texts, even at that most depressing of assemblies: Prime Minister's Questions in the House of Commons.

Etymologies and meanings

One approach to understanding the concepts is to consider their semantic histories. First appearing in English usage in the 12th century, *humour* came to us from the Latin *hūmor* for *moisture, fluid, bodily fluid* via Old French and referring in ancient Greek and Roman medicine to the four fluids in the body which influenced a person's character and health. Hippocrates – who gave us the physicians' oath sometime between the fifth and third centuries BC – theorised that good health depended on the correct balance – eukrasia – of the four humors: blood, yellow bile, black bile and phlegm. Of these, blood gave us the sanguinity of our nature, being enthusiastic, social and active, while black bile (in the ancient Greek, *melaina kholé*) was associated with melancholy. Hippocrates' theory was adopted and adapted in Persian and southern Indian medicine and prevailed in Europe for many centuries before microbes were discovered. In addition to the Oath, numerous Hippocratic techniques are still practised today, including, unfortunately, the use of ligation and cauterising in the treatment of haemorrhoids. In the 16th century, in Christopher Marlowe's *Tamburlaine the Great*, Bajazeth talks of his empty stomach, which

DOI: 10.4324/9781003638773-3

"Draws bloody humours from my feeble parts" (1590/1997, Part 1, 4.4.94). William Shakespeare variously uses *humour* in the sense of a temporary inclination, mood or feeling, as in *King Henry V*, in which Nym, a soldier in the king's army, uses two senses in the same speech: "I have an/humour to knock you indifferently well" (1600/1995) and "I would prick your guts a little, in good terms, as I / may, and that's the humour of it" (1600/1995), with the latter meaning "that's the way things are" (Shakespeare, 1995).

It is not until the 17th century that *humour* makes the semantic leap to denote the ability to "appreciate or express what is funny or comical; a sense of what is amusing or ludicrous" and "the quality of being amusing, the capacity to elicit laughter or amusement" (Oxford English Dictionary, n.d.), and *sense of humour* first appears in usage in the mid-18th century.

The somewhat older word *mirth* derives from the Old English *myrgth*, with a similar meaning to today. *Merry* has a similar origin: *myrige* meaning *pleasing*, *delightful*, and also *short*, *brief*, *sudden* and can be traced via Old High German to the Sanskrit *muher* (Oxford English Dictionary, n.d.). The supposition is that we entertain ourselves to pass the time, to shorten it. Or perhaps that joy is only ever short-lived.

The verb *amuse* first appeared in usage in the late 15th century, from Old French, but in the sense of *distract*, *delude* and *deceive* and also *muse*, rather than *entertain* and *occupy*, which appear a century later (Oxford English Dictionary, n.d.).

Finally, the Ancient Greek word for *laugh* – *γελάω* (*gelaō*) – belongs to a family of words with the *γελ-* (*gel-*) root, which includes *laughable*, *laughter* and also *mock*, *scorn*, *deride*, *ridiculous* and *absurd* (Naas, 2016). As we will now see, this lexical affiliation is not accidental or inconsequential.

ὄρνις διαβαίνει ὁδόν (a chicken crosses a road) A very brief history of humour (Figure 1.1)

We consider humour an essential part of our lives. We swap jokes, visit comedy stores, watch sitcoms, romcoms, game shows, chat shows and funny cat videos, we listen to comedy on the radio, on podcasts and we see it in advertisements. Without these art forms, our lives would be much impoverished, unrecognisably so. We see humour, too, in life's absurdities, coincidences and mishaps.

And yet, humour has not always enjoyed such an elevated status in society. In the literature of the ancient Greeks, tragedy and comedy are never far apart.

Plato, for example, wrote a number of comedies, but he and his philosopher-mentor Socrates called for comedy to be state-controlled because ordinary (i.e. uneducated) folks – and youths especially – might be inspired to violence by the spectacles they witnessed. In *Philebus*, written around 360 BC, Plato argued people laughed at others' ignorance – especially their self-ignorance – "but in doing so we commit an injustice. Ignorance is bad, and in laughing at it we delight in what is bad" (Duplessie, 2020). Thus, our

Figure 1.1 Why did the chicken cross the road?

enjoyment is underscored by malice and also envy: seeing others' fall from grace – a slip on the banana skin – constitutes a relief from the pain of seeing them succeed and is all the more enjoyable if we consider them "enemies" or not "one of us" (Zillmann, 1983). Plato is often held up as the progenitor of the superiority theory of humour, but his view of humour – at least in the fragments of his writing that have survived – appeared to have been coloured by the treatment of Socrates, who was tried before a jury of some 500 Athenian citizens and sentenced to death by drinking hemlock. And, as Sheila Lintott highlights, "Plato and Aristotle spoke of humor and laughter largely in terms of ethical considerations" (2016), proposing reasons we might *laugh* rather than what constitutes *funny*.

Perhaps we laugh because we feel superior to the butt of the joke, but does that explain all laughter? What about puns and wordplays, or events that surprise and delight us? Or the chicken crossing the road? We should, in many respects, feel superior to a chicken, even one clever enough to abscond from the battery, but in explaining this joke Aristotle would argue in favour of surprise and paradox (Sachs, 2009), or, in other words, *incongruity*. The mental image of a chicken crossing a road alerts us to an unexpected – and potentially dangerous – situation. We know it's a joke, though, which perhaps adds to the tension. This is where Funny Peculiar here overlaps with Funny Ha-Ha.

It is a joke. We expect a satisfying resolution. The chicken has "To get to the other side", and this comforts us: the universe is once again in good order. The resolution contained here is a release. Which brings us to *Relief* theory:

> tragedy provides *catharsis*; comedy provides *relief*. Both genres reflect mankind's accumulated experience and wisdom in dealing with the basic and

> perennial problems in living: love and hatred, collaboration and opposition, truth and falsehood, candor and hypocrisy, gentleness and aggression, warfare and dialogue, social equality and inequality, democracy and dictatorship. In short, both address the antinomy between good and evil, morality and immoral, social and antisocial.
>
> (Lothane, 2008, emphasis in original)

The ambivalent attitude towards humour – the sense of it being a guilty pleasure – continued for a millennium. In the Bible, we see humour offered as a medicine to guide an individual to health: "a merry heart doeth good like a medicine but a broken spirit drieth the bones" (*Proverbs* 17:22, KJV). In *Kings* (2:23–24), Elisha is mocked by some young people from Bethel, presumably pagans, who deride him for not having joined his mentor Elijah in his ascent to heaven in a whirlwind. "Go up, thou bald head", they say. In response, Elisha curses them in the name of the Lord, whereupon two bears appear and maul 42 of them. It isn't entirely clear whether the youths are divinely punished for using superiority-theory humour or because they were non-believers or simply because Elisha was surrounded by at least 42 scary youths and was frightened that he might be joining Elijah sooner than he had hoped. In *Genesis*, God promises to Abraham, who is 100 years old, that his wife Sarah, 90, will bear his child, and tells him that the child will be called Isaac. This is Hebrew for *laughter*, taken by commentators to be symbolic of the joy a child brings its parents and/or a rebuke at Abraham's temerity for laughing at the idea that Sarah might still be able to bear a child. In *Ecclesiastes*, Solomon advises us how pointless a life without faith is: "It defends the life of faith in a generous God by pointing to the grimness of the alternative" (Eaton, 1983). Comparing the non-believer to a weak, babbling fool, he warns that "Sorrow is better than laughter: for by the sadness of the countenance the heart is made better" (7:3 KJV).

Judging by John Morreall's account (2024), the Christian church took up the Old Testament cynicism with a good deal of enthusiasm, along with the Puritans in England, who, in 1642 banned comedies and went on to demolish the Globe Theatre and Blackfriars Theatre in London (Croal, 2020). With the Enlightenment thinkers such as the third Earl of Shaftesbury argued that the suppression of wit and free inquiry undermined religion and truth rather than protected them, comparing the zealots who would ban humour, laughter and comedy to "those Grotesque Figures, and Dragon-Faces, which are seen often in the Frontispiece, and on the Corner Stones of old Buildings" (Cooper, 1709).

Henri Bergson's *Laughter: An essay on the meaning of the comic* (*Le Rire. Essai sur la signification du comique*), first published in 1900, proposed the *mechanical theory*, drawing on the three classical theories, which challenges our rigid thinking about how the world should be. Comedy, he says, is both phenomenological and essentially human:

> A landscape may be beautiful, charming and sublime, or insignificant and ugly; it will never be laughable. You may laugh at an animal, but only because you have detected in it some human attitude or expression. You may laugh at a hat, but what you are making fun of, in this case, is not the piece of felt or straw, but the shape that men have given it, the human caprice whose mould it has assumed. It is strange that so important a fact, and such a simple one too, has not attracted to a greater degree the attention of philosophers. Several have defined man as "an animal which laughs." They might equally well have defined him as an animal which is laughed at...
>
> (Bergson, 2008)

In the Monty Python film *The Life of Brian*, we laugh at the centurion guard who disturbs Brian daubing "Romanes eunt domus" on the wall of Pontius Pilate's palace. In a scene reminiscent of a public school Latin lesson, the centurion terrifyingly corrects Brian's poor grasp of Latin grammar, which ends:

Centurion: So we have... *Romani, ite domum*. Do you understand?
Brian: Yes, sir.
Centurion: Now write it out a hundred times.
Brian: Yes sir, hail Caesar, sir.
Centurion: Hail Caesar.
Brian: Yes, sir.
Centurion: And if it isn't done by sunrise, I'll cut your balls off.

(Chapman et al., 1979/2001)

Some among the audience may have felt superior to Brian if they were au fait with the vocative (plural) and locative cases and the imperative mood. There is plenty of incongruity, too, with a centurion correcting the culprit's grammar in his graffiti. Possibly, there is a sense of release, or relief, when morning comes, and we see Brian has covered almost all of the huge wall with *Romani ite domum*. Bergson's mechanical theory suggests we find comedy when people behave in a way that is contrary to how they should behave. Here, instead of arresting the villain, the centurion behaves like an overbearing, authoritarian, old-school (I hope) teacher. For his part, Brian stops behaving like a protester against Roman occupation and acts like a schoolboy, obediently following his teacher's absurd command to write out the phrase a hundred times. "The rigidity is the comic", Bergson wrote, "and laughter is its corrective". *The Life of Brian*, initially banned by 39 local councils in the United Kingdom, stands in a long line of comedies that achieve what Molière professed: "Le devoir de la comédie étant de corriger les hommes en les divertissant" (1910) – "The duty of comedy is to correct men by amusing them". The playwright, who is widely viewed to have granted comedy equal status with tragedy in the French arts, was here addressing King Louis XIV after his comic play *Tartuffe* was banned for sacrilege. The eponymous anti-hero is a religious hypocrite and *imposteur*, who inveigles his way into a wealthy Parisian family. Everyone sees through the false piety but the head of the household, Orgon. It falls to his wife, Elmire, to prove to Orgon the extent of Tartuffe's hypocrisy: she arranges for him to hide under a table while she pretends to yield to Tartuffe's lascivious advances:

Elmire: Won't Heaven frown upon us, though?
Tartuffe: Heaven an obstacle to love?
If so, it's one I can remove.
Elmire: I thought the ten commandments said…
Tartuffe: Why are you bothering your head
With such inane concerns? Look here:
You haven't *anything* to fear,
God's outlawed certain pleasures, true,
But he grants dispensations, too.

(Bolt, 2002)

Watching Tartuffe paw at Elmire and making his pious *raisonnements* while Elmire signals in vain to Orgon with pantomime coughing fits, is pure farce. Molière's portrayal of religious hypocrisy is timeless; it gives us the term *Tartuffian* and the play was recently revived by the Royal Shakespeare Company in Anil Gupta and Richard Pinto's relocation of the drama to present-day Birmingham's Pakistani Muslim community (2018), with Tartuffe recast as a "holy man" going by the name Tahir Taufiq Arsuf.

SchadenFREUDEe

A review of what makes us laugh that omits mention of Sigmund Freud would be like visiting Paris and not taking in a stop at the Mona Lisa. So, in a similar vein to the 30-second viewing rule at the Louvre, we will permit just a brief survey of the great psychoanalyst's contribution to our understanding.

In *The Joke and its Relation to the Unconscious* (2002), Freud argued that jokes serve as a socially acceptable outlet for unconscious desires and repressed thoughts. Originally published in 1905, the work extended Freud's theories of the unconscious mind into the realm of everyday social interaction. Jokes operate through similar mechanisms to dreams, employing techniques such as condensation, displacement and representation to disguise forbidden or anxiety-provoking content. He drew a distinction between "innocent" jokes, which derive pleasure purely from wordplay and technique, and "tendentious" jokes, which express aggressive or sexual impulses that would otherwise have been socially unacceptable (in Vienna). The latter category particularly interested Freud, as these jokes allow the unconscious to momentarily bypass the ego's censorship.

The pleasure derived from tendentious jokes comes from the "psychical economy" achieved when repressed material finds expression without triggering guilt or anxiety. Laughter represents the discharge of psychical energy that would otherwise be expended in maintaining repression.

An example of this is the following joke – one of the many he analysed:

> His Majesty is travelling through his provinces and notices among the crowd a man who looks remarkably like his own sublime personage. He beckons to ask him: "Was your mother once in service at the palace, perhaps?" – "No, Your Highness," came the reply, "*but my father was.*"
>
> (Freud, 2002, emphasis in original)

Freud approaches this joke from two angles, the technical and the psychological. The technique used is an example of "unexpected unities" created by the inversion of the potential parentages of the commoner, where the attacker becomes the attacked. The release of repressed aggression is also highlighted. The commoner would "surely like to knock the insolent questioner down for daring to cast aspersions on the memory of his beloved mother with such an insinuation", Freud explains. But to do so would cause him to lose his "whole existence". He could suppress his anger and stay silent, but the joke "shows the way to repaying the insult unscathed" and causes us to forget that the aggressor's question was itself a joke. To Freud, the joke is amusing because it represents a rebellion against authority – "a creditable thing". In telling or listening to a joke that puts down an individual or group we dislike, we let out the hostility we might otherwise repress. And in telling a sexual joke or listening to one, we bypass our internal censor and give vent to our libido. In both cases, Freud argued, the psychic energy normally used to do the repressing becomes superfluous and is released in laughter.

Of course, jokes are just one form of humour and we are unlikely to be hearing a joke in any therapy room (though Chapters 3 and 4 describe a few). Freud also explored the connection between jokes and other mental phenomena, particularly dreams and parapraxes (AKA Freudian slips). These, he argued, reveal the workings of unconscious processes through their linguistic construction and symbolic content.

Reflection

In a former life, I developed and presented workshops for a major multinational company. The workshops took place at various locations around the world and were always hosted in an upmarket hotel in whichever city's business district. The workshops lasted five days, and participants were generally given no option but to attend since the subject matter was Very Important For Their Professional Development. And that subject matter? The practical application of International Financial Reporting Standards. In plain English: advanced accounting.

The reader will appreciate that not all participants were looking forward to those five days. Similar workshops delivered by my predecessors were known for stretching to breaking point the time/space continuum.

So, in some trepidation, I started each workshop with a welcome and a reflection on the luxurious surroundings we found ourselves in. The hotel rooms were sumptuous, the beds unbelievably comfortable, but best of all were the bath towels. I told the by now somewhat baffled participants that I had never seen such huge, fluffy, radiantly white bath towels in my life. "My only worry", I added, "is that I won't be able to fit them all in my suitcase".

The release of collective tension in the room was as loud as the laughter. Maybe the week wouldn't be so long after all.

Wider perspectives

If the theorists cannot agree entirely on what humour represents, are there any common denominators across cultures? An admittedly narrow-scope review of the dictionary definitions of *humour* reveals some curious agreements and divergences.

The Western Europeans in my random sample (French, Spanish, German and Basque) emphasise the cognitive element of *humour*, with the French definition of *humour* "highlighting the comic, ridiculous, absurd or unusual character of certain aspects of reality" (Larousse, transl.). This is also reflected in Basque, one of the oldest European languages and one whose roots are not shared with any other known language. The Basque definition additionally emphasises the absence of ill will, which is shared with the German *Humor*, while all four definitions and etymologies are traced back to the Latin *humor*, discussed earlier.

If we look further afield, we notice shifts in the relational emphasis. In Japanese, for example, ユーモア (pronounced *yuomo*) is depicted as "A kind of funniness that soothes people's hearts" (Digital Daijiten, transl.) and "Refined wit that is not offensive, accompanied by a sense of ease and generosity in intelligent wit and deliberate satire" (Seisen-ban Nihon Kokugo Daijiten, transl.).

The Hindi concept most closely associated with *humour* is हास्य (*hāsya*), one of the nine *rasas* (essential aesthetic essences) codified in the Nāṭyaśāstra, a seminal text of Indian performing art dating from around the 2nd century B.C.

Humour and comic sentiment are thus understood as both an emotion felt by the audience and an artistic technique used by the creator. In Swahili, the etymology of the word for *humour*, *ucheshi*, comes from the verb "to make someone laugh" (Oxford Languages) and translates as the "quality of being cheerful and joyful towards people". The root of the Arabic, فُكَاهَة (*fukāha*) is shared with the words for *fruit*, *enjoyment* and *pleasure* (Dictionary of Contemporary Arabic Language), reflecting a tradition of storytelling, wit and the removal of sadness. Two of the most widely spoken indigenous language groups of South America, Quechua and Guaraní, seem not to have developed an abstract conceptual term for *humour*. Quechua is the language of the Inca Empire – from which we have "loaned" (as linguists put it) the words *puma*, *condor*, *coca*, *quinine* and *llama* – and is spoken across Andean South America, where it is an official language in Peru and Bolivia. Guaraní is spoken by most of the population of Paraguay, where it has equal official status with Spanish, as well as parts of neighbouring countries. Instead, the two languages emphasise actions and emotions with rich vocabularies for expressing mirth's nuances. In Quechua, *asiy* translates as *laughter*, *to laugh*, *to smile* and *who walks cheerfully* (Academia Mayor de la Lengua Quechua, 2005). The Guaraní verbs *puka* – to laugh and to laugh at oneself – and *pukavy* – *to smile*, *to laugh a little* and *to half-laugh* (Roman, 2012; Glosbe) – equally emphasise an embodied conception of the expression of humour.

In summary, the theme of positive emotion underlies each of the meanings and etymologies of this (randomly selected) sample of languages. In addition, social connection, benevolence, the expression of humour and mirth and cognitive perceptions feature widely, with each culture understanding and expressing humour through its own unique lens.

In closing, it is also worth noting that a number of these sources also reference the local adoption of *humour* as a loan word from the English! Imagine it: football, cricket, trains, the internet... and humour!

Pause for thought

The banana skin – do we laugh at someone who has suffered a misfortune because we feel superior to them?

Perhaps our laughter is a way of expressing "phew, that could have happened to me, and I'm glad it didn't!"

In which case, how much does the person planting his foot on the plantain have to suffer before it stops being funny?

Modern conceptions

The last hundred years or so have seen the task of understanding humour taken up by psychologists, anthropologists and even neurobiologists.

Writing in 1922, Max Eastman initiated a systematic exposition of our senses of humour, and many other psychologists followed, eschewing the apparently unattainable – a definition of humour that synthesised the various theories that came before it – in favour of systematically induced concepts grounded in empirical research. These are explored in detail in Chapter 2.

Still more recently, research into the psychological and physiological benefits of humour by Norman Dixon at University College London culminated in *Humor: A cognitive alternative to stress* (1980). He proposed that humour was a way of coping with social and cognitive stress by creating a beneficial "cognitive-affective shift", enabling the individual to re-frame a stressful situation as less threatening and thus reduce its negative emotional consequences. Arguably a continuation of work in previous centuries, such as that of the 13th-century surgeon Henri de Mondeville (Lefcourt, 2003), Dixon's work went on to become a foundational element in the psychological literature on the relationship between humour and well-being. These and other perceived benefits are also discussed in later chapters.

Physical anthropologists have shed some light on the evolutionary and socialising aspects of humour. In a challenge to Freud's theory that laughter represents a release of psychic energy, V. S. Ramachandran and Sandra Blakeslee proposed the "False Alarm Theory" (1999). They argued that laughter has a social function, that it is a means of telling others in the laughing individual's social group that the danger is spurious:

> A band of early humans is walking across the savanna, when they spot a lion in the clearing ahead. They freeze in their tracks for a moment, but then they see that the lion is feasting on a zebra and doesn't even look up at them. With the sudden realization that the lion is not a threat, they laugh, signaling to each other "We're safe. We can enjoy this."
>
> (Morreal, 2009)

Jokes typically lead "the listener along a garden path of expectation, slowly building up tension" (Ramachandran & Blakeslee, 2005), and the tension that builds during the telling of a chicken-crossing-the-road joke is analogous to the dread-filled moments of suspense in horror films and, arguably, the plot of every story ever conceived (Storr, 2020). This is because our brains keep a ceaseless vigil for any incongruity or disturbance in the distance: we are wired to expect the unexpected. Every few seconds of the day, the core of our eyes – the small central fovea that possesses higher acuity than the rest of the retina – flits in a movement called a "saccade" (Blackmore, 2013), on the lookout for prey or predator. The moment something out of place is spotted, our attention is drawn to establishing whether the irregularity is a promise or a threat. If neither, the eye and brain return to their previous states of vigilance. And, following Ramachandran and Blakeslee's thinking, we might also laugh to signal to our fellow hunter-gatherers that normal service has been restored.

Again drawing on neurological studies, Matthew Hurley et al. (2011) reveal that the reason we crave humour is because our brains reward us with pleasure when we figure out the punchline, just as they do when we have an inspirational thought or have successfully worked through a puzzle. Or when we've finished the first chapter of a book.

Summing up

The word *humour* originated in early medical teaching about the *corporeal fluids* that governed a person's character and health, a concept that survived to the plays of Marlowe and Shakespeare.

The nature and power of humour have to this day evaded precise *definition* despite the efforts of philosophers and scientists. *Socrates* called for humour to be state-controlled, the Puritans banned comedies and demolished the Globe Theatre. *Freud* analysed jokes and theorised that they served several social and psychopathological needs. In cultures *beyond Europe*, humour is embodied in storytelling and the arts.

Recent *neurological studies* shed light on how we respond to jokes.

References

Amuse; Merry; Mirth; Humour. (n.d.). *Oxford English Dictionary*. https://www.oed.com. Retrieved 13October2025.

Aristotle. (2009). *Rhetoric* (J. Sachs, Trans.). Focus Philosophical Library.

Bergson, H. (2008). *Laughter: An essay on the meaning of the comic* (C. Brereton & F. Rothwell, Trans.). The Floating Press.

Blackmore, S. J. (2013). *Consciousness: An introduction* (2nd ed.). Hodder Education.

Chapman, G., Cleese, J., Gilliam, T., Idle, E., Jones, T., & Palin, M. (2001). *Monty Python's The life of Brian (of Nazareth)*. Methuen (Original work published 1979).

Cooper, A. A. (1709). Sensus communis: An essay on the freedom of wit and humour. Printed for Egbert Sanger at the Post-Office in Fleetstreet.

Croal, J. (2020). From pandemics to puritans: When theatre shut down through history and how it recovered. *The Stage*, April 2. https://www.thestage.co.uk/long-reads/

from-pandemics-to-puritans-when-theatre-shut-down-through-history-and-how-it-recovered

Dixon, N. F. (1980). Humor: A cognitive alternative to stress. In I. G. Sarason & C. D. Spielberger (Eds.), *Stress and anxiety*, Vol. 7. Hemisphere.

Duplessie, D. (2020). Socrates' analysis of comedy in Plato's Philebus. *The Review of Metaphysics*, *74*(1), 3–20.

Eastman, M. (1922). *Wit and humor*. Charles Scribner's Sons.

Eaton, M. (1983). *Ecclesiastes*. Inter-Varsity Press.

Freud, S. (2002). *The joke and its relation to the unconscious* (J. Cricke, Trans.). Penguin. (Original work published 1905).

Gupta, A. & Pinto, R. (2018). *Tartuffe*.Oberon Modern Plays.

Hurley, M. M., Dennett, D. C., & Adams, R. B., Jr. (2011). *Inside jokes: Using humor to reverse-engineer the mind*. The MIT Press.

Lefcourt, H. M. (2003). Humor as a moderator of life stress in adults. In C. E. Schaefer (Ed.), *Play therapy with adults* (pp. 144–165). John Wiley & Sons Inc.

Lintott, S. (2016). Superiority in humor theory. *The Journal of Aesthetics and Art Criticism*, *74*(4), 347–358. https://doi.org/10.1111/jaac.12321

Lothane, Z. (2008). The uses of humor in life, neurosis and in psychotherapy: Part 2. *International Forum of Psychoanalysis*, *17*(4), 232–239. https://doi.org/10.1080/08037060701549861

Marlowe, C. (1997). *Tamburlaine, parts one and two* (A. B. Dawson, Ed.). Bloomsbury. (Original work published 1590).

Molière. (1910). *Œuvres complètes de Molière* (Vol. 2). Charpentier.

Molière. (2002). *Tartuffe* (R. Bolt, Trans.). Oberon Books.

Morreal, J. (2009). *Comic relief: A comprehensive philosophy of humor*. John Wiley & Sons, Inc

Morreall, J., (2024). Philosophy of humor. In E. N. Zalta & U. Nodelman (Eds.), *The Stanford Encyclopedia of philosophy (Fall 2024 edition)*. https://plato.stanford.edu/archives/fall2024/entries/humor/

Naas, M. (2016). Plato and the spectacle of laughter. *Angelaki: Journal of Theoretical Humanities*, *21*(3), 13–26. https://doi.org/10.1080/0969725X.2016.1205253

Ramachandran, V. S., & Blakeslee, S. (1999). *Phantoms in the brain: Human nature and the architecture of the mind*. Fourth Estate.

Ramachandran, V. S. & Blakeslee, S. (2005). *Phantoms in the brain: Human nature and the architecture of the mind*. Harper Perennial.

Shakespeare, W. (1995). *King Henry V* (T. W. Craik, Ed.). Routledge. (Original work published 1600).

Storr, W. (2020). *The science of storytelling*. William Collins.

Zillmann, D. (1983). Disparagement humor. In P. McGhee & J. Goldstein (Eds.), *Handbook of humor research: Basic issues* (Vol. 1, pp. 85–108). Springer Verlag.

Chapter 2

Humour senses and styles

Introduction

The last century has seen the emergence of a new science: the measurement of people's humour and how people prefer to express and experience humour. We examine the pioneering research into humour sensitivity and affinity and how those assessments have evolved. Chapter 3 expands the study to how universal – or not – humour is, across genders, ages, cultures and the neurological variances.

Early years

Many of the studies carried out from the 1920s to the 1980s focused on the idea of humour being an indicator of personality. Attempts were made to categorise what made people laugh and what it said about their characters, intellect and ability.

In one of the earliest studies of its kind, Polyxenie Kambouropoulou tasked 70 students at the eminent, all-female Vassar College in New York State, USA, with keeping "humour diaries" for a period of one week to find out, "if possible, whether certain individuals laugh at certain situations, rather than at certain other situations, consistently enough to be grouped into types" (1926). The diaries were kept free-form and varied in volume between eight and 119 laughter instances, with the average being 30.1. The instances were then categorised using the following characteristics, together with the proportions recorded:

- a No obvious cause (4%), for example, pleasant weather, because others laughed;
- b Physical causes (25%), for example, someone fell over, or was ugly;
- c Mental inferiority of others or self (37%), for example, a mistake, naïve remark;
- d As for c) (11%), but with a remark or teasing directed at the inferior person;

DOI: 10.4324/9781003638773-4

e An unexpected (18%), incongruous event or situation; and
f Puns and clever remarks (5%), directed at no one in particular, nonsense.

The results were then cross-tested using jokes indicative of the above characteristics. For example, for the most popular type of humour, the following joke was included in the 16 that were ranked by the students:

Miss N.: What is it that you just played?
Violinist: An improvisation, Madam.
Miss N.: Ah, one of my old favorites!

Kambouropoulou found that the students were fairly consistent in the types of humour that they remembered enough to make note of in their diaries and their preferences in jokes. A correlation between intellect and volume of humour instances diarised was also attempted, with more gifted students tending to note a higher number of humour instances, or, at least, to document those instances more diligently.

This study was influential in its approach and methods. Later studies focused on what types of jokes were found to be amusing, dividing participants into groups for comparative analytical purposes, for example, by gender and by nationality (e.g. Omwake, 1937; Wells, 1934). They were limited in four important respects. Firstly, participants were nearly always recruited from within colleges and universities, often psychology students. Despite this, researchers drew conclusions that were applied more universally. Secondly, the focus of the studies relied on whether the participants laughed or not, this being regarded as definitive evidence that the joke was perceived to be amusing. Thirdly, jokes and cartoons were used to assess how much participants laughed. Curiously – in the spirit, perhaps, of *the old ones are the best* – researchers tended to "recycle" a number of jokes previously used by other researchers for their own studies. Apart from the possibility that participants might already have heard a particular joke, it is possible that a given person might not find any of the jokes especially amusing and would have been categorised as lacking in humour, when in fact what was missing was good, that is, *funny material.* Finally, many of the studies asked participants to assess themselves with respect to their sense of humour, leading to suggestions of bias in the results.

One study that looked at how others perceived our sense of humour was carried out by Jacob Levine and John Rakusin, who studied two groups of men: 40 college undergraduates at a New England college and 65 psychiatric patients at a hospital for veterans. The two groups differed from each other in terms of average age, education, intelligence and social class as well as mental health, but intra-group homogeneity was reasonably strong. In addition to asking participants to rate a selection of "popular cartoons taken from magazines like the New Yorker and the Saturday Evening Post" (1959), they were tasked with rating themselves and their group peers on two questions: "(a)

How humorous was he? and (b) How well does he appreciate humour?". Levine and Rakusin found that, overall, the college students rated themselves and one another higher than the psychiatric patients in being humorous and in appreciating humour, but more significantly, the individuals in both groups rated themselves more highly than they were rated by their peers.

Humour studies did not want for imaginative approaches. The Blacky Pictures, published in 1950 by Gerald Blum at the University of Michigan, USA, were a series of 12 cartoons featuring Blacky the Dog and its family. The cartoons depicted aspects of Freudian psychosexual development. In one of them, Blacky is furiously chewing the collar belonging to one of its parents: the test subject's response to the scene depicted was taken to indicate the extent of his Oedipus complex or her Electra complex. The cartoons also attempted to assess other "syndromes", including anal retentiveness, oral sadism and castration anxiety/penis envy; however, few of the cartoon cards have survived, so we must only imagine how Blacky was depicted in them. Another study (Brody & Redlich, 1953) compared the responses of schizophrenic patients to comic cartoons before and after they were subjected to prefrontal lobotomy, a psychosurgical procedure estimated to have been carried out on around 40,000 people in the United States and 17,000 in the United Kingdom between 1935 and 1965 (Raz, 2008; Tranøy & Blomberg, 2005). The study's co-author, Eugene Brody, was an eminent psychiatrist who was both a life fellow of the American Psychiatric Association and President and Secretary-General of the World Federation for Mental Health. He was also chief psychiatrist for the Yale lobotomy project from 1949 to 1952 (Rasmussen, 2010). In the study's report, Brody correlated:

> the ability "to gain pleasure and to respond to the cartoon humor" with "regression in the service of the ego".
>
> (Raz, 2008)

Perhaps, in response to the discrediting of psychosurgical procedures such as lobotomies (as well as electroconvulsive, insulin shock and malarial therapies) as a method of extracting – literally in some cases – data from patients, questionnaires were increasingly used as an assessment tool. The Norwegian Sven Svebak (1996) formulated a number of hypotheses about humour styles in the late 1960s, which led to the creation of the Sense of Humor Questionnaire (SHQ). Svebak's aim was to explore a person's sense of humour as an aspect of his or her personality, split into three distinct areas of focus:

- Sensitivity to humorous messages, an example question being, "Would you say that you have much cause for amusement during an ordinary day?"
- Affinity for comical situations and humorous others, an example question being, "It is my impression that those who try to be funny really do it to hide their lack of self-confidence".

- Tendency to permit or suppress emotional impulses of mirthfulness and joy in general, an example question being, "Do you sometimes find yourself laughing in situations where laughter is quite out of place?"

Revised several times, the SHQ was used in a number of prominent research studies from the 1970s to 1990s, enabling distinctions between styles of humour, particularly based on the individual's sensitivity to humour and affinity for comical situations and humorous others.

Responses to each of the 21 questions/statements were rated depending on how much the correspondents felt about them, with the results processed to "measure" their sense of humour. Other research at the time, such as Raymond Cattell and Donald Tollefson at the Institute for Personality and Ability Testing in Illinois, developed the IPAT Humor Test (1966), which assessed different personality characteristics associated with humour preferences using – once again – jokes, 104 pairs of them spread across 13 "humor dimensions" ranging from "introversion–extraversion" and "dry wit–good natured play" to "theatricalism–cold realism", "rebound against feminine aggression–scorn of ineffectual male" and "dullness–general intelligence".

Humour as a predictor of personality

With the introduction of computers onto more university campuses, psychometric studies grew in complexity and ambition. At the University of Waterloo in Canada, Rod Martin and Herbert Lefcourt used no less than four separate questionnaires (and a checklist), which were completed by volunteer first-year psychology students at the university, to investigate whether or not humour mitigated the harmful effects of stressful experiences (1983):

- The two strands (subscales in the parlance) of the SHQ noted above;
- Profile of Mood States, used to assess the students' predominant mood level;
- The Situational Humor Response Questionnaire (SHRQ), developed specifically for the study by Martin and Lefcourt;
- The Coping Humour Scale (CHS), also developed by the two researchers; and
- A checklist of positive and negative life events experienced by students during the preceding twelve months.

The SHRQ comprised a number of hypothetical situations to which participants rated their response, from seriousness (e.g. "I would not have been particularly amused") to hilarity ("I would have laughed heartily"). Examples of situations included having an accident and being rendered bed-bound for a few days, a date with a special someone and trying to get a "computer error" fixed at work.

The Coping Humor Scale was developed to examine the degree to which people used humour as a means of coping with seven stressful experiences:

1 I often lose my sense of humor when I'm having problems.
2 I have often found that my problems have been greatly reduced when I tried to find something funny in them.
3 I usually look for something comical to say when I am in tense situations.
4 I must admit my life would probably be easier if I had more of a sense of humor.
5 I have often felt that if I am in a situation where I have to either cry or laugh, it's better to laugh.
6 I can usually find something to laugh or joke about, even in trying situations.
7 It has been my experience that humor is often a very effective way of coping with problems.

Processing, analysing and comparing the responses from the various questionnaires suggested a "moderate" correlation between possessing a strong sense of humour and coping with adversity, indicating that humour reduced "the impact of negative life experiences on moods" (Martin & Lefcourt, 1983). Interestingly, there was no significant difference observed between the outcomes for men and for women. The researchers performed further related studies throughout the 1980s, confirming these findings.

Reflection

Coping with adversity with the aid of humour is a feature of many memoirs and autobiographies.

When Simon Boas, an aid worker at the UN, was diagnosed with terminal cancer in his mid-40s, he set down his thoughts in the bestselling book *A Beginner's Guide to Dying* (2024). The book was successful because Boas spoke to people in a language they understood and could relate to, and because he spoke with cheerful and inspirational stoicism about a subject we in the United Kingdom are not generally equipped to face up to – our own mortality. Characteristic of his humour is the description of how he learned the cancer was incurable, in the chapter "My cancer situation has developed not necessarily to my advantage", a paraphrasing of Japanese Emperor Hirohito's response to the bombing of Hiroshima and Nagasaki:

> …although the chemo and radiation did a good job on the tumours in my throat and neck, my lungs are now riddled with the bloody

things. The prognosis is not quite 'Don't buy any green bananas', but it's pretty close to 'Don't start any long books'.

(Boas, 2024)

In innumerable sessions with clients who are processing the loss of a loved one, I've found that the darkness of the tears is interspersed – eased and underlined – by laughter, our most powerful pain-reliever.

A 1993 study by Martin et al. at the University of Western Ontario in London, Canada, extended the scope of investigation to encompass the discrepancy between the "actual and ideal self-concept". These terms are familiar to person-centred counsellors: the self-concept refers to how an individual perceives him- or herself, essentially, "who am I?"; the ideal self, then, is "who I would most like to be". The 1993 study also assessed participants' self-esteem and found that those whose sense of humour was strongest also enjoyed a more positive – and more realistic – self-concept with lower discrepancies with the ideal self, and higher self-esteem.

A significant step forward in the categorisation of how and why people use humour came with the publication of the Humor Styles Questionnaire (HSQ) (Martin et al., 2003). The conceptual foundation of the Questionnaire is a model of humour styles that cuts across two axes: the self versus others and benign versus detrimental. Thus, the four elements of the model are:

"Self-enhancing" humour draws on the earlier study (Martin et al., 1993) of an individual with a humorous outlook on life, open to amusement at life's absurdities and able to keep a generally positive perspective even when confronted with stress or a threat. It is assessed in the questionnaire with items such as:

- If I am feeling depressed, I can usually cheer myself up with humor.
- I don't need to be with other people to feel amused – I can usually find things to laugh about even when I'm by myself.

"Affiliative" humour is also self-affirming in that it is seen in people who are amusing to others (e.g., because they can tell jokes) and do not take themselves too seriously. There is also less emphasis on resilience and more on relationships with others, with humour used to help defuse conflicts or increase one's attractiveness. Thus, the affiliative style of humour is associated with extrovert personalities, with self-enhancing humour preferred by introverts. It is assessed in the questionnaire with items such as:

- I don't have to work very hard at making other people laugh – I seem to be a naturally humorous person.
- I enjoy making people laugh.

Conversely, "self-defeating" humour takes self-deprecating humour to the extreme, disparaging oneself in order to maintain or enhance relationships with others. It is defensive, avoidant, hides underlying negativity and can suppress the individual's needs or wants. The humour may be amusing to others, but it is tainted with neediness and low self-esteem. It is assessed in the questionnaire with items such as:

- I often try to make people like or accept me more by saying something funny about my own weaknesses, blunders, or faults.
- If I am having problems or feeling unhappy, I often cover it up by joking around, so that even my closest friends don't know how I really feel.

"Aggressive" humour behaviours such as sarcasm and ridicule are reflective of the "superiority" theory discussed previously and may even convey veiled threats to others. This humour disregards the feelings of others and may be intentionally offensive, even if the speaker defends it with "It was only a joke". It is assessed in the questionnaire with items such as:

- If someone makes a mistake, I will often tease them about it.
- If I don't like someone, I often use humour or teasing to put them down.

Since its publication, the HSQ has enjoyed extensive usage, having been translated and adapted into languages including Arabic, Armenian, Chinese, French, German, Italian, Lebanese and Turkish (Ruch & Heintz, 2016). Repeated evaluations have confirmed its usefulness in psychometric assessments and that the four humour styles are indeed distinct from one another (Kuiper, 2012).

A significant feature of the HSQ is the recognition that not all uses of humour are positive, either in intention or in effect. While the research points to the correlation between the adaptive (self-enhancing and affiliative) humour styles and "good" mental health: lower depression and anxiety and higher self-esteem, the maladaptive (self-defeating and aggressive) styles are linked to increased depression and anxiety and lower self-esteem.

A 2007 study by Sarah Erickson and Sarah Feldstein at the University of New Mexico, USA, which measured the coping and defence strategies and depressive symptoms of 94 adolescents aged 12–15. They found that self-defeating humour was predictive of depressive symptoms, which suggested that the need at that stage of development to build and sustain friendships risked leading youths to mistakenly adopt a style of humour that they believed enhanced their relationship with others but acted to their own detriment (2007). A later study (Kuiper et al., 2016), on young adult students at the University of Western Ontario, Canada, confirmed these findings, observing that the development of the students' identities was enhanced with greater use of self-enhancing and affiliative humour and less use of self-defeating humour. At the same time, their capacity for intimacy in their relationships was enhanced by greater use of affiliative humour and less use of self-defeating humour. A third study (Hampes, 2016) established a significant positive relationship between the self-enhancing humour style and the capacity for forgiveness. Likewise, it found that the aggressive style of humour negatively correlated with forgiveness capacity. Nicholas Kuiper (2012) similarly found that humour styles affected how satisfied people were with their relationships.

Humour as a predictor of behaviour

The use of the HSQ has extended to studies of other aspects of behaviour, often in conjunction with other psychometric tools. A study carried out by Virgil Zeigler-Hill and Avi Besser of 200 Israeli undergraduates combined the use of the Questionnaire with the Pathological Narcissism Inventory (Pincus et al., 2009) to examine the relationships between self-esteem, humour styles and pathological forms of narcissism. Most people would associate narcissism with arrogance, conceitedness and/or unjustifiably entitled attitudes, expressed overtly through a range of behaviours such as exploitation, aggression and exhibitionism, as well as more covertly, for example, falsely supporting or untruthfully empathising with others. This "grandiose" narcissism contrasts with narcissistic vulnerability, where the individual ideates the possession of a special status that others cannot appreciate and which often leads to withdrawal through shame or denial. Thus, a pathologically grandiose narcissist might say "I often fantasise about being recognised for my accomplishments", (so-called, "grandiose fantasy"), while a pathologically vulnerable narcissist might say "It irritates me when people don't notice how good a person I am" ("entitlement rage") (Pincus et al., 2009).

The study's results suggest a darker side to humour use. Zeigler-Hill and Besser found a strong correlation between people displaying grandiose narcissism and high self-esteem and their preference for adaptive forms of humour, which allowed them to enhance themselves and others. Conversely, people with vulnerable narcissism and low self-esteem were found to refrain from adaptive humour and instead use humour to hurt both themselves (i.e. self-defeating humour) and others (i.e. aggressive humour). Zeigler-Hill and Besser suggested that the use of maladaptive humour was motivated by a "misguided attempt to gain the approval and acceptance of others" (2011).

And not a million miles apart from the subject of narcissism, perhaps, Serkan Sari at the Recep Tayyip Erdogan University in Turkey (2016) examined the humour styles of cyberbullies – bullies who use the internet and/or mobile phones – using the HSQ alongside the Revised Cyberbullying Inventory (Topcu & Erdur-Baker, 2010). Sari found that the preference for aggressive humour was a significant predictor of cyberbullying perpetration. Not surprisingly, perhaps, Sari also noted a prevalence of self-defeating humour among many of this cohort; he speculated that cyberbullies often suffer low self-esteem, may have themselves been victims of bullying in one form or another, and so are replicating their experiences. Another possible explanation is that such humour is used as a form of avoidance or distraction from emotional problems they are unable to address.

Still relevant?

The longevity of the HSQ is a testament to both its usefulness and its general reliability. By 2017, it had been used in over 120 published studies worldwide, as diverse as suicide risk, marital divorce and body dysmorphia (Baisley & Grunberg, 2019).

It has also been used to develop other tools, such as the Relational Humor Inventory (De Koning & Weiss, 2002), which was developed to ascertain positive and negative behaviours in intimate relationships with questions such as "When my partner is angry with me, I can usually change his/her mood by making him/her laugh" and "My partner uses humor to avoid facing issues that concern us". In addition to confirming that positive humour can be viewed as a strength in a relationship, with negative humour being the opposite, the Inventory provided an indication of how a couple "may deal with sensitive issues, which can be positive or negative, depending on the context" (De Koning & Weiss, 2002).

Pause for thought

How does the concept of the four humour styles resonate with you?
Do you feel that we favour one humour style, all of the time?
If we accept that the HSQ is an effective tool for predicting behaviour, how much do you think the tool establishes a cause-and-effect relationship?

Summing up

The *psychology of humour* has been studied intensely over the last century. Many of the studies carried out from the 1920s to the 1980s focused on the idea of humour being an indicator of personality and relied on subjects' responses to *cartoons* and *jokes*. With greater availability of computer processing power, studies evolved using questionnaires, of which the *HSQ* (Martin et al., 2003) was the most widely used. It is still considered a useful framework within which the multidimensionality of humour can be examined, enabling us to consider its impact on our *mental and physical health and our relationships* with other people. Other approaches are gaining prominence, especially in the field of neuroscience, which we will examine in later chapters.

References

Baisley, M. C., & Grunberg, N. E. (2019). Bringing humor theory into practice: An interdisciplinary approach to online humor training. *New Ideas in Psychology*, *55*, 24–34. https://doi.org/10.1016/j.newideapsych.2019.04.006

Blum, G. S. (1950). *The Blacky pictures: A technique for the exploration of personality dynamics*. Psychological Corp.

Boas, S. (2024). *A beginner's guide to dying*. Swift Press.

Brody, E. B., & Redlich, F. D. (1953). The response of schizophrenic patients to comic cartoons before and after prefrontal lobotomy. *Folia Psychiatrica, Neurologica et Neurochirurgica Neerlandica*, *56*, 623–635.

Cattell, R. B., & Tollefson, D. L. (1966). *The IPAT humor test of personality*. Institute of Personality and Ability Testing.

De Koning, E., & Weiss, R. L. (2002). The relational humor inventory: Functions of humor in close relationships. *American Journal of Family Therapy*, *30*(1), 1–18. https://doi.org/10.1080/019261802753455615

Erickson, S. J., & Feldstein, S. W. (2007). Adolescent humor and its relationship to coping, Defense strategies, psychological distress, and well-being. *Child Psychiatry and Human Development*, *37*(3), 255–271. https://doi.org/10.1007/s10578-006-0034-5

Hampes, W. (2016). The relationship between humor styles and forgiveness. *Europe's Journal of Psychology*, *12*(3), 338–347. https://doi.org/10.5964/ejop.v12i3.1012

Kambouropoulou, P. (1926). Individual differences in the sense of humor. *American Journal of Psychology*, *37*(2), 267–278. https://doi.org/10.2307/1413696

Kuiper, N. A. (2012). Humor and resiliency: Towards a process model of coping and growth. *Europe's Journal of Psychology*, *8*(3), 475–491. https://doi.org/10.5964/ejop.v8i3.464

Kuiper, N. A., Kirsh, G., & Maiolino, N. (2016). Identity and intimacy development, humor styles, and psychological well-being. *Identity: An International Journal of Theory and Research*, *16*(2), 115–125. https://doi.org/10.1080/15283488.2016.1159964

Levine, J., & Rakusin, J. (1959). The sense of humor of college students and psychiatric patients. *Journal of General Psychology*, *60*(2), 183–190. https://doi.org/10.1080/00221309.1959.9710219

Martin, R. A., Kuiper, N. A., Olinger, L. J., & Dance, K. (1993). Humor, coping with stress, self-concept, and psychological well-being. *HUMOR: International Journal of Humor Research*, *6*(1), 89–104.

Martin, R. A., & Lefcourt, H. M. (1983). Sense of humor as a moderator of the relation between stressors and moods. *Journal of Personality and Social Psychology*, *45*(6), 1313–1324. https://doi.org/10.1037/0022-3514.45.6.1313

Martin, R. A., Puhlik-Doris, P., Larsen, G., Gray, J., & Weir, K. (2003). Individual differences in uses of humor and their relation to psychological well-being: Development of the humor styles questionnaire. *Journal of Research in Personality*, *37*(1), 48–75. https://doi.org/10.1016/S0092-6566(02)00534-2

Omwake, L. (1937). A study of sense of humor: Its relation to sex, age, and personal characteristics. *Journal of Applied Psychology*, *21*(6), 688–704. https://doi.org/10.1037/h0055199

Pincus, A. L., Ansell, E. B., Pimentel, C. A., Cain, N. M., Wright, A. G. C., & Levy, K. N. (2009). Initial construction and validation of the pathological narcissism inventory. *Psychological Assessment*, *21*(3), 365–379. https://doi.org/10.1037/a0016530

Rasmussen, F. (2010). Eugene B. Brody. *Baltimore Sun*, March 17. https://web.archive.org/web/20150321035139/http://articles.baltimoresun.com/2010-03-17/news/bal-md.ob.ci.brody17mar17_1_dr-brody-psychiatry-slave-labor

Raz, M. (2008). Between the ego and the Icepick: Psychosurgery, psychoanalysis, and psychiatric discourse. *Bulletin of the History of Medicine*, *82*(2), 387–420. http://www.jstor.org/stable/44448553

Ruch, W., & Heintz, S. (2016). The German version of the humor styles questionnaire: Psychometric properties and overlap with other styles of humor. *Europe's Journal of Psychology*, *12*(3), 434–455. https://doi.org/10.5964/ejop.v12i3.1116

Sari, S. V. (2016). Was it just joke? Cyberbullying perpetrations and their styles of humor. *Computers in Human Behavior*, *54*, 555–559. https://doi.org/10.1016/j.chb.2015.08.053

Svebak, S. (1996). The development of the sense of humor questionnaire: From SHQ to SHQ-6. *Humor*, *9–3*(4), 341–361. https://doi.org/10.1515/humr.1996.9.3-4.341

Topcu, Ç., & Erdur-Baker, Ö. (2010). The revised cyber bullying inventory (RCBI): Validity and reliability studies. *Procedia Social and Behavioral Sciences*, *5*, 660–664. https://doi.org/10.1016/j.sbspro.2010.07.161

Tranøy, J., & Blomberg, W. (2005). Lobotomy in Norwegian psychiatry. *History of Psychiatry*, *16*(1). https://doi.org/10.1177/0957154x05052224

Wells, R. E. (1934). A study of tastes in humorous literature among pupils of junior and senior high schools. *The Journal of Educational Research*, 28(2), 81–91. https://doi.org/10.1080/00220671.1934.10880466

Zeigler-Hill, V., & Besser, A. (2011). Humor style mediates the association between pathological narcissism and self-esteem. *Personality and Individual Differences*, *50*(8), 1196–1201. https://doi.org/10.1016/j.paid.2011.02.006

Chapter 3

Is humour universal and eternal?

Introduction

Everyone's sense of humour is different... or is it?

COVID-19 didn't give us much to laugh about. A review of 49 research studies from across the planet into the use of humour in social media during the pandemic (Alkaraki et al., 2024) revealed a great deal of commonality despite the diversity of formats and platforms used. On the positive side, humour was found to serve as an important coping mechanism for alleviating distress caused by quarantine, travel restrictions, the negative effects of social distancing, shortages in shops and, of course, death anxiety. Humour mitigated anxiety and fear and aided psychological well-being in the creators of the humour as well as in the beneficiaries, who enthusiastically shared humorous content they received or encountered. Despite the diversity of the studies surveyed, including their methodologies, their results are especially noteworthy in their consistency across all the world's continents. Not knowing whether the world was about to end, the world laughed at much the same material.

Which begs the question: are the perceived differences in sense of humour enjoyed by women and men mere myths? Can we perceive differences in attitudes towards humour between cultures? And how does having a neurological difference affect someone's sense of humour?

Gender differences

It is interesting – possibly even amusing – to look back from this twenty-first-century vantage point at the early days of research into the differences that were hypothesised between humour as understood and used by men and women.

In a study carried out by Alice Heim (1936), a specialist in intelligence research with the British Psychological Society, 50 English-speaking female and male students from the United Kingdom, United States, Germany, France, Italy, India and Japan (including one described as a communist) were presented with 32 jokes, of which three were controls (i.e. not intended to be

DOI: 10.4324/9781003638773-5

funny) and asked to rate the jokes' funniness. A mixture of written and "pictorial" jokes was used, with some of the material originating outside the UK and/or translated from another language. The responses of the participants to the material, as well as their ability to remember the jokes, were observed.

The research's conclusions are tentative, but noteworthy. None of the jokes was considered funny by everyone, but a few respondents laughed at the non-jokes. Every joke was considered not funny by at least three respondents, though they generally could not explain why they found a joke funny or not funny. Men and women usually found the same things amusing or not amusing. However, in response to one of the jokes, "several men said 'this does not appeal to me, but it would probably appeal to women'; several women said of the same joke 'I don't find this funny, but I expect it would appeal to a man'". In fact, few men or women found this particular joke amusing.

Another study, carried out by Carney Landis and John Ross in the United States, recruited 278 male psychology undergraduates and 112 "incorrigible or delinquent girls under 21 years of age" at a state institution (1933) to assess 100 jokes. The participants' personalities and intelligence were also assessed with the aim of discovering how they influenced humour appreciation and comprehension.

The results reveal some of the challenges of attempting a quantitative study of what is a complex and highly subjective phenomenon. Landis and Ross believed they found a significant difference between how the male and female participants evaluated the "quality" of the jokes. The two jokes rated highest by the male students were:

> "You should be more careful to pull the shades down at night. Last night I saw you kissing your wife." "Ha, ha, ha! The joke is on you. I wasn't home last night."

And:

> The attorney for an electric light company was making a popular address. "Think of the good this company has done!" he cried. "If I were permitted a pun, I would say in the words of the immortal poet — 'Honor the Light Brigade.'"
>
> Voice of the consumer from the audience: "O, what a charge they made."

These contrast, perhaps, with the joke favoured among the incorrigibles:

> An elderly farmer drove into town one day and hitched his team to a telegraph post. "Here," exclaimed a burly policeman, "you can't hitch there."
>
> "Can't eh?" shouted the irate farmer. Well why have you got a sign up, 'Fine for hitching?'

The researchers also highlight significant differences between how the male and female participants categorised the jokes according to the type of humour they expressed, with the females often incorrectly categorising them. The lack of comprehension was ascribed to the fact that men had compiled the jokes and that, had they been compiled by women, the results would have been different. It does not seem to have occurred to the researchers that other differences between the two groups might have come into play, not least their social standings and their education levels. Or, perhaps, they had simply assumed that the incorrigibles were less intelligent by virtue of their having been institutionalised.

The celebrated psychologist Hans Eysenck, whose academic interests included genetics, intelligence, personality and race, followed up on the research by Landis and Ross with a UK-based study in 1942. With just 16 participants, the study was smaller in scope than Landis and Ross's experiment (there was, after all, a war on), but the population was somewhat more representative, comprising equal numbers of university students and non-academics and men and women, aged between 17 and 35. As with the previous surveys, participants were tasked with assessing the same jokes as in the Landis and Ross study, along with cartoons and other graphic humour, the latter items hand-picked by Eysenck from publications as diverse as the satirical *Punch* and the pin-up magazine *Razzle*. Also included were a number of controls, or "jokers". Eysenck's findings correlated with Heim's regarding the similarity between the genders in their tastes for humour. He also considered personality traits, reporting that extroverts tended to prefer "simple" jokes (as well as jokes containing sexual content) compared with introverts, who preferred theirs to be "complex" and non-sexual. Mercifully for the introverted among us, he found that:

> the assertion often made which attributes a better sense of humour to the extraverts than to the introverts is wrong, and that we are dealing rather with differences in the manner of appreciating humour than with differences in the amount of sense of humour possessed by the two types.
>
> (1942)

Men create it more, and women enjoy it more

Not my words, but a quotation from Auner Ziv, a professor at Tel Aviv University, from 1984, based on the entirely scientific observation that "women are scarce among professional humorists". And if you thought this kind of trope was confined to the history dustbin of the twentieth century, ask yourself this: are women funny? I know the answer to this question. More importantly, my wife knows the answer to this. So, it was inevitable, perhaps, that the article "Why women aren't funny", written by the journalist Christopher Hitchens and published in 2007 in the leisure and current affairs magazine *Vanity Fair*, attracted much (and no doubt much hoped-for) public opprobrium.

The article eschews sharing any evidence to support claims such as, "As every father knows, the placenta is made up of brain cells, which migrate southward during pregnancy and take the sense of humor along with them." Instead, Hitchens offers a perfunctory review of the Rudyard Kipling's 1911 poem "The female of the species" and a derisory reference to the only "decent joke about the death of an infant", made by the "queer" Oscar Wilde.

A more informed – and more informative – approach to the question is offered by the research carried out by Mary Crawford at the University of Connecticut. She has questioned whether the academic and non-academic foraging for inter-gender differences misses the bigger picture:

> It encourages us to think of women and men as opposites, when there is much more gender similarity than difference. When researchers choose to focus on the differences, they are making a value judgment about what is important. Even when a reliable difference is found, we know little about its causes. Despite the most careful matching of samples, women and men who are in "identical" situations may be functioning in different social worlds because of others' social reactions to them as women or men.
>
> (2003)

She has also highlighted misconceptions about the kind of language used by the two genders and how they reflect a paradigm of essential difference between them, including, for example, the belief that women lack a sense of humour and are more affiliative, resulting in humour used by women (with other women) to build solidarity and intimacy, while men use humour to compete with each other for status. These myths are debunked by a study in New Zealand by Jennifer Hay, which found that men also used humour to create solidarity, for example, in stories about their shared experiences. Most striking perhaps is the emergence of "feminist humor", which Crawford portrays as having formed a distinctive identity. Today, identity politics shapes a great deal of public discourse, and feminism – now in its "third wave" – is just one of many identities formed to fight social injustice. In the early days of the feminist movement, however, when resistance to change was perhaps greatest, humour was used to get the message out. That humour was often irreverent: a feminist aphorism from the 1970s, cited by Crawford, read, "A woman without a man is like a fish without a bicycle" (though, interestingly, not originally a feminist slogan). The movement also saw aggressive humour, a style of humour favoured – according to many psychologists – by men rather than women. A bestselling book by Regina Barreca (1992), *They used to call me Snow White… but I drifted: Women's strategic use of humor*, reviewed by the Chicago Tribune as "An impassioned, wily and often hilarious argument for women to unleash their sense of humor on the world" and boasted chapters titled, "How many feminists does it to take to change a light bulb?" and "She who laughs, lasts". The book's cover reads "A guide for any woman who wants to respond forcefully yet appropriately to a boor's come-on or a boss's put-down".

Children's humour

A child's humour development is argued to go through five distinct stages (Honig, 1988; Loevinger, 1976; McGhee, 1979; Piaget, 1963; Tamashiro, 1979). In the first year or so, while the baby is ascertaining a sense of itself, the humour is primarily non-verbal: tickling, wriggling and smiling. In the next stage, the child is predominantly concerned with acquiring basic language and physical coordination and mastering its bodily functions. Those bodily functions are often a source of hilarity, as are slapstick humour, nonsensical expressions and singing. At the toddler stage, when children become capable of forethought, delay of gratification, and they establish and defend the ego boundary, humour begins to include practical jokes, as well as insults and put-downs. By the time children are attending pre-school, kindergarten and the like, the distinctions between different social groups – predominantly family and peers – become apparent to the child. Social acceptance and belonging become important, as does pleasing others. The humour evolves to include jokes and riddles, word plays, but also ridicule of "undesirables", which can cross over to bullying behaviour – probably not the most appropriate stage, then, to be letting them loose with smartphones. In their review of media entertainment designed for 10- to 14-year-olds, Amber van der Wal et al. (2020) found that aggressive humour featured most frequently. Coping and self-defeating humour were least prevalent, which the researchers argued reflected the stage of this age group's psychological development. A poignant recollection is told by Najla Said, actress, playwright and daughter of the famous intellectual and outspoken Palestinian advocate Edward Said, in her candid memoir, *Looking for Palestine*. Her younger brother, Wadie, is trying to impress their father by correcting Najla's rendition of a Christmas carol she is singing:

> "Noel, Noel, Noel, Noel, born is the *kiiiing* of *Iiiiis*–"
> My pleasure was abruptly cut short by a swift smack on the arm.
> "*Owww– Wad-ee– uh–* why'd you *hit* meeeeeee?"
> "*Naj*, you're *supposed* to say '*Occupied Palestine*'!!!"
>
> (2013, emphasis in original)

The fifth and final stage of development commences around later adolescence, when self-selected standards and values acquire greater importance than group norms. Children also gain a comprehension of their impact on others. Humour that the child itself invents comes to the fore, and it can be good-natured, tongue-in-cheek and satirical.

At which point then, do boys' and girls' humour diverge, if at all? It seems that differences begin to appear once children leave the home and socialise with other children. This is when they form groups, begin competing with others and form a sense of group identity. Boys were found to be more aggressive, to show off with clowning and slapstick humour and, later, indulge in sexual jokes (Honig, 1988). Other influences also come into play, including traditional gender modelling: girls behaving with greater passivity and self-control, boys encouraged towards dominance.

Pause for thought

What is your experience of humour in childhood (either as a child or a parent)?
Were you forever playing practical jokes on other people?
What cartoons did you (do you!) enjoy most? Perhaps more revealingly, which did you like least?

Global humour?

How global is humour? The comic antics of Charlie Chaplin, Marcel Marceau, Mr Bean, Jacques Tati and even Benny Hill are enjoyed the world over. The meme is a concept coined way back in 1976 by evolutionary biologist Richard Dawkins to represent a unit of cultural information that spreads from person to person through imitation, "Just as genes propagate themselves in the gene pool by leaping from body to body via sperms or eggs" (2006). An example of this, in Figure 3.1, is Kilroy, a graffito which became popular with American troops during the Second World War. Today, memes take the form of images, videos and texts – usually humorous in intent – and are shared on the internet, capable of reaching millions and adapted so that they evolve as they spread through online communities. Much like natural selection, the humorous and relatable memes get shared the most; they "go viral", while unsuccessful ones fade away. And Shakespeare's comedies have been translated into most of the

Figure 3.1 An example of an analogue meme.

languages on the planet, including Esperanto, Latin and, venturing where no man has gone before, even include a "Klingon restoration" of *Much Ado About Nothing* (2001).

Of course, the humorous atlas is much like the physical one: land masses marooned on drifting tectonic plates, causing ruptures when they collide, separated by fathomless oceans and divided into cultures defined by the mountains, rivers and other borders that separate them.

While humour is generally considered a positive trait in "Western" societies, such that humorous people are considered more attractive, creative and well-adjusted, attitudes in China are more ambivalent (Jiang et al., 2019). Studies suggest that Chinese people might consider humour important but tend not to consider themselves humorous, or that humour is necessarily a desirable personality trait. Tonglin Jiang et al. point towards a tension between two dominant Chinese philosophies: Confucianism, which devalues and denigrates humour; and Taoism, which equates wit with peacefulness and harmony with nature. Further differences emerge when the use of humour in different societies is compared. For example, using humour as a coping mechanism was observed to be more prevalent in the United States and Canada than in China, Japan and Singapore. Using the Humor Styles Questionnaire (HSQ) (Martin et al., 2003) discussed in Chapter 2, comparisons of humour styles indicated that maladaptive humour usage was more prevalent among "Westerners" and adaptive humour usage was more prevalent among "Easterners". Intra-regional differences were also observed: "Hong Kong students reported more use of aggressive and self-defeating humor and less use of affiliative and self-enhancing humor than mainland Chinese students" (Jiang et al., 2019), which is ascribed to the former colony's bicultural history. Comparing humour usage in the United States, Lebanon and Egypt, Morris Kalliny et al. (2006) found that Americans use significantly more self-defeating and self-enhancing humour than Lebanese and Egyptians, while there was no significant difference in the use of affiliative and aggressive humour. They suggest that the hierarchical and collectivistic cultures prevalent in Lebanon and Egypt could explain the lower usage of self-defeating and self-enhancing humour.

Research by Guo-Hai Chen and Rod Martin into how Canadian and Chinese students used humour using the Coping Humor Scale (Martin & Lefcourt, 1983) indicated that the latter group was less likely to use aggressive humour as a coping mechanism (Chen & Martin, 2007). A possible explanation for this was that because "North American jokes are sexual and aggressive, Chinese jokes deal more with social interaction", and that "Chinese are generally less aggressive than Canadians on average".

Interpreting the results in studies such as these is far from straightforward. Chen and Martin noted that one of the questions in the HSQ was open to interpretation:

> If I am having problems or feeling unhappy, I often cover it up by joking around, so that even my closest friends don't know how I really feel.

A positive response to this question might be considered self-defeating in Canada but self-enhancing in China, where "mien-tsu" – face – is an important facilitator of social interactions.

The two studies by Jiang, Kalliny and their colleagues both mention that the men in their samples used aggressive humour more than the women. Chen and Martin also looked into coping humour (i.e. humour used as a coping mechanism) differences between the genders, finding no significant difference between Canadian men and women, but the Chinese women tended much more than men to use humour in a self-deprecating way to please others and maintain group cohesion.

Figure 3.2 Contextuality of a joke.

Pause for thought

Humour is often dependent on a number of different contexts at the same time. Take, for example, the cartoon in Figure 3.2. To get the joke, one must be able to identify the Dutch painter Van Gogh's self-portrait (which *some* might consider "famous") and be aware that the artist (sort of) cut off his right earlobe. One must also be aware of the use of medical facemasks during the Covid-19 pandemic. Of course, Van Gogh didn't live through Covid-19, so this is fictional, and we have to imagine what he might think about facemasks if he did. And if we understand Dutch, we will understand the disgruntled thought going through his mind, but if we don't, we can hazard a reasonable guess as to his state of mind.

A common feature of all of these studies is that they draw their conclusions from a sample population made up entirely of students at universities and colleges. Although this practice might seem odd to a non-academic, it is not unusual, and one does wonder if psychology researchers should get out more.

A different perspective comes to us from the Indian subcontinent. Humaira Jehangir and Musarrat Azher in Pakistan recently reported gender differences in their review of satirical cartoons published online in Pakistan and India (2025). These cartoons were produced by both men and women and generally critiqued various social and political issues. The differences apparently arise in the styles of humour used, such that "Female cartoonists use bright, emotive styles to point out the ridiculousness of how society expects you to be". Male cartoonists, on the other hand, tended to use dialogue which directly challenged the system. What unites these cartoonists is their aim of challenging "the objectification and oppression of women while drawing attention to societal expectations of gender roles".

Humour, of course, is only one tool in the fight for justice and sadly not sufficient to protect women such as the young (unnamed) doctor raped and murdered at a medical college and hospital in Kolkata in 2024, which led to thousands of angry women taking to the streets on Independence Day singing the national anthem in protest (Telegraph India, 15 August 2024). The case was brutal, but not unusual: In 2022, the Indian National Crime Records Bureau reported an average of 86 rape cases every day, and a total of 2,118 gang rapes (2022), these being the assaults actually reported. This despite initiatives such as the satirical video "*It's your fault*" by the comedy group All India Bakchod, featuring well-known actress Kalki Koechnlin and TV presenter Juhi Pandey. Styled as a public education film, the video opens with an actress stating:

> Ladies, do you think rape is something men do out of a desire for control empowered by years of patriarchy? You've clearly been misled by the notion that women are people too, because, let's face it, ladies, rape, it's your fault.

The anger is evident in the vitriol of the sarcasm. Viewers are *advised* that. "If you're tired of being humiliated by rape you can always go to the cops and be humiliated by them instead", and "Fun fact: If he is your husband, it's not rape". To date, the video, posted on AIB's YouTube channel in 2013, has been viewed around eight million times; it even has its own Wikipedia page.

By contrast, the deleterious power of humour is revealed in research into jokes made about women by Romanian men. As discussed in Chapter 1, humour can mask the lowering of inhibitions around talking about certain topics, for example, race or, indeed, gender. Iulian Apostu and Bianca Surdu found that jokes covertly reinforced the legitimacy of sexist views: "they rely on the innocence of the jokes and on the idea that their purpose is merely to entertain society" (2025). The perpetuation of sexual stereotypes succeeds, Apostu and Surdu find, because the humour insulates them from challenge: literally, *it's just a joke, no need to make a fuss, dear*. The humour also defends men's own status, which the researchers conclude is a greater motivation for their use than amusement alone.

Reflection

The very real intersectional distinctions in humour appreciation that are touched on here do not detract from the fact that humour is entirely individual. I recall a performance of one of the Shakespearean comedies I saw many years ago in what was then West Germany. The actors played it straight. Deadpan. The experience was comical for all the wrong reasons, and of course, it reinforced the stereotypical view (in Britain) of the Germans having no sense of humour. Yet, I also have German friends who are huge Monty Python fans; one of them does a hilarious impression of John Cleese's man from the Ministry of Funny Walks (Monty Python, 1970). When I look back on such experiences, my sense is that we meet each other, first and foremost, as individuals.

Humour difference disorder

The studies we've reviewed so far have concentrated on humour appreciation and creation differentiated by age, gender and culture. But one section of society that is rarely considered and which can tell us a great deal about the essence of humour – of what it is that makes us laugh and smile – comprises folks we refer to as *neurodivergent*. A term that is arguably more euphemistic than it is inclusive, *neurodiversity* recognises that there exists a range of cognitive and neurological conditions that *diverge* from what we understand as *normal*.

Reflection

When it comes to humour, the irony is that people tend to assume people with ASD and/or ADHD have the same issues with humour, that is, that they suffer from a *humour deficit*. Which, of course, assumes also that those from the *neuronormative* side of town all have a sense of humour. Unless they're women. Or German. Or those people in uniform at JFK and Heathrow who regard with such obvious distate your attempt to enter their countries.

The term *autism* was first used by Swiss psychiatrist and eugenicist Paul Bleuler in 1911 to describe a form of childhood schizophrenia. Curiously, the term described much the opposite of how we understand autism today: extreme fantasising and hallucinations, which infants contrived to block out unattractive realities (Evans, 2013). Of course, the condition did not appear overnight: documentation of the symptoms – varied though they are – dates back centuries.

A related condition, Asperger's syndrome, identified by the Viennese paediatric psychiatrist Hans (Johann) Asperger in the 1940s but not coined as such until 1976 by the British psychiatrist Lorna Wing, described children with an incredibly wide range of differences in intellect, thinking and temperament:

> The range encompasses all levels of ability from the highly original genius, through the weird eccentric who lives in a world of his own and achieves very little, down to the most severe contact-disturbed, automaton-like mentally retarded individual.
>
> (Asperger, 1991)

Not until the 1970s did schizophrenia and autism come to be considered different conditions, with Asperger's syndrome and childhood autism brought under the same label – autism spectrum disorder (ASD) – in 2013. In the United Kingdom, 1 to 2% of the population is believed to be autistic (according to autistica.org.uk), presenting any of various characteristics, including strong preferences for routine, anxiety when confronted with change or uncertainty, different levels of sensory intensity, an intense focus on certain topics and differences in, and challenges with, communication. Some people with autism have support needs and may "stim" to help with feelings of anxiety or to express emotions (from "self-stimulation", examples of which include rocking, flapping hands and jumping).

For many years, people with ASD were considered to be humourless. Hans Asperger (1991) perhaps contributed to this perception:

> Another characteristic of autistic children is *the absence of a sense of humour*. They do not 'understand jokes', especially if the joke is on them. This is another reason for their often being the butt of teasing: if one can laugh at oneself, one can take the edge off ridicule. However, autistic children are rarely relaxed and carefree and never achieve that particular wisdom and deep intuitive human understanding *that underlie genuine humour*.
>
> (emphasis in original)

Research evidence published since the turn of the century presents a clearer view: that the humour of people with ASD is in some ways *different* rather than in some way *defective* or *absent*. This picture was recognised even by Asperger, who acknowledged that autistic children had a sense of fun, albeit "unpleasant... exaggerated and immoderate. They jump around the room, infringe other people's space, are aggressive and annoying" (Asperger, 1991). Much like any and every child, perhaps. "When making puns, however, autistic people sometimes shine, and may even be highly creative. This can range from simple word-play and sound associations to precisely formulated, truly witty remarks".

In-depth research carried out in Sweden by Hanna Bertilsdotter Rosqvist used interviews with people with Asperger's to identify three forms of expression of humour they favoured. Surprisingly perhaps, there are distinct echoes with Asperger's findings. Firstly, they enjoyed "plays on words" and "weird puns", which were described by participants as "typical Asperger humour" (2012). Secondly, they allowed themselves to release the inner child, for example, by "doing 'fun' things... viewed as contrary to norms of adulthood, such as swinging on a swing, playing hopscotch, not stepping on lines, skipping, and balancing" and taking simple pleasures in the minutiae of the world around them. These preferences were also observed in studies in other countries, in Taiwan, Ireland, Germany as well as the United Kingdom, which Shaun May (see below) suggests indicates a degree of cross-cultural homogeneity.

More surprising, perhaps, is the third category of humour identified by Bertilsdotter Rosqvist, namely black humour. This was described by participants as a form of self-acceptance when used among other people with Asperger's, as observed by Johanna:

> ...it's pretty nice here to sort of be able to joke about with each other about their problems and so on. And I also think, like you [Mikael], that it's a really good way of playing it down, joking about your problems.
>
> (2012)

In one respect, this black humour might be viewed as comforting, possibly even confirmatory. But the participants in Bertilsdotter Rosqvist's study also viewed the humour as grounded in a kind of bitterness at the burden of being in a minority, having to reach out to neurotypical people and educate them. Described by one of the participants as "deformity comedy", this humour is disabling, and often angry, an attitude confirmed by Alex, an autistic adult quoted on the Autistica website:

> Many traits associated with autism are characteristics that most people exhibit to a greater or lesser extent but it's their intensity and impact that makes someone autistic. It frustrates me when neurotypical people say, 'We're all a little bit autistic, aren't we?' It's like saying we're all a little bit pregnant. Just like pregnancy, autism is a clear medical diagnosis – you either are or you aren't; there's no halfway house, no grey areas.
>
> (autistica.org.uk, 2025)

In the United Kingdom, a pilot project by Shaun May at the University of Kent's School of Arts (2017) took the debunking of the "humour deficit" model myth further by undertaking a series of comedy workshops with young adults, five of whom were diagnosed with ASD and a further four who did not. The workshops focused on the production of humour and explored stand-up comedy and clowning. May reviews three traits typically ascribed to people with autism: inflexibility, taking things literally and social anxiety (a "hallmark" of the condition according to the American Psychiatric Association (2013)). May reframes these traits as differences rather than deficits, for example, when an autistic artist "depicts a robbery and plays with the phrase 'this is a stick up', which is shown literally with a character holding a stick in the air" (2017).

The findings of a recent similar research project undertaken by Nathan Keates add further weight to May's arguments. Keates recruited eight male, five female and four non-binary autistic adults between the ages of 25 and 56 years from five different countries to take part in an online four-week improv course. "Improv" – short for improvisational comedy – requires performers to spontaneously create comedy in front of a live audience, often in collaboration with other performers. Thus, a high degree of "meta-communication" (e.g. being able to perceive and respond to cues) is demanded, as well as creativity.

In post-training session debriefs, participants expressed feeling gains in mental health, specifically emotional wellbeing, contentment, self-concept and decreased stress. Participants also reported feeling accepted by other autistic people in an environment that held an autotelic purpose rather than a support group, summed up by one member as being "inclusive by being exclusive" (2025). Another member suggested that neurotypical people should join people with autism because they have more fun, "… the things I laugh at, and my world is amazing, except we've gotta go into your [neurotypical] world". Participants' improved sense of self-determination empowered them to acquire skills they could use in other aspects of their lives. This might perhaps represent the most significant benefit, given that participants were unlikely to go on to become professional improv performers. It also highlights the challenge of having to live, work and interact with neurotypical people in an environment that to a great degree does not accommodate neurodivergence. Although adamant that they did not value neurotypical "social skills training", the participants nonetheless found it beneficial to gain insight into how autistic people are perceived by others, and valued improved communication skills, which could help them "in the *obligatory* conversations that they have at work or in their personal lives" (my emphasis). Furthermore, they recognised that spontaneity was not an attribute found in some autistic people and that improv helped them "go with the flow", as well as working on a fear of failure – something that arguably most people would benefit from.

A common theme in these studies is the participants' anger at the barriers to opportunities not experienced by neurotypical people. In 2025, the Ugly Bucket Theatre Company and arts charity Random Acts of Wildness Disability (RAWD) combined to stage a new play, *Don't Call Us, We'll Call You*. Inspired by the 1990s' "Piss on Pity" block telethon protests against the demeaning portrayal of disabled people, the show confronts the audience with a Molotov cocktail of deafening satire and hilariously rebellious clowning. The play's cast comprised 35 disabled performers living with a number of different conditions. The show was performed against a backdrop of continued cuts in state-funded social support for the disabled, and it is important, Artistic Director Grace Gallagher told me, that their voices are heard: "When people are laughing, they're listening".

Attention deficit hyperactivity disorder (ADHD) is estimated by the UK National Institute for Health and Care Excellence to affect 3% to 4% of adults in the United Kingdom and 5% of children worldwide (NICE, 2025). Symptoms comprise an inability to maintain attention, persistence and focus for a reasonable period of time and/or hyperactive and impulsive behaviour. They are considered to manifest themselves in childhood and interfere with the individual's day-to-day functioning and/or development.

As with autism, the causes of ADHD are as yet unknown, and there are no "cures"; and there is a long history of individuals with ADHD having been treated as somehow behaviourally and socially deficient: forgetful ("scatter-brained!"), for example, unable to focus or to see tasks through to completion. This stigmatising continues to a great extent, exacerbated in the United Kingdom by a lack of mental health service resources allocated to it. As a consequence, adults especially find themselves left with no alternative but to self-diagnose. One of the "tools" being employed is the video-sharing platform TikTok. Reporting in 2024, Abigail Leveille noted that *#adhd* was the seventh most popular health-related hashtag on the platform but that at the same time the overwhelming majority of videos were created by "non-health care providers". And while (at the time of writing) UK-based visitors to TikTok are signposted to the information service provided by the NHS, medical researchers found that around half the videos posted on the platform were factually misleading.

With respect to both ASD and ADHD, humour is cited as a form of coping mechanism. Leveille highlights that much of the TikTok video content used humour – predominantly self-defeating and coping humour. Through revealing the often-hidden struggles of people with ADHD, the humour debunks prevailing medical and wider public misconceptions; the content also fosters "a sense of connection among viewers who share similar experiences" (2024). Leveille draws parallels with a study of autistic Twitter users by Justine Egner in 2022, who found:

> Most narratives and media representations about living life as an autistic person are oversimplified, highly medicalized, rely on stereotypical depictions, and present autism as a series of deficits. Autistic people are thus using Twitter to try to make meaning of their experiences that are not represented within these very medicalized notions of what it means to be autistic by establishing virtual learning communities.

Leveille warns that the self-advocacy championed in social media can dilute the importance of obtaining a formal ADHD diagnosis, which can be arduous and expensive. However, the accessibility of the content – aided no doubt by the use of humour – provides relief to the many people who have not been able to get help, or to obtain any educational information at all.

Another feature of the humour in these videos – as well as the tweets posted by people with ASD – is the countering of these conditions as defects and the people living with them as defective with alternative, attractive and affirmative conceptions of people who are simply different. This was confirmed by a study in Switzerland among outpatients with ADHD (Canela et al., 2017), who were striving to reconceptualise their coping mechanisms. For them, their sense of humour was part of what made them fun to be with. Jane Sedgwick et al. (2019) similarly found in the United Kingdom that the people with ADHD they surveyed said that of all the things they would miss if their condition went away, their sense of humour would be the thing they missed the most.

Reflection

In these explorations, I have resisted reciting or recycling some of the tropes about neurodivergents' relations with humour, but not out of well-meaningness or what some people might describe as "wokeness". Before setting out with this book, a couple of friends and colleagues asked me what I was going to say with respect to people with neurodivergence. I really didn't know. I spoke at some length with Jo, a student friend who lives with both ASD and ADHD, and she told me that she struggled with non-literal humour such as metaphors and sarcasm, which could perhaps be ascribed to her autistic side. She also said she was very empathic (which I knew already), and that this was an ADHD trait (which I didn't know). She laughed her head off at TikTok videos as well.

Was that her ADHD or her ASD?

Summing up

Research into the differences in humour preference among *men and women* carried out since the 1930s suggests some differences, but other social influences cannot be eliminated. *Children's humour* evolves with their powers of perception and increasing socialisation. *Westerners* are found to use humour more aggressively than their counterparts in the *Middle East and Asia. Neurodivergent people* possess divergent types of humour.

References

Alkaraki, S. M. S., Alias, N. B., & Maros, M. (2024). Exploring the impact of social media humor related to the COVID-19 pandemic: A systematic literature review on themes, coping mechanisms, critiques and linguistic devices. *Cogent Arts & Humanities*, *11*(1), 2322227. https://doi.org/10.1080/23311983.2024.2322227

All India Bakchod (2013). *It's your fault*. Video clip, YouTube. https://www.youtube.com/watch?v=8hC0Ng_ajpY&t=8s

American Psychiatric Association (2013). *The diagnostic and statistical manual of mental disorders (DSM-5)* (5th ed.). American Psychiatric Association.

Apostu, I., & Surdu, B. (2025). The image of the woman in Romanian jokes. *Journal of Social Sciences and Innovation*, *1*(1). https://epejournals.com/index.php/jssr/article/view/26

Asperger, H. (1991). Autistic psychopathy in childhood. In I. H. Asperger & U. Frich (Eds.), *Autism and Asperger syndrome* (pp. 371–392). Cambridge University Press.

Barreca, R. (1992). *They used to call me snow white… but I drifted: Women's strategic use of humor*. Penguin.

Bertilsdotter Rosqvist, H. (2012). The politics of joking: Narratives of humour and joking among adults with Asperger's syndrome. *Disability & Society*, *27*(2), 235–247. https://doi.org/10.1080/09687599.2011.644933

Canela, C., Buadze, A., Dube, A., Eich, D., & Liebrenz, M. (2017). Skills and compensation strategies in adult ADHD – A qualitative study. *PLoS One*, *12*(9), e0184964. https://doi.org/10.1371/journal.pone.0184964

Chen, G.-H., & Martin, R. A. (2007). A comparison of humor styles, coping humor, and mental health between Chinese and Canadian university students. *Humor International Journal of Humor Research*, *20*(3), 215–234. https://doi.org/10.1515/HUMOR.2007.011

Crawford, M. (2003). Gender and humor in social context. *Journal of Pragmatics*, *35*(9), 1413–1430. https://doi.org/10.1016/S0378-2166(02)00183-2

Dawkins, R. (2006). *The selfish gene* (3rd ed.). Oxford University Press.

Evans, B. (2013). How autism became autism: The radical transformation of a central concept of child development in Britain. *History of the Human Sciences*, *26*(3), 3–31. https://doi.org/10.1177/0952695113484320

Eysenck, H. J. (1942). The appreciation of humour: An experimental and theoretical study. *British Journal of Psychology*, *32*(4), 295–309. https://doi.org/10.1111/j.2044-8295.1942.tb01027.x

Heim, A. (1936). An experiment on humour. *British Journal of Psychology*, *27*(2), 148–161. https://doi.org/10.1111/j.2044-8295.1936.tb00826.x

Hitchens, C. (2007) Why women aren't funny. *Vanity Fair*, January 1.

Honig, A. S. (1988). Humor development in children. *Young Children*, *43*(4), 60–73. https://www.jstor.org/stable/42726102

Jehangir, H. & Azher, M. (2025). Representation of south Asian women in online cartoons: Unfunny realities, *Pakistan Journal of Gender Studies*, *25*(1), 55–78. https://www.socialsciencejournals.pjgs-ws.com/index.php/PJGS/article/view/805

Jiang, T., Li, H., & Hou, Y. (2019). Cultural differences in humor perception, usage and implications. *Frontiers in Psychology*, *10*, 123. https://doi.org/10.3389/fpsyg.2019.00123

Kalliny, M., Cruthirds, K. W., & Minor, M. S. (2006). Differences between American, Egyptian and Lebanese humor styles: Implications for international management. *International Journal of Cross Cultural Management*, *6*(1), 121–134. https://doi.org/10.1177/1470595806062354

Keates, N. (2025). The experience of participating in improv comedy for autistic adults. *Neurodiversity*, *3*. https://doi.org/10.1177/27546330251323154

Landis, C., & Ross, J. W. H. (1933). Humor and its relation to other personality traits. *The Journal of Social Psychology*, *4*(2), 156–175. https://doi.org/10.1080/00224545.1933.9921567

Leveille, A. D. (2024). "Tell me you have ADHD without telling me you have ADHD": Neurodivergent identity performance on TikTok. *Social Media + Society*, *2024*, 1–9. https://doi.org/10.1177/20563051241269260

Loevinger, J. (1976). *Ego development*. Jossey-Bass.

Martin, R. A. & Lefcourt, H. M. (1983). Sense of humor as a moderator of the relation between stressors and moods. *Journal of Personality and Social Psychology*, *45*(*6*), 1313–1324. https://doi.org/10.1037/0022-3514.45.6.1313

Martin, R. A., Puhlik-Doris, P., Larsen, G., Gray, J. & Weir, K. (2003). Individual differences in uses of humor and their relation to psychological well-being: Development of the Humor Styles Questionnaire. *Journal of Research in Personality*, *37*(*1*), 48–75. https://doi.org/10.1016/S0092-6566(02)00534-2

May, S. (2017). Autism and comedy: Using theatre workshops to explore humour with adolescents on the spectrum. *Research in Drama Education*, *22*(3), 436–445. https://doi.org/10.1080/13569783.2017.1329651

McGhee, P. E. (1979). *Humor: Its origin and development*. W. H. Freeman.

National Crime Records Bureau. (2022). *Crime in India 2022: Statistics Vol. 1*.

NICE (National Institute for Health and Care Excellence) (revised February 2025). Attention deficit hyperactivity disorder: How common is it? Clinical knowledge summaries. https://cks.nice.org.uk/topics/attention-deficit-hyperactivity-disorder/background-information/prevalence/
Piaget, J. (1963). *The psychology of intelligence*. Adams.
Said, N. (2013). *Looking for Palestine: Growing up confused in an Arab-American family*. Riverhead Books.
Sedgwick, J. A., Merwood, A., & Asherson, P. (2019). The positive aspects of attention deficit hyperactivity disorder: A qualitative investigation of successful adults with ADHD. *Attention Deficit and Hyperactivity Disorders*, *11*(3), 241–253. https://doi.org/10.1007/s12402-018-0277-6
Shakespeare, W. (2001). *Much ado about nothing: The restored Klingon text*. Trans. N. Nicholas). Klingon Language Institute Press.
Tamashiro, R. T. (1979). Children's humor: A developmental view. *The Elementary School Journal*, *80*(2), 68–75. https://doi.org/10.1086/461174
van der Wal, A., Piotrowski, J. T., Fikkers, K. M., & Valkenburg, P. M. (2020). More than just a laughing matter: A coding framework of humor in media entertainment for tweens and teens. *Journal of Broadcasting & Electronic Media*, *64*(3), 478–498. https://doi.org/10.1080/08838151.2020.1796389
Ziv, A. (1984). *Personality and sense of humor*. Springer Verlag.

Part II

Better than an apple a day?

Can humour be therapeutic?

Chapter 4

Models of therapeutic humour

Introduction

In Part I, we definitively answered the age-old question of what humour is. We also examined the work of pioneering psychologists exploring how humour affects our emotions and behaviour.

We now turn our gaze to the therapy space, to approaches to humour that have (or claim to have) the power to heal: *therapeutic humour*.

Two distinct themes emerge. Firstly, what do we mean by humour having therapeutic power? How is it defined? And is it the same as watching a sitcom or visiting a comedy club? Secondly, we see how models of humour are applied in therapeutic relationships generally and also in specialist settings.

The distinction between models of therapeutic humour and humour-based therapies – which are reviewed in Chapter 5, is not always obvious. Here, we are concerned with the concept that humour can be intended to have a therapeutic impact on the client.

What is therapeutic humour?

According to the dictionary, a thing is therapeutic if it has a healing effect. We might call to mind therapeutic massages, for example, which address specific health problems to improve physical function and reduce pain. A quick search on Google offers up therapeutic pads, blankets, books, apps, journeys, light-therapy lamps, even a weighted vest, and many, many lotions and oils. But not humour.

An early description of how therapeutic humour might appear came from American psychologist Harvey Mindess:

> Deep, genuine humor – the humor that deserves to be called therapeutic, that can be instrumental in our lives – extends beyond jokes, beyond wit, beyond laughter itself to a peculiar frame of mind. It is an inner condition, a stance, a point of view, or in the largest sense an attitude to life.
>
> (1971) [cited in Franzini, 2001]

DOI: 10.4324/9781003638773-7

He later writes (1976) that the therapist having a humorous outlook and an awareness of life's absurdities and creating a space for humour in the therapy room can facilitate therapeutic change.

Pause for thought

We might assume that *therapeutic humour* is like an apple a day: *good for us*. But can we be so emphatic?

The apple might be sour, or you might discover a worm has taken up residence.

And some people just don't like apples.

Another depiction of the kind of humour that possesses therapeutic potential comes from the *Handbook of Humor and Psychotherapy*:

> constructive, empathic humor, which is totally unrelated to sarcasm, racist or sexist humor, deformations, put-downs and other abuses of humor.
>
> (Fry & Salameh, 1987)

This description better conveys what William Fry and Waleed Salameh considered therapeutic humour *is not* rather more than what it *is*. We will review some of the humour-based therapies promoted by the *Handbook's* contributors in Chapter 5, but what does seem clear is that the kind of humour envisaged here should be only beneficial and in no way detrimental to the client or, indeed, to anyone.

Bernard Saper at Florida International University, USA, describes therapeutic humour in a roundabout way, using algebra to formulate the therapeutic process (see Figure 4.1).

The formula describes: *C* – change, cure or outcome (desirable or undesirable) as being the product of:

- the therapist, *T*,
- the client, *Cl*,

$$C = (T_{123}\ r\ Cl_{123}\ x)E$$

(Saper, 1987)

Figure 4.1 Therapeutic humour formulated.

- the relationship, *r*, and
- *x*, "numerous happenings, variations in settings and paraphernalia within the session that importantly influence the course of therapy but about which therapists have very little, if any, dependable research or experiential knowledge"

(1987)

All of this is subject to the influence of external environmental factors, *E*. The components *T* and *Cl* are overlaid by: (1) the therapist and client's personality traits and demographic attributes, their experiences, (2) the therapist's training and the client's dilemma and (3) by whatever is said and/or done during the sessions.

Saper proposes that humour may be introduced into one or more of these components, suggesting, for example, that the therapist may be "a basically funny person, prone to wit, flippancy, joking and clowning (T_1)". Further, the client may have a sense of humour or may not (Cl_1) or may not be in a frame of mind to receive the humour as it is intended (Cl_2).

Louis Franzini's definition of therapeutic humour was rather less algorithmic, more process-oriented:

> Therapeutic humor includes both the intentional and spontaneous use of humor techniques by therapists and other health care professionals, which can lead to improvements in the self-understanding and behavior of clients or patients.
>
> (2001)

Here we see two relatively new components: first, that humour can arise spontaneously in the therapy session, that is, without the therapist necessarily intending to introduce it. Secondly, while earlier theorists cautioned that humour has the capacity to damage the therapeutic relationship, Franzini also acknowledges that positive therapeutic change may simply not occur in the client. One imagines this might happen, for example, if the client does not realise the therapist has been – or attempted to be – humorous.

Writing in 2013, "Mirthologist" and Clinical Psychologist Steven Sultanoff precluded the possibility of such spontaneity: therapeutic humour is promoted as a tool or a technique which is *intended to promote* the client's therapeutic change.

Arguably, the most comprehensive definition of therapeutic humour comes from the Association for Applied and Therapeutic Humor, established in 1987 as the American Association for Therapeutic Humor. A not-for-profit organisation, the association's mission statement is "We elevate and nourish the human spirit through the intentional use of humor and laughter". Its website (www.aath.org) promotes membership, an annual conference, the opportunity to become a Certified Humor Professional by attending its Humor Academy and a merchandise store. Members can access a research library which addresses humour usage in numerous settings, including in therapy. In 2005, it published this definition of therapeutic humour, which, curiously, is no longer accessible on its website:

> Any intervention that promotes health and wellness by stimulating a playful discovery, expression or appreciation of the absurdity or incongruity of life's situations. This intervention may enhance health or be used as a complementary treatment of illness to facilitate healing or coping, whether physical, emotional, cognitive, social or spiritual.
>
> (cited in Sultanoff, 2013)

Less a definition of therapeutic humour and rather more an itemised summary of how humour has informed his work with the aged and dying, Joseph Richman (2006) observed ten features of therapeutic humour:

- First, the humour emerges spontaneously, *usually*.
- Second, humour is used "when it is most relevant and meaningful".
- Third, humour fosters social cohesion, especially when everyone laughs together.
- Fourth, humour can help reduce stress and affirm life.
- Fifth, death is less frightening when we do not have to face it alone.
- Sixth, humour allows us to gain perspective and distance, making "the imminence of death bearable".
- Seventh, we acknowledge our fears rather than deny or sugar-coat them.
- Eighth, having someone to communicate our humour to helps us distance ourselves from our fears.
- Ninth, "the therapist must possess the temperament and experience to master the principles of humor and their applications. The principal personal requirement for working as a humor therapist – in fact for all the health services – is empathy".
- Tenth, we need each other, or we could not laugh, have fun or use humour therapeutically.

While the first and second features might be considered contradictory, Richman's features, taken as a whole, offer an existentialist outlook on how humour consoles us and consolidates the relationship between therapist and client.

Pause for thought

How do you feel about the idea of therapeutic humour?
Does it align with your understanding of the therapeutic process?
If you are a person-centred counsellor, does the concept of therapeutic humour help or hinder your work?

Humour in the toolkit

We see humour used to enhance therapeutic practices in many ways, some more subtle than others. As we will see, all the approaches described below have the client's needs as their focus; they also help practitioners cope with what can be difficult working conditions.

A paradoxical intention

Logotherapy, a modality originated in the 1930s by the celebrated Viennese neurologist and psychiatrist Viktor Frankl and heavily informed by his experiences as a prisoner at four Nazi concentration camps. This existentialist approach to therapy was founded on the beliefs that our primary motivator is the search for meaning and that, no matter what the circumstances – even the most miserable – we have free will. A technique of logotherapy is the therapeutic humour model *paradoxical intention* (translated from the German *paradoxe Intention*). In order to disrupt the cycles of clients' fears becoming fears of their fears, so-called self-fulfilling prophecies, Frankl instead encouraged his "phobic" clients to do the thing they feared and his "obsessive-compulsive" clients to wish the things they feared would happen (1975). This approach deliberately evokes humour in the relationship, usually absurd exaggeration. Although there is surprisingly little research evidence to support the technique's efficacy, Frankl illustrates it with numerous case studies, including a client who is frozen with fear before taking an exam. Recalling Frankl's counsel, the client resorted to the paradoxical intention:

> I said to myself, "Since I'm going to fail anyway, I may as well *do my best at failing!* I'll show this professor a test *so* bad, that it will confuse him for days! I will write total garbage, answers that have nothing to do with the questions at all! I'll show him how a student *really* fails a test! This will be the most ridiculous test he grades in his entire career! With this in mind, I was actually giggling when the exam came. Believe it or not, each question made perfect sense to me – I was relaxed, at ease, and, as strange as it may sound, actually in a terrific mood!
>
> (emphases in original)

The client went on to pass the exam with flying colours, and noted that paradoxical intention also cured hiccups: "If one *tries* to keep hiccuping, one can't!" [emphasis in original].

Pause for thought

Frankl's memoir, *Man's search for meaning* (1946/2004), describes how he made (some) sense of his and his fellow prisoners' experiences in Nazi concentration camps. The unimaginable despair is most profoundly illuminated with the kind of humour captured by Thomas Mann's words: "*Das Lachen ist ein Erglänzen der Seele*" - Laughter is a sunbeam of the soul (1924).

How do we make light of our troubles? It seems we let ourselves be depressed by trivialities (though they might not seem trivial to us), but people like Frankl are able somehow to *keep calm and carry on.*

Towards scoring the counsellor's humour

We saw in Part I various approaches developed by psychologists to measure and categorise a person's sense of humour. Person-centred counsellors will also be aware of attempts to score a therapist's empathy, unconditional positive regard and congruence (Barrett-Lennard, 1962; Mearns et al., 2013; Merry & Haugh, 2020; Truax & Carkhuff, 1967). It should not be surprising, then, to see the therapist's humour enjoying a similar level of scrutiny. A five-point scale was developed by James Foster for assessing the quality and therapeutic potential of the counsellor's humour:

- Level 1: the humour is hostile in intent and causes the client obvious harm;
- Level 2: the humour is misplaced and potentially or actually disrupts the client's process;
- Level 3: the humour may elicit some form of appreciation from the client, but does not demonstrably assist in improving the client's self-awareness;
- Level 4: the humour is well received and the therapeutic relationship is strengthened, with the client feeling "greater willingness to explore fully his or her predicament"; and
- Level 5: the humour facilitates a breakthrough in the client's perception leading to a deeper self-awareness.

(Foster, 1978)

Foster took a generally affirmative view of humour in therapy, considering it a "creative expression" and went on to propose adding humour to the therapeutic conditions identified by Robert Carkhuff (incidentally, one of Carl Rogers' students) in the late 1960s.

An antidote to "mastodonic manifestations"

Integrative Short-term Psychotherapy (ISTP) was a short-lived technique developed by Waleed Salameh, co-editor of the *Handbook of humor and psychotherapy* (1987) as an antidote to what he described as "mastodonic manifestations of high priest psycho-babble", applying a six-part process that begins with the "Archaeological Stage" and progresses through the "Subjectivization" and "Integraction" (a "harmonious blend of integration and action") stages to conclude with the "Humor Stage".

Salameh additionally proposed a "Humor Rating Scale" to "rate therapists' use of humor in psychotherapy". Curiously similar to the earlier model proposed by Foster, it also comprised five levels, albeit with different descriptors. The first two levels are "destructive humor" and "harmful humor" respectively, which were likely to elicit responses "usually characterized by a preponderance of giggling, tittering, forced laughter, or short anxious laughs". The upper three levels, he claimed, usually elicit "predominantly diaphragmatic or abdominal gut-level laughter". Salameh introduced the scale for the first time in the 1983 *Handbook of humor research*, additionally promoting it as a tool for measuring the use of humour by the "patient". As was the case with Foster's earlier proposal, Salameh seems to have been inspired by Carkhuff's attempts to assess patients' levels of functioning (he also suggested adding humour to Carkhuff's list of core therapeutic conditions). Indeed, he goes further, speculating that the Humor Rating Scale could also be used to assess how closely therapists are aligned with their clients:

> What happens to therapeutic process when a patient employing level 4 or 5 humor ["very" and "outstandingly" helpful respectively] is matched with a therapist is showing lower levels of humor use? How do humorous therapists respond to clients who are nonhumorous?
>
> (Salameh, 1983)

It is not clear why, writing in 1987, Salameh limits the use of the Scale to assessing therapists. Instead, he promotes a workshop he called *Humor Immersion Training*™ for "therapists and other individuals interested in exercising their 'humor muscles'" (Salameh, 1987). We can all be trained to be more humorous, he asserted. The workshop starts with explorations into the "holy trilogy of humor-making", how to tell jokes and humorous stories and is followed up by "membership" of Laughers Anonymous, an organisation founded by Salameh to provide therapeutic humour resources. We will return to the subject of training in Chapter 10.

Although humour is an important – possibly integral – element to Salameh's ISTP technique, such that its overall objective appears to be the restoration (or installation) of the client's sense of humour, it is nonetheless peripheral, a therapeutic tool. It is also worth noting that short-term therapy was not new, having been developed during the Second World War as a means of treating trauma among returning combatants.

Writing in 1988, Ben Furman and Tapani Ahola at the Brief Therapy Institute of Helsinki, Finland, suggested that humour in therapy can facilitate the therapeutic co-creation of new ideas and alternative perspectives, but stopped short of claiming *humour speeded therapy up*. They used humorous anecdotes, comments and questions, challenges to clients' thinking to expose and "deframe" beliefs and introduce new concepts, fantasies and tasks. An example of shedding light on repressed thoughts or fears, which Furman and Ahola suggested be done "in a respectful way, by using humorous exaggeration" is offered:

> So this is the first time you have been to speak to a psychiatrist. Did you ever think, that you would end up sitting face to face with a shrink? You know, they have a saying, that anybody who goes to see a psychiatrist should have his head examined.
>
> (1988)

In an interesting counter to the person-centred approach of walking alongside the client to see the world through his or her frame of reference, the authors suggested that:

> Humour serves as an indispensable antidote to the hypnotic pull of the clients as the clients unavoidably try their best to influence the therapist to see their problem in the same way that they themselves understand it.
>
> (1988)

Brief therapy of one form or another is widely practised today, not surprisingly perhaps in a society where quick fixes are craved and where, if called for at the same time, a pizza will most likely arrive sooner than an ambulance. Salameh's approach, however, seems not to have survived the passing years.

Positive psychology

Not a therapeutic modality as such, Positive Psychology is an approach that is underpinned by a focus on identifying and promoting people's innate and acquired strengths. It is largely attributed to Martin Seligman, a professor and founder of the Positive Psychology Center at the University of Pennsylvania, USA, whose early career was distinguished by his work in developing (with the help of man's best friend) the theory of *learned helplessness* (1967), which informs contemporary thinking around post-traumatic stress, Stockholm syndrome and emotionally abusive relationships. A 180-degree turnaround in his thinking led to the co-authoring (with Christopher Peterson) of *Character Strengths and Virtues* (2004), intended as a counterpart to the Diagnostic and Statistical Manual of Mental Disorders (DSM) by classifying positive human strengths rather than deficits and disorders. Using the Values in Action (VIA) Inventory of Strengths, a questionnaire-based survey, readers can assess their 24 character strengths, of which humour and playfulness are one (2004). For Seligman and Peterson, humour must:

> serve some moral good – by making the human condition more bearable by drawing attention to its contradictions, by sustaining good cheer in the face of despair, by building social bonds, and by lubricating social interaction.
>
> (2004)

Today, Positive Psychology is a significant player in the self-help industry, and not only has its own base at the University of Pennsylvania, but a whole website promoting training and self-help materials; there is even a *Positive Psychology for Dummies* book (Leimon & McMahon, 2009).

Humour in healthcare settings and in group and family therapy

Primary healthcare settings are typically uninviting, often decidedly anti-therapeutic. In the United Kingdom, where healthcare is taxation-funded and provided by the state, budgets rarely run to initiatives that take emotional needs into account alongside the physiological priorities. Not all attempts at ameliorating the sterility of healthcare settings need be prohibitively expensive, however. A drug treatment institution for young people in Denmark, for example, displayed posters with Winnie the Pooh characters in cartoons that suggest they were on drugs:

> Christopher Robin thinks he can talk to various animals (hallucinogens), Tigger can't ever calm down, he's always bouncing and never gets tired (Ecstasy), Eeyore, doesn't care about anything, he lacks motivation and has very slow reactions (marijuana)....
>
> (Andersen, 2015)

The cartoons described here juxtapose the innocence embodied in the Winnie the Pooh stories and the Disney films they inspired with the less benign world of illegal drugs and how they affect users. One wonders if seeing the cartoons caused the young clients to reflect on their own loss of innocence.

You talking to me?

Also in Denmark, a different approach is used by a group of drug treatment practitioners, who adopt a joking style of interaction with their young clients. Banter and teasing by practitioners, of both clients and other colleagues, with content that ranges from politics to sexual innuendo, are used with the intention of lightening the atmosphere in the institution, breaking down barriers between professionals and clients and promoting openness. It is an approach that must seem risky to the external observer, and it does not always amuse the clients, even if they compare it favourably with other institutional experiences (Andersen, 2015).

Banter is a particular form of humour that might not always seem suitable in a therapeutic setting. Originally a slang term, banter is defined by the Oxford English Dictionary as "teasing, joking, or humorously mocking remarks exchanged playfully with another person or group, esp. among men" and it goes on to highlight "In recent use, the word is sometimes characterized as a means of justifying or excusing humour or behaviour considered boorish or chauvinistic" (n.d.). Banter then appears to defy neat categorisation, particularly if viewed through the lens of the Humor Styles Questionnaire (HSQ, see Chapter 2). "Affiliative" humour, for example, facilitates the fostering of relationships with others, the strengthening of interpersonal bonds and the alleviation of tension in social settings, situations in which – according to Chia-Yueh Chang et al. at the National Tsing Hua University in Taiwan – spontaneous good-natured bantering neatly fits (Chang et al., 2025). However, studies of banter occurring in therapeutic settings paint a more complex picture of what it reveals about the protagonists and their relationship. Helga Kotthoff at Bern University describes "humour orgies", rituals of verbal putdowns by in-group members – predominantly male – in the presence of others, which present a sense of solidarity (Kotthoff, 2022). Here, the humour is expressed through ridicule and sarcasm and conveys a disregard for the other's feelings, a humour style better characterised perhaps as "aggressive". Ordinarily, the ridiculed party could expect to feel some degree of distress at being put down, but as Peter Blundell found in social work settings, relationships improved rather than deteriorated: in one case, Fred explained that "being the subject of a joke told by his teammates or colleagues meant he felt accepted within the team irrespective of whether those jokes may be viewed as unprofessional from others" (Blundell, 2023).

Banter then can be a verbal joust: confrontational, competitive, macho even. It can be used by the therapist to challenge the client to view issues in a different, more positive way, to break down resistance and create the energy needed to change. Or the banter can be gentler, playful and harmonious, a means of consolidating the therapeutic relationship (Brooks et al., 2020).

Group therapy: You laughing at me?

Teasing clients also occurs non-verbally, it seems, in the Minnesota Model of addiction treatment. Developed at the Hazelden Foundation (now Hazelden Betty Ford Foundation) in the United States in the 1950s, the Minnesota Model is still widely used in the treatment of addiction to alcohol and other substances as well as behavioural addictions. An important feature of the model is the use – alongside treatments delivered by doctors, psychologists and social workers – of group therapy from counsellors who are themselves in recovery.

At the core of the group therapy process is the breaking of clients' denials concerning their addiction, considered a significant hurdle for them to overcome at the commencement and throughout their treatment: "The problem of patients not recognizing their problems is a genuine one" (Arminen & Halonen, 2007). The peer counsellors use confrontational techniques in attempting to break those denials; however, as with any intervention, there are risks which may instead reinforce clients' resistance to diagnosis and/or treatment. To mitigate these risks, laughter – with the client and at the client – is used. Group therapy sessions observed by Ilkka Arminen and Mia Halonen at an inpatient clinic for addicts in Finland reveal a number of different approaches to the way laughter is used. One is in "laughing off" the client's perceived difficulties as being less worrisome than the client initially felt. This might be considered an attempt at denying the client's feelings, but done empathically – by both the peer counsellors and the other group members – the laughter reportedly soothes and comforts the client, and a shift in perception can be achieved. An example is given of a newly arrived client who has slept badly and ends up in the communal smoking room in the night. The therapist says:

> Recent studies have shown that one sleeps better, like erm... in bed than... for example in a smoking room.
>
> (Arminen & Halonen, 2007)

The client laughs at this, and that laughter is accompanied by the other members of the group.

At other times, the counsellor may use laughter to highlight something the client has missed. In another session, a client expresses confidence in being able to overcome any setbacks that might threaten his recovery. The counsellor signals her greater understanding that recoveries are far from straightforward by countering with laughter and the phrase "Let's see". The laughter is echoed by other group members, who also understand what the counsellor means when she says "Let's (i.e. *let us*) see". Interestingly, the client in this vignette does not laugh along with the counsellor and other members, and only later acknowledges the thrust of the confrontation. Again, there is a risk that this laughter-confrontation is perceived as mocking, but the group members' laughter suggests – with empathy – that they themselves may have been in the same frame of mind as the client.

Thirdly, laughter is shown to help overcome a client's passive resistance and lead everyone present – client, the other group members and the counsellor – out of an interactional dead-end. Here, the counsellor's laughter defuses the tension and allows a return to greater therapeutic collaboration.

Couples and families

Research indicates that couples who use affiliative humour rather than aggressive humour in their interactions with each other will experience closer bonding and achieve greater success in resolving relationship problems

(Campbell et al., 2008). This style of humour has also been found to mitigate disagreements and relieve tension by communicating feelings of affection, and as a safe way of saving face (Long & Graesser, 1988; Kane et al., 1977.

Reflection

An estranged couple came for counselling, wanting to explore the possibility of getting back together. During the first three sessions, they argued incessantly about who needed to compromise more. Neither side appeared willing to give way, and my attempts at mediation seemed not to be helping.

Finally, one of the partners said to me: "It's hopeless, isn't it?"

"This is such a waste of time", the other partner countered.

"You would say that, wouldn't you? Too easy to give up".

One of them then asked me, "I know we can't ask you for advice, but what do you do?"

"What do *I do*?"

At the time I was living with my partner, before we were married.

"Yeah. When you have to compromise".

"It's not always easy", I replied. "But it's like this: my partner doesn't like watching football, and I don't want to die alone. So we don't watch football".

The couple laughed in recognition. Somehow, the reflection shifted something in their connection with each other. Once one of them showed a willingness to give ground, the other reciprocated.

If relationships with a partner are compared with minefields, then perhaps families constitute an entire warzone. This is because working with children presents a number of challenges to the therapist that do not appear to such an extent with (most) adults.

The first challenge is to establish a trusting relationship with the child, whose experience of adults may be tainted and who may be fearful of a continuation or repetition of previous experiences. With adults, it is relatively easy to find common ground on which to build a sense of mutuality. Children, however, don't worry much about household bills, job security, or whether the England men's football team will ever lift the World Cup again. The therapist's efforts at ingratiation may fall flat or worse if they trigger recollections of painful memories. Adolescent children may be struggling to assert their developing personalities in the face of hostility or even indifference, and so resort to controlling behaviours, leaving the counsellor with the problem of the balance of power in the dyad, particularly if working in institutional settings.

If the child is uncommunicative, the therapist may have a hard time gaining an understanding of the child's emotional and mental state. William Bernet suggests the therapist might instead make fun of the non-communication by parodying it to the point of ridiculousness. In doing so, the therapist and the client laugh together while the client is thrown off-balance in a non-threatening way, realising that the therapy session is not what he or she expected. A comically ridiculous introductory statement, such as "Good morning doctor, did you wish to consult me about a patient?" communicates to the child that the therapist is "genuinely enjoying his company" (1993).

Children's responses to humour introduced by the therapist can help to reveal how resilient they are. Depressed or psychotic children are unlikely to respond to humour in a positive way, for example, but Bernet observes that their unresponsiveness tells us something about their mental states. While a depressed child may recognise the therapist's humour and make some attempt at smiling only to revert immediately to the depressed state, a schizophrenic child will be most likely to be puzzled or confused by the humour.

Kate Rutherford, a counsellor and professor, told of how, when counselling adolescents, she would often encounter "I don't know" when she asked them a question:

> The counselor may ask, "How are you getting along with your classmates this year?"
>
> "I don't know," the student says.
>
> Or, "How are you feeling about not being allowed to play football because of your grades this fall?"
>
> "I don't know," he says.
>
> So, the counselor says, "But, if you did know, how would you feel?"
>
> (1994)

Rutherford observes drily that more often than not, this approach worked when others failed.

As highlighted in Chapter 3, a child's response to humorous stimuli – what the child appreciates and understands – can also help the therapist understand the child's cognitive and social development. One approach by therapists working with children is to ask them to share their favourite joke. Whether or not the child is able to do this tells the therapist how strong the child's social awareness is and/or how willing the child is to opening up his or her personal world. In another case, two unrelated boys came to therapy with the same favourite joke, concerning an ogre of a father who strictly forbade talking at the dinner table. At one particular meal, the father scolded his child repeatedly and told him he could not speak until the meal was finished, and when it was finished he asked the child what he had wanted to say. The child replied, "I was only going to say that there was a bug on your plate".

It emerged that one of the children had a "tyrannical" grandfather and the other a "very strict" father (Bernet, 1993).

> **Pause for thought**
>
> Psychiatrists Robert Reynes and Arnold Allen report (1987) the challenge of having to assess as quickly as possible the mental states of the many troops returning from action in the Second World War; they did this by chatting briefly with their patients and asking them if they had heard any good jokes lately, an approach they later incorporated in their routine work.
>
> How would you feel if in your first session your psychotherapist asked you for your favourite joke? Would you be able to call one to mind? What do you think it would reveal about you? Could you contemplate approaching your own clients with this technique?

Jokes are also used as a way of facilitating change in the child client. The levity is not intended at cheering the child up, but to establish a fun and, above all, non-threatening atmosphere where the child becomes receptive to learning serious stuff. Many of us will recall how we eagerly traded jokes in the school playground. The cleverer the better, because we knew the punchline and they didn't, the fools. And in the back of our minds lurked that fear that they would guess the answer or had already heard it. To be funny was to be popular, and in some schools it kept the bullies at bay. Bernet suggested helping children develop their sense of humour by giving them special homework: go out and "learn some new jokes from children at school or in the neighbourhood" (1993).

Summing up

Definitions of therapeutic humour: Humour used in therapy to promote healing, health and wellness. It may be spontaneous or planned and aims to improve the client's self-understanding and facilitate therapeutic change. The humour should be constructive and empathic, never sarcastic or harmful.

Measuring therapeutic humour: Assessment scales developed: Foster's and Salameh's five-level scales rated therapeutic humour from destructive/hostile (lowest) to breakthrough-facilitating (highest).

Key therapeutic techniques: Paradoxical intention (Frankl) motivates clients to do what they fear by using absurd exaggeration. Brief therapy uses humorous challenges to "deframe" beliefs.

Specialist settings: Laughter can be used to break denial, "laugh off" difficulties, highlight missed points, and defuse tension. Humour establishes trust and facilitates change through playful approaches; favourite jokes reveal cognitive development and social awareness. Banter and teasing can break down professional barriers. Affiliative humour in couples therapy strengthens bonds and aids problem-solving.

The approaches described in this chapter are tools used to facilitate therapeutic change – what Frankl described as components in the therapist's "armamentarium". In Chapter 5, we review whole methodologies built on the promise that humour alone can bring healing to our clients.

References

Andersen, D. (2015). What's so funny? Towards a client perspective on professionals' use of humour in drug treatment. *Drugs: Education, Prevention and Policy*, *22*(3), 263–271. https://doi.org/10.3109/09687637.2015.1016399

Arminen, I., & Halonen, M. (2007). Laughing with and at patients: The roles of laughter in confrontations in addiction group therapy. *The Qualitative Report*, *12*(3), 484–513.

Banter. (n.d.). *Oxford English Dictionary*. Retrieved 30October2025.

Barrett-Lennard, G. T. (1962). Dimensions of therapist response as causal factors in therapeutic change. In N. L. Munn (Ed.), *Psychological monographs: General and applied* (pp. 1–36). American Psychological Association.

Bernet, W. (1993). Humor in evaluating and treating children and adolescents. *Journal of Psychotherapy Practice and Research*, *2*(4), 307–317.

Blundell, P. (2023). Humour as a boundary-breaker in social work practice. *Ethics and Social Welfare*, *17*(2), 206–220. https://doi.org/10.1080/17496535.2023.2204448

Brooks, A. B. J., Herrmann, P. L., & Andreas, S. (2020). The use of banter in psychotherapy: A systematic literature review. *Counselling & Psychotherapy Research*, *21*, 570–586. https://doi.org/10.1002/capr.12361

Campbell, L., Martin, R. A., & Ward, J. R. (2008). An observational study of humor use while resolving conflict in dating couples. *Personal Relationships*, *15*(1), 41–55. https://doi.org/10.1111/j.1475-6811.2007.00183.x

Chang, C.-Y., Chan, Y.-C., Chen, I.-F., & Chen, H.-C. (2025). Sex differences in resting-state fMRI functional connectivity related to humor styles. *Biological Psychology*, *194*. https://doi.org/10.1016/j.biopsycho.2025.108983

Foster, J. (1978). Humor and counseling: Close encounters of another kind. *Personnel and Guidance Journal*, *57*(1), 46–49. https://doi.org/10.1002/j.2164-4918.1978.tb05094.x

Frankl, V. E. (1975). Paradoxical intention and dereflection. *Psychotherapy (Chicago, Ill.)*, *12*(3), 226–237. https://doi.org/10.1037/h0086434

Frankl, V. E. (2004). *Man's search for meaning*. Rider. Original work published 1946.
Franzini, L. R. (2001). Humor in therapy: The case for training therapists in its uses and risks. *The Journal of General Psychology*, *128*(2), 170–193. https://doi.org/10.1080/00221300109598906
Fry, W., & Salameh, W. (Eds.). (1987). *Handbook of humor and psychotherapy: Advances in the clinical use of humor*. Professional Resource Exchange.
Furman, B., & Ahola, T. (1988). The use of humour in brief therapy. *Journal of Strategic and Systemic Therapies*, *7*(2), 3–20.
Kane, T. R., Suls, J., & Tedeschi, J. T. (1977). Humour as a tool of social interaction. In A. J. Chapman & H. C. Foot (Eds.), *It's a funny thing, humour* (pp. 13–16). Pergamon Press.
Kotthoff, H. (2022). Gender and humour. The new state of the art. *Linguistik Online*, *118*, 6. https://doi.org/10.13092/lo.118.9084
Leimon, A., & McMahon, G. (2009). *Positive psychology for dummies* (1st ed.). Wiley.
Long, D. L., & Graesser, A. C. (1988). Wit and humor in discourse processing. *Discourse Processes*, *11*(1), 35–60. https://doi.org/10.1080/01638538809544690
Mann, T. (1924). *Der Zauberberg, Zweiter band*. S. Fischer.
Mearns, D., Thorne, B., & McLeod, J. (2013). *Person-centred counselling in action* (4th ed.). SAGE.
Merry, T., & Haugh, S. (2020). *Learning and being in person-centred counselling* (3rd ed.). PCCS Books.
Mindess, H. (1971). *Laughter and liberation*. Nash.
Mindess, H. (1976). The use and abuse of humour in psychotherapy. In A. Chapman & H. Foot (Eds.), *Humour and laughter: Theory, research and applications* (pp. 331–341). Wiley.
Peterson, C., & Seligman, M. E. P. (2004). *Character strengths and virtues: A handbook and classification*. Oxford University Press.
Reynes, R. L., & Allen, A. (1987). Humor in psychotherapy: A view. *American Journal of Psychotherapy*, *41*(2), 260–270. https://doi.org/10.1176/appi.psychotherapy.1987.41.2.260
Richman, J. (2006). The role of psychotherapy and humor for death anxiety, death wishes, and aging. *Omega*, *54*(1), 41–51. https://doi.org/10.2190/D0NX-7V03-W1H0-4614
Rutherford, K. (1994). Humor in psychotherapy. *Individual Psychology*, *50*(2), 207–222.
Salameh, W. A. (1983). Humor in psychotherapy: Past outlooks, present status, and future frontiers. In P. McGhee & J. Goldstein (Eds.), *Handbook of humor research: Applied studies* (Vol. 2, pp. 61–88). Springer Verlag.
Salameh, W. A. (1987). Humor in integrative short-term psychotherapy (ISTP). In W. Fry & W. Salameh (Eds.), *Handbook of humor and psychotherapy: Advances in the clinical use of humor* (pp. 195–240). Professional Resource Exchange.
Saper, B. (1987). Humor in therapy: Is it good or bad for the client? *Professional Psychology: Research and Practice*, *18*(4), 360–367.
Seligman, M. E. P., & Maier, S. F. (1967). Failure to escape traumatic shock. *Journal of Experimental Psychology*, *74*(1), 1–9. https://doi.org/10.1037/h0024514
Sultanoff, S. (2013). Integrating humor into psychotherapy: Research, theory, and the necessary conditions for the presence of therapeutic humor in helping relationships. *The Humanistic Psychologist*, *41*, 388–399. https://doi.org/10.1080/08873267.2013.796953
Truax, C. B., & Carkhuff, R. R. (1967). *Toward effective counseling and psychotherapy: Training and practice*. Aldine Publishing Co.

Chapter 5

Humour-based therapies

Introduction

In Chapter 4, we looked at theories promoting the idea that humour – along with laughter – can be therapeutic. Some psychotherapists have gone further still and developed methods of therapy that rely heavily on humour, laughter and mirth. These methodologies are the focus of this chapter, which should perhaps be prefaced with a warning:

> The following contains details of therapeutic modalities which some counsellors might find upsetting.

Although some humour-based therapy modalities are as elaborate in their design as they have proved to be controversial, particularly among more dynamically inclined psychotherapists, it is worth remembering that their proponents worked in the United States around the same time as Carl Rogers, and some were students of his. They may have felt the same urge as he did to break free of the yoke of their teaching. That so many psychoanalysts express a borderline "phobic" (Shearer, 2016) aversion to the expression of humour seems ironic given that their theoretical ancestor was not only a keen collector of jokes but also wrote a book and – 20 odd years later – a paper on the subject (see earlier chapters). That irony is underlined by Robert Pierce:

> Ideally in psychotherapy people are dealing with conflictual material and are trying to extend mastery to areas of their lives where they have had uncertain control. This is exactly what humor is about, achieving mastery, however briefly, over rules, impulses, or the limitations life imposes on us.
>
> (1994)

Rational emotive behaviour therapy, AKA rational-emotive therapy, AKA rational psychotherapy

Albert Ellis's work is a direct precursor of cognitive behavioural therapy. A Freudian psychoanalyst active in the 1940s, Ellis questioned the effectiveness

DOI: 10.4324/9781003638773-8

of his work and in 1955 introduced the world to Rational Psychotherapy (later, Rational-Emotive Therapy (RET); later still, Rational Emotive Behaviour Therapy (REBT).

This approach was colourfully promoted as a departure from Freud "and his chief followers" who, he said, were preoccupied:

> ...with the assumption... that if psychotherapists discover and effectively communicate to their clients the main reasons why these clients originally became disturbed, they will thereby discover how their neuroses are being perpetuated and how they can be helped to overcome them. This is a dubious assumption.
>
> (Ellis, 1958)

Rational Psychotherapy operated on a different assumption, namely that our emotional processing and our thought processes coincided to such an extent that by changing how we think, we can change how we feel. Our emotions, Ellis said, are really "a certain kind – a biased, prejudiced, or strongly evaluative kind – of thinking". A rational person who sees that a piece of bread is partly mouldy and recalls having fallen ill after eating mouldy bread will cut the mouldy part off and eat the non-mouldy part. But an "emoting individual", Ellis argued, will "remember so violently or prejudicedly his previous experience with the mouldy part that he will quickly throw away the whole piece of bread and therefore go hungry".

The influences here of the modern philosophers Alfred Adler and Erich Fromm are clear. Ellis also took from the teaching attributed to the Greek Stoic philosopher Epictetus that we are disturbed, not by things, but by the views we take of things. This he translated into a framework: The ABCs of RET.

In summary:

A is an Activating Experience or Event.
B is the individual's belief system.
C is the emotional or behavioural impact of A, as influenced by B.

Ellis illustrated the framework, taking the loss of a job as the activating experience. How we might feel about losing a job (C) is governed, not by the loss of the job itself (A), but by what we tell ourselves we should feel (B). If we let "irrational" beliefs govern our thinking – for example, telling ourselves we'll never find another good job again –we are suffering from "can't-stand-it-itis", and we are letting ourselves "awfulize" the situation. If, on the other hand, we view the situation through the lens of "rational" belief, we would perhaps tell ourselves that while it's not desirable to lose a job and have to search for another, the next one might be better, and if it isn't, we can keep trying and something will eventually turn up.

Irrational beliefs, he said, emanated from a "hidden *must*urbatory agenda" (Ellis & Grieger, 1977, emphasis in the original). Those beliefs take one or more forms:

> (1) you think that someone or something *should*, *ought*, or *must* be different from the way it actually does exist; (2) you find it *awful*, *terrible*, or *horrible* when it is this way; (3) you think that you can't *bear*, *stand*, or *tolerate* this person or thing that you concluded should not have been as it is; (4) you think that you or some other person (or people) have made or keep making horrible errors and that because you or they must not act the way they clearly do act, you or they deserve nothing good in life, merit *damnation*, and can legitimately receive the label of *louse*, *rotten person*, or *turd*.
>
> (Ellis & Grieger, 1977, emphases in original)

Ellis's delivery did not lack gusto: "a major purpose of psychotherapy is to undermine people's over-seriousness" (Ellis & Grieger, 1977). Therapy confronted the client's irrational beliefs and replaced them with rational, more realistic and adaptive beliefs. Humour featured frequently and included ebullient trumping of the client's thinking with exaggerated ripostes. An example of this is offered in a recollection by Ellis of working with clients with eating disorders: "What do you keep telling yourself immediately before you cram that stuff down your gullet…? 'I hate food?'… 'I'll fix my dead mother by showing her that I can eat all I want without getting fat?'" (Ellis, 1987). Ellis also wrote alternative, parodic lyrics to numerous well-known songs, such as *Glory, glory, hallelujah, people love ya till they screw ya!*, which he used in sessions as well as at weekly group workshops.

The humour deployed in Ellis's approach was aligned with the ABCs referred to earlier:

> Humor, quite naturally and because of its very nature, works in all three of these basic ways. Cognitively [A], it presents new ideas to the absolutistic, rigid client in an insightful, hard-hitting way. Emotively [B], it brings enjoyment and mirth, makes life seem more worthwhile, and dramatically intrudes on gloom and inertia. Behaviorally [C], it encourages radically different actions; it constitutes an anti-anxiety activity in its own right; and it serves as a diverting relaxant.
>
> (Ellis & Grieger, 1977)

One might think Ellis's unashamedly polemic style would alienate most people. He often took aim at Freud, whom he dismissed as having "become anally fixated on the notion of having to bugger his mother" and:

> …retreated into a loony transference-schmansference routine from which most of his followers, not to mention Carl Rogers (1961) and his followers, have not yet recovered.
>
> (Ellis & Grieger, 1977)

Nevertheless, he wrote on the subject of psychology and therapy throughout his life and by the time of his death in 2007, aged 93, he had produced 78 books and many more articles. Among his bestsellers are *How to live with a neurotic* (1956) and *Sex without guilt* (1958), published just in time for the sexual revolution of the 1960s. Other titles proved to be more controversial. *Homosexuality: Its causes and cures* (1965) set out to portray homosexuality as a treatable psychological disturbance, a view he later moderated. His works also filled the self-help bookshelves, including *How to master your fear of flying* (1977), *How to make yourself happy and less disturbable* (1999) and *The myth of self-esteem* (2005). In 2003, the American Psychological Association voted him the second-most influential psychotherapist of the twentieth century, after Carl Rogers, and ahead of Freud, who came third (Burkeman, 2007). And on his 90th birthday in 2003, he received congratulatory messages from, among many others, the then-President George W. Bush, former President Bill Clinton and the Dalai Lama, the latter sending him a blessed silk scarf.

Pause for thought

At first glance, it might seem that Ellis's approach is far removed from person-centred thinking, but do you think any of the so-called core conditions of empathic understanding, unconditional positive regard and congruence are present in this modality?

Imagining humorously

The Humorous Imagery Situation Technique (HIST, 1985) was developed by Frank Prerost, a psychologist in the United States, as a "safe yet therapeutic vehicle" (1994) to induce humour in sessions with clients. He described it as a method that "formalizes the use of humor in therapy by combining imagery techniques as a companion for humor in therapy". This guided imagery technique, drawing on Scheidler and Schorr's directed daydream work in the 1970s, was aimed at breaking cycles of anxiety and allowing humour to be "restored in daily activity".

The therapist begins by suggesting a scene to the client, who then describes that scene as vividly as possible. The therapist then asks the client to focus on humorous reactions of others in the scene, asking questions such as "What is everyone laughing about?" and "Do you feel like joining them?". The specific aim here is to immerse the client in the humorous aspects of the scene. The therapist brings in an incongruity to the scene that touches on the source or cause of the client's anxiety, which is then humorously resolved. The ensuing laughter defuses the anxiety and brings the client towards a better mental state for appreciating humour.

An example might be a client who is experiencing undue tension at work, say, due to the demands of an overbearing boss. The therapist might direct the client to picture a works party that takes place on a boat. Once the client has described the scene and the characters in it, the therapist asks the client to focus on the playful interactions of those characters: why they are laughing and how the client can contribute to the light mood. Once the client has successfully described this, the therapist then introduces the incongruity, for example, having the boss say something idiotic in a speech, or fall off the side of the boat or picture a seagull flying overhead and diving down to steal the boss's toupé.

Prerost advised that the success of HIST depends on the therapist's skill in developing appropriate client-specific imagery, requiring the therapist to be conversant with the antecedents to humour, as well as a competent "script writer and director". As a therapeutic technique that is used in practice, HIST seems to have lapsed, although imagery techniques do feature prominently in cognitive behavioural therapy.

Provoking therapeutic change

A modality originating in the same era is Provocative Therapy, developed by Frank Farrelly, a psychiatrist originally of the Freudian school. While working with hospitalised psychotic "patients", he experienced an epiphanic breakthrough when, on the recommendation of his colleagues, he tried the approach described in *Client-Centered Therapy* (Rogers, 1951) for the first time. The experience is described in effusive terms:

> For the first time in seven months I began to see how things were for her, not just from the hospital staff's standpoint or my standpoint or that of her family and the community at large. From her perspective it made sense for her to act the way she did. It was a very frightening experience, but exhilarating too, to go into another person's world, into whatever limbo or "corner or the universe" she inhabited... and to see people, places, things, feelings, ideas, attitudes, etc. from her viewpoint. Then her behavior made sense, it all hung together, it was eminently "rational."
>
> (Farrelly & Brandsma, 1974)

The conversion to person-centred thinking was instant. Farrelly applied the modality to all his patients and wrote to Rogers that he felt that he was "wading knee-deep in diamonds" (Farrelly & Brandsma, 1974). In 1958, he moved to Chicago and got a job at the Mendota State Hospital, where Rogers and his group were working (more on this in Chapter 7). During that time, he found that some clients moved him towards "radical congruence", which:

> ...if held constant, was very helpful to patients in interviews; that I could not only laugh at patients without detriment to them but even with help to

> them; that laughter towards patients was not inevitably "demeaning their dignity".

A second epiphany came in 1963 during his participation in Rogers' project with chronic schizophrenics. Having applied the client-centred approach over 91 sessions with "Bill", conveying to him that he was (1) worthwhile and had value; (2) he could change; and (3) his life could be different, Farrelly became tired of Bill's responses, which were:

> 1) I am worthless; 2) I'm hopeless and can never change and 3) My life will always be one long psychotic episode and hospitalization. It was becoming increasingly clear that empathic understanding, feedback, warm caring, and genuine congruence were simply not enough and were getting us nowhere. At this point I "gave up" and said to him, "Okay, I agree. You're hopeless. Now let's try this for 91 interviews. Let's try agreeing with you about yourself from here on out."

Farrelly reports that the client responded immediately that "he was not *that* bad, nor *that* hopeless" (emphases in original). Farrelly persisted with, essentially, taunting Bill with the prospect of never leaving the hospital; predicting that he would have to be fed baby cereal, that he'd lose control of his bowels and bladder and need to wear a nappy made from "bedsheets because you've got such a fat ass". Six interviews later, Farrelly writes, Bill was discharged and did not return.

Pause for thought

It is possible that Bill was not "cured" by Farrelly's radical congruence but checked himself into another institution – I think I might have.

But is Farrelly's approach antithetic to person-centred thinking? Does our congruence as therapists always have to be communicated *gently*?

Four months later, Farrelly switched over to his newfound approach entirely, though not sure how his clients would react:

> I had visions of all my clients leaving, threatening malpractice suits while muttering through their clenched teeth, "Why the hell should I stay here and listen to you insult me when I can go home and get my spouse to do it as well?"
>
> (Farrelly & Brandsma, 1974)

Between 1974 and 1987, Farrelly honed the framework of Provocative Therapy, which comprised ten *assumptions*, two *hypotheses*, a *rationale*, five *techniques* and four *languages*.

Starting with the *rationale*, Farrelly believed that deliberate, targeted humour was "an essential ingredient" in Provocative Therapy and that the Provocative therapist, rather than explicitly communicating concern or liking for the client, best expressed "positive regard" for the client using warmth, which is "communicated implicitly by humor, physical touch, affectionate banter, and a twinkle in the eye" (Farrelly & Lynch, 1987).

Farrelly's *assumptions* set out his views on why people behave in the ways they do and how the therapist ought best to respond (all references: Farrelly & Brandsma (1974), except where otherwise stated):

1 *People change and grow in response to a challenge*. When people are forced to cope with a challenge that cannot be avoided, they can and do change, but the therapist's mere accepting of the client does not, by itself, facilitate therapeutic change. Instead, the Provocative therapist attends to the client's impulse – the "constructive anger" – to change, to *get better* rather than just *feel better*.
2 *Clients can change if they choose*. Contrary to the prevailing view at the time (according, at least, to Farrelly) that clients were helpless victims of circumstance or genetics, people have autonomy and agency and holding them "responsible for their actions gives them hope and dignity". The Provocative therapist does not collude with clients who say they cannot change but instead transmits the message "Get your rear in gear", moving them to a point where they begin to recover their agency.
3 *Clients have far more potential for achieving adaptive, productive, and socialized modes of living than they or most clinicians assume*. Farrelly appears here to be admonishing therapists who conclude the clients can't be helped by anyone, including themselves.
4 *The psychological fragility of patients is vastly overrated both by themselves and others*. Farrelly asserts that therapists forget they are meeting their clients when they are in a state of extreme crisis and conflate this state with the clients' normal functioning state. As a result, therapists err on the side of caution when it comes to which intervention to use and when.
5 *The client's maladaptive, unproductive, antisocial attitudes and behaviors can be drastically altered whatever the degree of severity or chronicity*. Farrelly observes that clinicians routinely dismiss cases where "patients" improve beyond expectation and are not curious about understanding why. He later omits this critique and asserts instead that the Provocative therapist, believing that all clients are capable of change, "enters clients' inner worlds and utilizes the energy in these to help them bring about constructive change" (Farrelly & Brandsma, 1974; Farrelly & Lynch, 1987).

6 *Adult or current experiences are at least if not more significant than childhood or previous experiences in shaping client values, operational attitudes and behaviors.* Farrelly offers a passionate defence of the complex, adventitious and thankless task of parenting, as well as an equally passionate dismissal of researchers who "draw unwarranted and overgeneralized conclusions" such as "Mother didn't give me a sandwich, so she doesn't love me anymore. I must be worthless". Adults, he asserts, are just as shaped by their peers, mass media and society's values as by their past and capable of judging for themselves how they are feeling in the moment. The Provocative therapist stays in the present with clients, attempting "a 'living theatre' production with the spotlight on current causality and corrective experience" (Farrelly & Brandsma, 1974; Farrelly & Lynch, 1987).
7 *The client's behavior with the therapist is a relatively accurate reflection of his habitual patterns of social and interpersonal relationship.* Arguing that the tendency in clients to be defensive in confrontational social situations is typically replicated in group therapy settings, Farrelly suggests first telling clients in no uncertain terms how others perceive those self-defeating behaviours, then portraying the impacts of the behaviours and finally offering tongue-in-cheek suggestions of how the client might want to respond.
8 *People make sense; the human animal is exquisitely logical and understandable.* Farrelly writes that everyone he has ever met – in social and clinical settings – has made sense to him, and he has been able to relate to them in some way. People are not "uniquely mysteriously alien"; we simply have not obtained enough information to understand them properly; it is for this reason that the Provocative therapist questions and probes clients (Farrelly & Brandsma, 1974; Farrelly & Lynch, 1987).
9 *The expression of therapeutic hate and joyful sadism toward clients can markedly benefit the client.* Perhaps the most controversial of the ten *assumptions*, Farrelly initially argues that "mentally ill" people feel rejected and unloved precisely because they have experienced being rejected and unloved; furthermore, they feel hated and hatred towards themselves because some of their behaviours are hateful. Farrelly then asserts that the therapist's genuine rejection of the client was "more helpful… than a phony, constrained acceptance". He illustrates his argument (in the earlier text) with seven case studies on the theme of genuine rejection. The cameos are intended to justify the Provocative therapist's choice of "short term 'cruelty'" in order to counter long-term detriment. Their content is indeed cruel, and it includes a vignette of a mother rubbing her child's nose in his excrement to stop him from defecating on a rug when he expressed anger at his parents and the use of a cattle prod to "cure" an autistic child of his self-harming. The 1987 text is more moderate in tone and it does not duplicate these case studies, instead referring to the need for "tough love", conveying an "eminently human way of relating… warmth and

confrontation, caring and annoyance, compassion and limits" (Farrelly & Brandsma, 1974; Farrelly & Lynch, 1987).

10 *The more important messages between people are non-verbal.* The client's body language, Farrelly argues, conveys the "more (later: 'most') important messages". The therapist must therefore be able to register and interpret those non-verbal messages (Farrelly & Brandsma, 1974; Farrelly & Lynch, 1987).

Farrelly's language often echoes his former mentor Rogers, for example, in offering two *hypotheses*, "open to proof or disproof by each new client and by scientific methods" (Farrelly & Brandsma, 1974):

1 If provoked by the therapist (humorously, perceptively, and within the client's own internal frame of reference), the client will tend to move in the opposite direction from the therapist's definition of the client as a person.
2 If urged provocatively (humorously and perceptively) by the therapist to continue his or her self-defeating, deviant behaviors, the client will tend to engage in self- and other-enhancing behaviors that more closely approximate the societal norm.

(Farrelly & Lynch, 1987)

The *techniques* used by the therapist comprise expressing the client's unspoken or subconscious thoughts, accentuating the negative aspects of the client's thinking, emphasising the client's fear of change and (ironically) the positive aspects of avoiding change, giving instant feedback ("radical congruence") and using lists. The last technique is illustrated with this dialogue excerpt:

Client: *(patiently)* Mr. Farrelly, you *know* there are good things about me too, and you know…
Therapist: (interrupting flatly) Well, name three.

(Farrelly & Lynch, 1987)

These techniques are for the most part a form of reverse psychology, exaggerating something the client has expressed to force the latter to confront the apparent absurdity of what has been shared. For example, the therapist characterises the client's low self-esteem as irredeemable: "You have within you, they say, the total power to cure yourself, but obviously they weren't considering people of your ilk" (Farrelly & Lynch, 1987).

Concomitant with this approach, Farrelly argued, the therapist sees the world as the client does, an assertion that is analogous with the person-centred therapist's need to understand the client's "frame of reference" (Rogers, 1957; Merry, 2020). However, where Rogers' motivation is to empathise with his client, the Provocative therapist's aim is to strengthen "clients' inhibitions and resistances to their own dysfunctional behaviors" (Farrelly & Lynch, 1987).

We come finally to the four *languages*, a term Farrelly uses to capture the flavour of his provocations. They are challenging to summarise without decontextualising them. The quotations are from case studies offered by Farrelly. *Religious-moral* language is used as a form of shaming: "I can't figure out whether you are immoral or whether you have learned self-defeating acting-out, anti-social behavioral patterns of promiscuity", is told to a chronic schizophrenic with multiple behavioural problems. With the same client, indeed, in the same speech, he uses *professional jargon*: "…or whether you have a highly impaired ego functioning related to your significant early emotional deprivation…". Another flavour is *locker room language*, a euphemism for vulgarity. The fourth is non-verbal: *body language*, which is aimed at capturing the client's attention, facilitating the reception of the therapist's messages and communicating "warmth, acceptance, and positive regard". The Provocative therapist sits close to clients and, unusually, will also touch them: "a tap on the knee, a hand on the shoulder or forearm, or a gentle pat on a client's check à la 'The Godfather'".

It is not always obvious how wholeheartedly Farrelly rejected person-centred principles. His writings frequently echo his former mentor's words, including the oft-quoted aphorism "what is most personal is most universal". Farrelly is also at pains to emphasise the importance of walking alongside his clients:

> Metaphorically speaking, the Provocative therapist is not across the room shooting barbs of humor at the client. Rather, the therapist is with the client (within the client's internal frame of reference), using humor to push out from the inside the imprisoning walls of the client's habitually dysfunctional thought patterns. Thus the therapist can demonstrate that the client's mental prison has more exits than it has walls and that laughter, like Joshua's trumpet at Jericho, can bring these walls tumbling down (Farrelly & Lynch, 1987).

Pause for thought

In interviews in his later life, Farrelly made a startling claim: Rogers had apparently told a mutual colleague that, had he been younger, he would be doing what Farrelly was doing.

What do you suppose Rogers might have admired about Provocative Therapy?

Naturally high

A contemporary of Farrelly and Ellis, Walter O'Connell developed a humour-based modality of therapy originally labelled Action Therapy, but which –

influenced by his work with drug addiction – he renamed Natural High Therapy (O'Connell, 1981). Little is known about O'Connell's life and career; he was an Adlerian therapist practising in Texas and a clinical psychologist at the Veterans Administration Medical Center there. His early work included a 1960 study of differences in humour preferences between the genders, called the Wit and Humor Appreciation Test, or WHAT for short. This study used methods similar to those discussed in earlier chapters and found that college males appreciated hostile wit more than women, who preferred "nonsense wit" (such as puns) and, more critically, that "well-adjusted" individuals favoured humour more than "poorly adjusted" individuals (O'Connell, 1962). The latter observation informed a central tenet of Natural High Therapy; indeed, O'Connell later noted that a better name for his approach might be "humorous self-therapy" (O'Connell, 1987).

Natural High theory builds on Adlerian principles of the self-actualisation impulse and unity of self, finding that both the individual's self-esteem and communal orientation are enhanced by a (non-aggressive) sense of humour which embraces the paradox of life:

> Humorous psychotherapy (a synonym for 'natural high') is at odds with subtle teachings based on delusional demands for an instant, perfect, painless, and practiceless nirvana. Following quantum physics, humorous psychotherapy plays with boundaries, reconciles opposites, and re-solves apparent paradoxes of solid separateness in time. Everything can be anything else. Life is 'both/and' (e.g., life-death, male-female, pleasure-pain) and not 'either/or.' To the humorous psychotherapist, all phenomena are in a state of flux and process.
>
> (O'Connell, 1987)

Natural High Therapy is undertaken in three chronological stages. The first aims to confront the client with the need to be freed from "'demandments', the I-must and You-must of controls, goals, and roles ingrained early in life" (O'Connell, 1981) – in Rogerian terms, an external locus of evaluation created by conditions of worth (Rogers, 1957). In the second, didactic-experiential stage, the client practises Adlerian "encouragement", defined as "teaching ourselves and others that we and we alone constrict our worth and belonging no matter how discouraging the environment" (O'Connell, 1981). The third stage uses guided meditation to instil a connection with religious (Christian) faith.

Throughout the process, O'Connell employs an openly idiosyncratic, cheerfully aphoristic style. The Fifteen Affirmations for Natural High Actualization begin with:

1 Remember you are dying. Give up body and ego attachments, but not involvements.
2 Remember people can give only the love they are capable of at any time.

And so on. The penultimate and final affirmations read:

14. Remember that life is too serious a game to be taken gravely. You'll never get out of it alive.
15. Remember and accept that there are times when you'll forget all of the above.

(1987)

Therapeutic techniques included "stroking-for-strength", where self-esteem is reinforced in group sessions using soliloquy or alone using journals, emphasising effort rather than performance or perfection. These efforts can be facilitated by natural high therapists, using humour; eventually, "[p]roductive humorists learn to stroke themselves, noncompetitively, simply for existing or 'for no reason at all'" (1987).

Another technique is "humordrama", a variant of psychodrama "which attempts to put into action, through therapeutic structure, a flexible, optimistic, response-able way of life" (1987) using primarily empty chair soliloquy and mirror soliloquy. O'Connell asserted that humordrama aided clients in understanding that happiness came from the acceptance of life's paradoxes and that we function best when we "cooperate-as-equals" (1987). He also claimed clinical evidence showed overwhelmingly that "patients who become involved in humordrama change positively" (1987). According to O'Connell, spirituality was an "important ingredient of humour". (1987), and that "All successful psychotherapists are faith healers. They teach clients faith in self, others, and faith in a loving God".

Pause for thought

As we have seen, Walter O'Connell was a proponent of Adler's Individual Psychology, which emphasised the importance of social connection, cooperation and working for the common good – values that align with many religious teachings but were grounded in Adler's secular, humanistic worldview rather than religious faith. O'Connell, conversely, put religious – Christian – faith at the heart of Natural High Therapy.

Do you agree with O'Connelly that spirituality is so fundamental to humour? Would your thinking differ if you brought other religions into this argument?

Who laughs last?

> **Pause for thought**
>
> Having come to this point of the chapter, the reader might be forgiven for thinking that any and every model of therapeutic humour will work. According to Steven Sultanoff, for example, the therapist needs only to intend for the intervention "to be funny and have a therapeutic reason" (Sultanoff, 2022).
>
> What do you think?

Provocative Therapy is practised today in the United Kingdom, the Netherlands and Germany, but for the most part, interest in these methodologies has lapsed since the retirement and deaths of their innovators. And we will search the various therapist directories for practitioners of these modalities in vain.

So, we might conclude that the modalities themselves were lacking in effectiveness and, as a result, failed to inspire sufficient numbers of disciples to spread the message. The proponents of these tough-love therapeutic approaches emphasised acceptance of their clients "despite their errors and human fallibilities" (Martin & Ford, 2018). Farrelly, as we have seen, claimed to be walking alongside his clients, but it is hard to imagine a client not being intimidated by a barrage of his invective, even if Rogers did approve of his work. Therapeutic change will not happen until the client's resistance is set aside; every practitioner knows how hard it is for some clients to recognise this. And perhaps *irrational beliefs* are really a slightly different way of framing *conditions of worth*. O'Connell's approach is perhaps closer to existentialist than person-centred thinking – we're all going to die, so we might as well have fun while it lasts. In Emmy van Deurzen's words: "The existential practitioner is always entirely serious and earnest, but when possible uses humour, without malice" (2012). And something about Ellis, who rightly asserted that *feeling better* isn't the same as *getting better*, must have impressed the Dalai Lama.

Every good idea needs equally good PR to get it into the mainstream. Artists, inventors and politicians know this. Perhaps the innovators here missed that trick. Farrelly travelled widely to promote his work, and Provocative Therapy survives perhaps due to this.

A third factor to consider is the personalities of the innovators. None of them comes across as shrinking violets. However, it is surprising to learn that Ellis was "painfully shy and intimidated by public speaking". To overcome this, he apparently challenged himself, at the age of 19, to make daily visits to the Bronx Botanical Gardens in New York, where he spoke to every woman he saw, 130 attempts in total. His experiment, according to Oliver Burkeman, did not lead to true love, but that was beside the point. He had proved to himself that rejection, though unpleasant, was not unbearable: there was no need to 'awfulise' it. 'Nobody vomited and ran away,' he wrote. 'Nobody called the cops.'

(Burkeman, 2007)

Or perhaps Ellis, Farrelly and O'Connell were ahead of their time? Because, as we will see in Chapter 6, interest is growing in the phenomenon of humour in therapy.

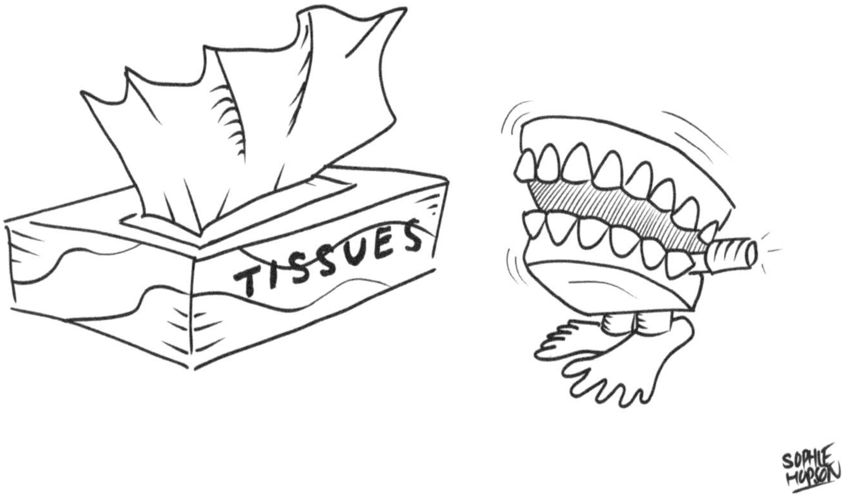

Doing therapy outside the box: Clown therapy and giggle doctors

Now, as they say, for something completely different…

Clown therapy, attributed to "Patch" Adams, originated in the 1970s as a way of reducing hospitalised children's anxiety (and, apparently, hospital-running costs) and has since spread from the United States to Europe, Africa and Asia (Adams, 2002; Finlay et al., 2014; Gomberg et al., 2020), including therapeutic treatments of adults. Research in Israel has found that "medical clowning" improved the pregnancy rate among women undergoing IVF (Friedler et al., 2011).

In something of a call to action, Adams listed ten "recommendations for doctors" (2002), exhorting them to add humour to their practise. The recommendations contain some practical tips, such as studying videos of funny people and stealing "bits" from each, wearing costumes, greeting people with a smile and a twinkle in the eyes and practising "public laughing". The most outrageous advice, perhaps, is Adams' assertion that farts are "universally funny in all countries" and for doctors to invest in a "glorious remote control farter". Or perhaps the most outrageous advice is Adams' final recommendation: for the medical clown to be an "instrument for peace, justice and care". In any case, the aim of these exhortations is not merely the reduction in patients' anxiety, but also a reduction in clinicians' stress levels.

Stephen King's 1986 novel and the films it inspired may have made clowns as popular with children as brussels sprouts, but the Patch Adams ethos lives on in the work of the Theodora Children's Charity, a member of the Foundation Théodora established in 1993 by the Poulie brothers in Lausanne, Switzerland. Active also in Italy, Spain, Belarus and Hong Kong, the organisation boasts over 100 "Giggle Doctors", including 25 in the United Kingdom. The two-year programme covers all the artistic elements and basic clinical training, such as infection control. Eschewing oversized footwear and Joker smiles in favour of comically pimped lab coats, Doctors Muddy Puddle, Teapot and Cowpat administer therapeutic *fun* to children in hospitals across England. In addition to hospital visits, virtual visits are possible, as well as "Giggle-a-Gram" video messages, a popular legacy of the pandemic lockdown. The charity's annual Impact Reports highlight many "case studies" such as Rory, a young boy admitted to hospital with a severe lung infection, who met Dr Fancy Pants and Dr Geehee and is quoted:

> The Giggle Doctors are like real doctors because they made me feel better but in a different way.
>
> (Theodora Children's Charity, theodora.co.uk, 2025)

The artistic training Giggle Doctors receive seems to draw somewhat on the non-directive approach to therapy, in that they "use play to understand the emotional state of the child by letting the child lead the sessions and adapting to their needs" (Sheffield Children's Hospital, sheffieldchildrens.nhs.uk, 2023). This helps ensure children – far from being intimidated or overwhelmed – feel less anxious. A positive "secondary" impact is also noted: on parents and carers and on medical and ancillary staff.

Today, hospital clowning programmes can be found all over the world: Le Rire Médecin (France), Die Clown Doktoren (Germany), Payasospital (Spain), Soccorso Clown (Italy), CliniClowns (Europe), Doctors of Joy (Brazil), Fools for Health (Canada) and Humour Foundation (Australia) (Spitzer, 2006).

Laughing all the way to the beach

Taking therapy even further away from the therapy room is Laughter Yoga. Much has been written about how infectious laughter is. Laugh, they say, and the whole world laughs with you. Scream, and well, it depends: stand up in the middle of a library and scream your head off and everyone around you will say

"Shhhh!". Do the same in a packed airliner 40,000 ft above the Atlantic Ocean, and they will join in.

The Laughter Club Movement began as a group of just five people who, led by Madan Kataria, met up in a Mumbai Park in 1995 to tell each other jokes and funny stories. When the group ran out of material, Kataria's research that the body cannot differentiate between genuine and forced ("acted") laughter inspired a change of method: to act at laughing. The group found that the acted laughter quickly turned to real laughter, and that they could keep it up for ten minutes. More people joined them. They began meeting on Apna Beach in the northern suburbs. Since then, Laughter Yoga has been taken up around the world. Laughter yoga clubs affiliated with Kataria's Laughter Yoga International meet in person in 26 countries, from Brazil, the United States and Canada to Qatar and Malaysia, and many more online. In England, at the time of writing, there are affiliated laughter yoga clubs in Stourbridge and Altrincham.

Laughter Yoga sessions last up to an hour and comprise four steps:

1 Clapping of hands: a warm-up exercise to stimulate acupressure points in the hand and increase energy levels, accompanied by dancing;
2 Deep breathing exercises commonly used in yoga to flush the lungs and bring about physical and mental relaxation;
3 Child-like playfulness: the cultivation of a playful mindset open to laughing without reason. Exercises include laughing while making animal noises or laughing while pretending to be riding on a roller coaster.
4 Further laughter exercises to reduce inhibitions and shyness and convert simulated laughter into unconditional laughter.

(Laughter Yoga International, n.d.; Hoffmann, 2013)

Reflection

There is a plethora of laughter club videos available on YouTube, one of which – from the Mumbai Laughter Club – I shared at a workshop on humour in therapy. When the video finished, one of the workshop participants voiced scepticism that English people would congregate en masse for the sole purpose of laughing. "We just don't do that sort of thing", she said.

After a short discussion, one of the other participants suggested we gave it a try and challenged ourselves to laugh for one minute. The sceptic sat with arms tightly crossed while the rest of us chuckled, tittered and guffawed. And at around the 40-second mark, her frown subsided and she smiled. And then she laughed.

Summing up

Rational Emotive Behaviour Therapy: Albert Ellis challenged Freud's "dubious assumption" that insight alone creates change, arguing instead that our emotions are really just "biased, evaluative thinking". REBT confronted clients' "*must*urbatory" beliefs with exaggerated ripostes and parodic songs ("Glory, glory, hallelujah, people love ya till they screw ya!"). Voted second-most influential psychotherapist of the twentieth century by the APA, ahead of Freud.

Former person-centred therapist Frank Farrelly's *Provocative Therapy* emerged after he tired of empathising with a client for 91 sessions and instead agreed the client was hopeless, whereupon the client immediately improved. His controversial "therapeutic hate" (later: "tough love") used reverse psychology, shaming, vulgarity and physical touch to provoke change.

Walter O'Connell's *Natural High Therapy* combined Adlerian principles with Christian spirituality and cheerful aphorisms in the belief that "all successful psychotherapists are faith healers". Remember you are dying!

Frank Prerost's *Humorous Imagery Situation Technique* used guided imagery to turn phobic ideas comically on their heads.

These modalities have mostly disappeared since their innovators' deaths, but *Clown Therapy* thrives globally with "Giggle Doctors" (Doctors Muddy Puddle, Teapot and Cowpat) reducing children's hospital anxiety, whilst *Laughter Yoga*, founded in a Mumbai park by Madan Kataria, now operates clubs in 26 countries.

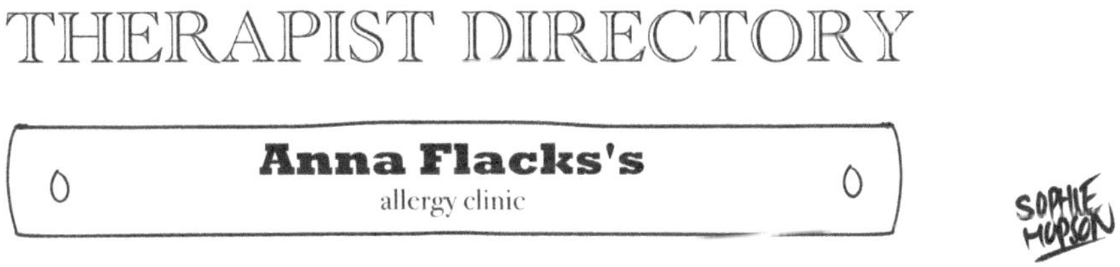

References

Adams, P. (2002). Humour and love: The origination of clown therapy; Compassion, joy, love, and humour are essential to build healthy and peaceful societies (the love strategy). *Postgraduate Medical Journal*, *78*, 922.

Burkeman, O. (2007). Influential American psychologist who led the revolution in cognitive therapy. *The Guardian*, August 11. https://www.theguardian.com/news/2007/aug/11/guardianobituaries.usa Retrieved 23June2025.

Ellis, A. (1958). Rational psychotherapy. *The Journal of General Psychology*, *59*, 35–49.

Ellis, A. (1987). The use of rational humorous songs in psychotherapy. In W. Fry & W. Salameh (Eds.), *Handbook of humor and psychotherapy: Advances in the clinical use of humor* (pp. 265–285). Professional Resource Exchange.

Ellis, A., & Grieger, R. (1977). *Handbook of rational emotive therapy*. Springer Publishing Company, Inc.

Farrelly, F., & Brandsma, J. (1974). *Provocative therapy*. Meta Publications.

Farrelly, F., & Lynch, M. (1987). Humor in provocative therapy. In W. Fry & W. Salameh (Eds.), *Handbook of humor and psychotherapy: Advances in the clinical use of humor* (pp. 81–106). Professional Resource Exchange.

Finlay, F., Baverstock, A., & Lenton, S. (2014). Therapeutic clowning in paediatric practice. *Clinical Child Psychology and Psychiatry*, *19*(4), 596–605. https://doi.org/10.1177/1359104513492746

Friedler, S., Glasser, S., Azani, L., Freedman, L. S., Arie Raziel, A., Strassburger, D., Ron-El, R., & Lerner-Geva, L. (2011). The effect of medical clowning on pregnancy rates after in vitro fertilization and embryo transfer. *Fertility and Sterility*, *95*(6). https://doi.org/10.1016/j.fertnstert.2010.12.016

Gomberg, J., Raviv, A., Fenig, E., & Meiri, N. (2020). Saving costs for hospitals through medical clowning: A study of hospital staff perspectives on the impact of the medical clown. *Clinical Medicine Insights. Pediatrics*, *14*, 1179556520909376. https://doi.org/10.1177/1179556520909376

Hoffmann, M. (2013). Benefits of humor and laughter: A brief introduction for rehabilitation Counselors. *Southern Illinois University Carbondale Research Papers*, *388*. http://opensiuc.lib.siu.edu/gs_rp/388

Laughter Yoga International (n.d.). https://www.laughteryoga.org

Martin, R., & Ford, T. (2018). *The psychology of humor: An integrative approach*. Elsevier Science & Technology.

Merry, T. (2020). *Learning and being in person-centred counselling* (3rd ed.). PCCS.

O'Connell, W. (1962) An item analysis of the wit and humor appreciation test, *The Journal of Social Psychology*, *56*, 271–276

O'Connell, W. (1981) Natural high therapy. In R. Corsini (Ed.), *Handbook of innovative psychotherapies* (pp. 554–568). Wiley.

O'Connell, W. (1987) Natural high therapy and practice: The humorist's game of games. In W. Fry & W. Salameh (Eds.), *Handbook of humor and psychotherapy: Advances in the clinical use of humor* (pp. 195–240). Professional Resource Exchange.

Pierce, R. (1994). Use and abuse of laughter in psychotherapy. In H. S. Strean (Ed.), *The use of humor in psychotherapy* (pp. 105–111). Jason Aronson.

Prerost, F. (1985). A procedure using imagery and humor in psychotherapy: Case application with longitudinal assessment. *Journal of Mental Imagery*, *9*(3), 67–76.

Prerost, F. (1994). Humor as an intervention strategy. In H. S. Strean (Ed.), *The use of humor in psychotherapy* (pp. 139–147). Jason Aronson.

Rogers, C. R. (1951/1999). *Client-centered therapy: Its current practice, implications and theory*. Constable.

Rogers, C. R. (1957). The necessary and sufficient conditions of therapeutic personality change. *Journal of Consulting Psychology*, *21*(2), 95–103.

Shearer, A. (2016). *Why don't psychotherapists laugh?* Routledge.

Spitzer, P. (2006) Hospital clowns – modern-day court jesters at work, *The Lancet*, *368*, 534–535.

Sultanoff, S. (2022). *Therapeutic humor or humor that is therapeutic: Is there a difference and does that matter?* Association for Applied and Therapeutic Humor. https://www.aath.org/post/therapeutic-humor-or-humor-that-is-therapeutic

van Deurzen, E. (2012). *Existential counselling and psychotherapy in practice*. SAGE Publications.

Chapter 6

What the research reveals

Introduction

We have, in previous chapters, considered a good deal of the research literature concerning humour and therapy. So far, however, we have not definitively answered the question:

> Do we know if humour and laughter positively impact therapeutic outcomes?

What follows is a decidedly unsystematic survey of the research corpus stretching across the ontological and epistemological spectrums. We begin with the philosophical underpinnings to research methodologies, moving on to consider qualitative, quantitative and mixed-method studies and systematic reviews to learn what they can tell us about this subject.

Approaching truth – the philosophies underlying our curiosity

As we saw in previous chapters, psychologists traditionally take a large group of people and subject them to various tests and measures with the aim of proving a theory and approaching a paradigm – a generalisable truth – about our behaviours, traits, beliefs and so on. These so-called quantitative studies apply a positivist ontological view, that there is a single objective world that we can come to know and understand through measurements and experimentation.

The opposite end of the ontological spectrum is occupied by the constructivist or interpretivist view that there is no such thing as a single objective world. Instead, what we perceive as reality is constructed – interpreted – through our minds, which are in turn influenced by our culture and language. Thus, because knowledge is not universal, meaning is created not by measurement and quantification but through language and through a qualitative grasp of individuals' lived experiences.

DOI: 10.4324/9781003638773-9

Figure 6.1 Ontology refers to the nature of reality. Epistemology refers to the nature of knowledge.

The qualitative evidence

The range and variety of research into humour in the therapy space reflect its complexity both in terms of its nature and how we perceive humour. Elizabeth Briggs and Alison Owen (2022) at Staffordshire University, UK, carried out semi-structured reflective interviews with six humanistic counsellors about how they had experienced laughter in therapeutic settings. All six counsellors were Caucasian females, half were trainees and half were qualified practitioners. Their research is significant: as well as being the most recent primary research specifically focusing on humanistic therapeutic modalities, it also considers the training of counsellors. Training is a topic we will return to in Chapter 10.

Patricia Talens (2020) at the University of Roehampton, UK, carried out a similar approach to collecting data, interviewing seven UK-based counsellors who worked with youths. Talens applied the descriptive phenomenological approach (DPA) in the analysis of the data she collected from interviews, while Briggs and Owen used interpretative phenomenological analysis (IPA).

Pause for thought

For therapists, all therapy is research. How we make sense of what we hear is influenced by our beliefs and philosophies.

On the surface, there might seem to be little to distinguish between the descriptive phenomenological approach (DPA) and interpretative phenomenological analysis (IPA), but the differences are significant.

In terms of their aims, DPA seeks to uncover the essential structures or essences of phenomena – what makes an experience what it is, stripped of individual variations and cultural interpretations. IPA, on the other hand, aims to understand how individuals make sense of their particular lived experiences within their specific contexts, acknowledging the role of culture, language and personal meaning-making.

Many of us unconsciously adopt an IPA-like approach to understanding our clients. For example, we might assume a female client will think in a particular way about a topic, drawing on our own experiences and beliefs, and potentially reflecting our prejudices as well. The DPA approach, however, does not view a phenomenon with preconceived notions of meaning and significance, but with a theoretical, philosophical open mind.

Two further qualitative studies have been undertaken in recent years. Devin Hussong and Joseph Micucci (2021) conducted a series of interviews with ten experienced "European-American" therapists (six males, four females) working in different settings with adults about their experiences with humour in the therapeutic setting. Their theoretical orientations varied: humanistic, psychodynamic, cognitive-behavioural, family systems and constructivist. The interviews addressed the participants' perceptions of the benefits, risks and contraindications of humour introduced by the therapist.

Neil Gibson (2014) interviewed six psychotherapists in the United Kingdom to investigate their experience of humour as both practitioners and clients of psychotherapy. The participants were 50:50 male/female and had between five and seven years' post-qualification experience. Half were British and half were EU-citizens residing and working in the United Kingdom. Four described their therapeutic practice as existential, one as integrative and one as psychoanalytic. As with the other studies, Gibson's interviews were semi-structured, and they opened with two questions:

- Can you tell me about any experiences you've had where humour has made an impact on the process of your clinical work?
- Can you tell me about any experiences you've had where humour has had an impact on the process of your own personal therapy?

(Gibson, 2014)

Unpacking the findings

The themes that emerged from these four studies fall into two very broad categories. The first theme addressed the role humour plays in the relationship between the therapist and the client. All of the researchers found that, overall, humour had a positive impact on the therapeutic alliance. Briggs and Owen spoke of humour contributing to fostering the relationship at its commencement, which can be "nerve-wracking" for clients, and to deepening the relationship in later sessions, where the most therapeutic humour is collaborative in nature:

> I think when you are able to share laughter together, you know you're both in on something together.
>
> (2022)

Talens (2020) confirmed this, humour helping her participants' youth clients relax and going on to strengthen the relationship between the therapists and their youth clients. The psychotherapists interviewed by Gibson (2014) and Hussong and Micucci (2021) also highlighted the beneficial impact the therapists' use of humour can have on the relationship.

The rapport-building effects of humour were found to contribute to a correction of the power imbalance in the therapeutic relationship. Gibson drew on the concept of superiority in humour discussed in previous chapters, arguing that, through humour, therapists simultaneously eroded their power status and boosted that of their clients. The image of the therapist as "human" and "fallible" is reported by Briggs and Owen (2022). Adolescents are also reported as needing humour in order to "engage in the treatment process" (Hussong & Micucci, 2021).

The therapist's humour, then, appears to contribute to the client's feeling of safety; researchers noted also that the client, with growing feelings of security, will often reciprocate the humour (Briggs & Owen, 2022). This, in turn, creates a stronger relationship, which in stressful environments such as prisons and hospitals (Talens, 2020) can already be an acute challenge. That these findings span the very wide range of therapeutic modalities reviewed is significant.

The second theme to emerge sheds light on the therapeutic work itself. As an emotion, humour:

> is felt as a lightness, and… offers relief from emotionally difficult moments or moments of stuckness.
>
> (Talens, 2020)

When the therapist uses humour, hidden depths in the client's consciousness can be unlocked. One therapist noted:

> He [the client] knew that I could appreciate his qualities, who he was, his skill in being funny, but also that I could see past that too and I don't think we could have gone deeper very easily without first being able to laugh together. So it was useful for his process, definitely.
>
> (Gibson, 2014)

Hussong and Micucci noted how humour can enhance the client's perspective and cognitive abilities:

> Humor takes some of the pressure off of [clients]. I think it allows them to feel safe looking at things that they otherwise wouldn't want to look at.
>
> (2021)

A participant in Gibson's study speaks of a client – a terminally ill patient – acquiring through humour the freedom to explore the "unknown" with greater bravery (2014). Other therapists highlight how the processes their clients go through are reflected in their use of humour; they find they are able to see humour in their situations and look back and laugh at themselves (Briggs & Owen, 2022). Humour also helps therapists model adaptive behaviours for their clients:

> It models for the client that two people can have a serious conversation and still have levity and compassion in those moments.
>
> (Hussong & Micucci, 2021)

Gallows humour is described in terms of a pain reliever, which can ease both the client and the practitioner (Briggs & Owen, 2022).

Reflection

A close relative of gallows humour is black humour, the kind of grim observational humour that conveys bitterness and truth rather than comedy. Living in central Europe in the 1990s, I encountered it many times and was reminded of it when I read an article interviewing female front-line soldiers in the Ukrainian military. In it, Evgeniya Emerald explains why women are favoured as snipers: "If a man hesitates whether to make a shot or not, a woman will never. Maybe that's why women are the ones giving birth, not men" (Malchevska, 2023). Statements such as this could perhaps be termed anti-humour: they challenge you to laugh. And yet, this is humour at its most profound and illuminating.

Caveats

All four studies recognised that there are risks with allowing humour into therapy spaces. The main risk is that the humour simply misfires, because it is felt to be hurtful or is otherwise misunderstood (Gibson, 2014), because the humour is contrived (Hussong & Micucci, 2021) or simply unnecessary:

> It's something you wait for the client to introduce, don't you? Because not everybody does need laughter.
>
> (Briggs & Owen, 2022)

Timing was also raised as a potential risk (Hussong & Micucci, 2021), such that the client's defensiveness might be increased if the therapist brought humour in too early in the relationship (Gibson, 2014).

The motives for introducing humour in the first place may not always be helpful. Clients may use humour, for example, to mask their emotions or avoid exploring them (Talens, 2020; Hussong & Micucci, 2021; Gibson, 2014). Also observed were clients' and therapists' attempts at ingratiating themselves with their dyad partner. Talens noted that "Humour can be used to get people to like you" (Talens, 2020), which could be a motivation for either party. The blurring of professional boundaries was also a risk identified (Talens, 2020; Hussong & Micucci, 2021; Gibson, 2014).

Discourse and content analyses

Three important studies explore the humour in verbal and non-verbal messages exchanged in the therapy room by examining and coding content in transcripts and recordings of sessions, including sessions involving Rogers.

Alberto Dionigi and Carla Canestrari (2018) studied audio recordings of eight first encounter "cognitive therapy" sessions for instances of humour. The sessions were conducted by two practitioners at mental health clinics in Italy.

Four different forms of humour are demonstrated by the therapists:

- A "rhetorical" ironic comment, which aligns the therapist with the client and which might be considered "affiliative" humour.
- In the same session, "surreal irony" is used, which again appears to be empathetic and affiliative in nature.
- With another client, the same therapist is interrupted by the client when explaining the symptoms of a panic attack, commenting that the therapist knows his stuff. The researchers suggest a role reversal has occurred when the therapist responds that he has studied the subject, as if in reply to a teacher's praise. It is a challenge to confirm this from reading the transcript; perhaps, the therapist is actually conveying sarcasm and/or displeasure at having been interrupted, particularly as the researchers note his eagerness to return to the matter at hand. Because of this uncertainty, it is not possible

to ascribe a particular humour style to the therapist's comment; it could be self-enhancing or, conversely, self-defeating.
- At a difficult emotional point for the client, the therapist initiates a change from the formal register of a clinical session to an informal one in an affiliative attempt to create a more relaxed atmosphere and help the client "overcome his resistance".

In all four instances, the client responded with laughter, which the researchers took as a signal that "they had understood that the therapist was trying to be humorous".

The three instances of humour initiated by clients that are reported here were categorised as follows:

- A client, explaining how he felt about a psychiatrist prescribing him lithium, makes the comment, "I said, 'Let's save lithium for car batteries…'". The researchers observed how the "therapist's alignment with and support for the client's humorous intent… represents a cooperative conversational activity".
- Another client is asked a question by the therapist, to which the answer seems negative. The client makes a humorous comment in the form of an absurd exaggeration and laughing, but the therapist does not reciprocate the laughter. The researchers noted that the therapist's silence signalled disalignment with the client.
- In something of a dance, a client suffering from panic attacks humorously echoes the therapist's words, and the latter reciprocates with the same humorous image, aligning himself with the client in the process of building a rapport.

Despite the limited scope of the research, the authors conclude from their work that humour has beneficial impacts on the therapeutic process. And perhaps, given Dionigi's position at the time at the Federazione Nazionale Clowndottori, this should come as no great surprise.

Kiersten Kneisel et al. at the University of Adelaide, New Zealand (Kneisel et al., 2022) analysed the content of 39 video-recorded counselling sessions to examine the frequency and features of humour. The videos – all filmed in the United States and featuring authentic, full-length one-to-one counselling sessions – were taken from the electronic academic database publisher Alexander Street. Different therapy modalities were included, including cognitive behavioural therapy, career counselling, Gestalt therapy, reality therapy, existential therapy, a person-centred session and four REBT sessions (see Chapter 5). The researchers noted a number of limitations to the generalisability of the study: all the sessions took place in the United States; the diverse range of modalities; and the presence of a recording camera in the sessions might have influenced how they progressed and/or the incidence of humour. In addition, the method for including/excluding videos was not made clear or how old the videos were.

Nonetheless, the results are noteworthy. The videos were studied to see who initiated humour, who laughed and how often and what the objects of the humour and laughter were. For the purposes of analysis, only humour that resulted in laughter was recorded on the assumption that laughter signified humour, though we know this is not always the case. Also, not all humorous exchanges give rise to laughter.

Laughter occurred 798 times in total, or about 25% less than in a typical daily conversation. Clients laughed nearly four times as much as counsellors and initiated nearly half the humorous exchanges. In a third of instances, the self was the target of the humour, which was reported as helping make the therapist appear less of an "authority figure". Other common humour targets included human nature, the other person present and other persons not present. No significant difference between the genders was noted.

Using text-mining and discourse analysis on session transcripts of Carl Rogers working with his clients, Pocholo Velasquez and Cristina Montiel (2018) at Ateneo de Manila University in the Philippines, attempted to understand how the core person-centred conditions are manifested in therapeutic discourse. The researchers obtained or created digital transcripts of 31 therapy sessions with 12 female and five male clients to arrive at a dataset of 1,790 utterances from Rogers, which were then notated and coded. This innovative approach to identifying "concrete ways in how to do Rogerian talk" revealed some surprising findings.

Rogers' congruence was coded as "tentative and affiliative", his language signifying the use of "careful, sensitive feedback". Common utterances included "I don't know…" as a means of seeking clarification, asking for feedback in "Is that it?", checking for agreement in "It sounds as though…" and reinterpreting the client's constructions with "In other words…". Most interestingly, however, the coders identified laughter as a significant and frequent signifier of congruence. They ascribe a number of clinical functions to the laughter: "modified meaning of utterance", "constructed affiliation" and "displayed authenticity". To illustrate this, they analyse a session with Jan, an unmarried woman anxious about approaching middle age. Towards the end of the session, Rogers proposes that Jan telephone her younger self, whom she has labelled "that naughty little girl". He precedes this suggestion with laughter, which the researchers observe as constructing the interpretation as unserious. He uses casual language: "Maybe you ought to look her up", which is followed by laughter. Jan responds in kind, jokingly asking Rogers if he would like to have the naughty little girl's number and also laughing. The discourse becomes distinctly affiliative at this point, anchored by the shared humour. The exchanges continue in their lightness, but not without purpose. Rogers references himself, "I'm only eighty, but I can still be a naughty little boy", in response to Jan's question: "even though I'm getting older, I can still be a naughty little girl?" The laughter recurs, reinforcing the "compatibility of these seemingly disparate experiences". Jan asks,

"Would that change my feelings about marriage?" and the response shows Rogers following the client's experiencing:

> I think that's a very significant question you're asking yourself. If you were a better friend of the little girl inside of you, would that make you less fearful of the risk of marriage? I feel badly that she's been missing for the last eighteen months, I really do.
>
> (Velasquez & Montiel, 2018)

Rogers' authenticity and the affiliative nature of the humour allow – and signal – a return to deeper emotional waters, which Jan duly affirms: "You're so right. You've really hit the nail on the head".

The complexity of the researchers' task is easily overlooked. They readily acknowledge the limitations of reviewing transcripts of utterances without reference to nonverbal utterances and body language, and the demand of the study for absolute categorisation of any given utterance to one of the core therapeutic conditions. They also note the relational semantic contexts of the sessions, where the therapeutic relationship is built up over time, allowing for things like mirroring of words and phrases, even in-jokes, as well as the cultural limitations of the analysis, meaning that the "core" conditions might be conveyed in different ways depending, for example, on the location of the therapy and the era in which it takes place. Nonetheless, what is clear from this study is that Rogers did not eschew humour or laughter in his work. Far from it, he appears confidently relaxed about allowing himself into the therapeutic relationship. Rogers' attitude towards humour in therapy is explored further in the next chapter.

Quantitative evidence

In Taiwan, Chuch Chang et al. (2013) carried out an old-school quantitative study of 67 adolescents, 33 of whom were control subjects, on the psychological, immunological and physiological impacts of Laughing Qigong therapy. Although not widely known in the West, qigong has been practised – in various forms – for centuries in China and neighbouring countries as a means of improving physical and mental health as well as longevity. The Laughing Qigong Program was established in the 1950s in Taiwan and, very briefly, comprises three main elements:

1 Warm-up stretching exercises to facilitate the flow of *qi* – a field of energy or "life force" considered to exist in and around the body of all living things.
2 Diaphragmic breathing combined with self-induced laughter to further unblock the body's meridians and release toxic *qi*.

3 A combination of physical gesturing, exclamations and self-induced laughter to release mental attachments, vent bottled-up negative mood states and transform negative *qi* into positive energy.

(Chang et al., 2013)

The experimental group took part in the Program once a week for eight weeks; the control group read books or did their homework instead. Immunological changes were derived from measurements of saliva cortisol levels; physiological indicators used blood pressure, heart rate and heart rate variability, while psychological changes were measured using three tools:

- a Chinese translation of Morris Rosenberg's Self-Esteem scale, a measure widely used with adolescents;
- the Chinese Humor Scale, derived from the Humor Styles Questionnaire (HSQ) discussed in Chapter 2 and adapted for Chinese contexts (Hsieh et al., 2005); and
- the Face Scale, a pictorial assessment tool using 20 sketched faces each depicting a slightly different mood state, from very happy to very sad, was developed for the non-verbal assessment of mood (Lorish & Maisiak, 1986).

Significant increases in subjects' mood states were noted over the duration of the experiment. Subjects also presented lowered cortisol levels. These changes, which were not observed in the control group, are attributed to subjects' improved stress management.

Refael Yonatan-Leus et al. (2018), studying therapeutic relationships of a year in length, found a perhaps unexpected result: clients with higher aggressive humour styles reported better outcomes than those who worked with therapists having lower aggressive humour styles. Less surprisingly, they also observed that therapists with self-defeating humour styles tended to lead to lower effectiveness. However, affiliative and self-enhancing humour styles, as well as playfulness and creativity, were observed to have little impact on therapeutic outcome. The unexpected outcomes appear to contradict the general view of effective therapists as warm and empathic, though it seems they remain congruent. It is not clear which therapeutic modalities were giving these results; equally, the sample size and demographic homogeneity may have distorted the outcomes, which nonetheless warrant further study.

Quantitative and qualitative evidence combined

In a relatively large-scale UK-based study, Mick Cooper and Rosanne Knox (2018) recruited 134 female and 34 male counsellors, of whom 70% were trainees and 93% considered their theoretical orientation to be person-centred, to examine how they used "chronic strategies of disconnection" in their day-to-day and therapeutic relationships. The four most common strategies of disconnection used in day-to-day life were physical avoidance (e.g. by leaving), mental withdrawal and switching off, falling silent and using humour. The latter included "'laughter' and 'making a joke'", which might be considered a "warm" way of disconnecting.

Olivia Longe (2018) at Dublin Business School, Ireland, explored the experiences of counselling clients and how they reacted when humour arose in the therapy room. 72 trainee therapists from humanistic and integrative programmes were recruited, and asked to report how often humour occurred, who initiated it and how it affected their appreciation of therapy overall. They were also asked to complete the HSQ and Coping Humour Scale (CHS) we saw in Chapter 2.

Three-quarters of the clients said their therapist initiated the humour, while a fifth said this never occurred. Just over half of the clients said they initiated the humour sometimes, and 38% frequently did. Four out of five clients stated they "sometimes" shared moments of laughter with their therapist; one in ten said they frequently shared such moments, and one in ten said this never happened.

13% of clients found the therapist's humour very helpful; 44% mostly helpful; 25% helpful sometimes. At the other end of the scale, 10% found the humour mostly unhelpful and 1% not at all helpful.

Longe found that, while the frequency of shared moments of laughter did not correlate with the subjects' ratings of the relationship with their therapists, she did ascertain that the ratings were strongly correlated with how well matched the humour styles of the therapist and client were and how helpful the clients found the therapists' humour.

Longe went on to apply a qualitative layer to the research by interviewing five of the participants to explore the topic in greater depth. The themes that emerged are summarised:

> ...the interview participants all gave examples of humour being an indicator of 'emotional and cognitive shifts' within their therapy, which they viewed as largely beneficial. These shifts were an ability of their humour: to bring relief; to reframe a situation; to reveal the unconscious; and for some, a sign of a return to mental wellness.
>
> (Longe, 2018)

Longe also explored the style of the clients' humour, observing that clients who reported self-defeating humour styles also reported weaker and less effective relationships with their therapists. This overlaps with Hussong and Micucci's research (2021), discussed earlier in this chapter, who found that clients with low self-esteem gravitate towards self-deprecating humour, while aggressive humour is favoured by more antagonistic clients. Affiliative and self-enhancing humour styles were found to indicate greater resilience. Noting these preferences can give therapists insight into not just the personalities of their clients but their coping strategies as well.

Systematic evidence

Two major reviews of the research carried out into the impacts of laughter were carried out in the last ten years.

The first, from C. Natalie van der Wal at the University of Leeds, UK, and Robin Kok at the University of Southern Denmark, exploring the potential benefits of "laughter-inducing therapies" (van der Wal & Kok, 2019), highlights some of the empirical challenges of researching humour, mirth and laughter.

The authors undertook the study to assess whether – in a climate of ever-increasing healthcare costs – sufficient evidence existed to be able to recommend the use of laughter-inducing therapies "as a cost-effective addition to regular healthcare". They identified nearly 100 studies published between 1995 and 2018 (with the overwhelming majority published between 2007 and 2015) for the first systematic review of the literature about the outcomes of laughter-inducing therapies.

Studies reviewed included quasi-experimental pre-test/post-test studies with a control group and randomised controlled trials, as well as pilot studies, field studies (without a control group) and studies with unknown study design. The studies assessed a mindbogglingly wide range of outcomes, from mental health and well-being (e.g. depression, coping responses, life satisfaction, mood, pain, self-esteem and anxiety) to physical health outcomes such as heart rate, immune function, pulmonary function, sleep quality and blood glucose level and blood pressure.

Despite the range and depth of this material, the researchers' most emphatic conclusion was that:

> …to our knowledge, there are few imaginable contraindications, which makes it universally safe to practice. The social aspect of laughing together seems to be an advantage to alleviate societal problems such as loneliness, bullying at schools, or aggression in general.

The review did report evidence of improvements overall in depression and reduced anxiety generated by laughter-inducing therapies, with greater improvements coming from "simulated" laughter (non-humorous, fake or self-induced) compared with "spontaneous" laughter (humorous, triggered by a stimulus such as a joke). However, the authors reported that

> Overall, reporting quality was low or very low, and crucial information to assess risk of bias was often missing from the studies.

Considering that the vast majority of the research identified by van der Wal and Kok was carried out in the twenty-first century this is surprising. Concomitantly, they found it impossible to offer anything more than tentative conclusions as to the efficacy – or otherwise – of laughter-inducing therapies. The authors could not recommend their use in "clinical practice on anything other than a complementary, patient-preference basis". More positively, van der Wal and Kok do conclude that laughter therapies benefit certain people and circumstances, including patients with serious or terminal conditions. Because watching funny videos and doing laughter exercises can be done in relaxed positions, people with reduced mobility might also benefit, while the elderly or cognitively impaired could benefit from non-humorous laughter therapies since they do not rely on verbal skills.

A second study, carried out by Freda Gonot-Schoupinsky et al. (2020) at the University of Derby, UK, included research into humour and laughter and the impact of both on personal development and mental health. For the purposes of their study, personal development was defined as "a way to develop, manage, or optimise our Biological, Psychological, Social [& Socioeconomic], Environmental, and Behavioural (BPSE-B) needs and conditions throughout the life cycle". The study, a compound scoping review in that it included both primary and secondary research, encompassed 564 articles and over half a million participants, with the majority of the research focused on humour rather than laughter. The researchers hoped to be able to use the research findings to "unify" the various definitions of humour and laughter (explored in Chapter 1) to facilitate future research into both phenomena. The resulting definitions supplement rather than replace those existing definitions:

> **Humour** is predominantly a cognitive process, often involving perceptions of funniness, occurring alone or socially. It can be created, appreciated, reminisced, arise spontaneously, or enacted e.g. clowns, and serves diverse personal development functions including social bonding. It may be induced by a range of emotions, playfulness, and, or, laughter, or induce these. It is influenced by motives, circumstances, and cultural and individual differences.
>
> **Laughter** is predominantly a physical behaviour, occurring alone or socially. It is often used as a form of verbal expression or communication. It can be spontaneous, provoked, or self-induced, and serves diverse personal development functions including social bonding. It may be induced by a range of emotions, playfulness, and, or, humour, or induce these. It is influenced by motives, circumstances, and cultural and individual differences.

As definitions go, these may not be the pithiest, but they support the collation of 15 characteristics shared by both humour and laughter:

1. Universal; likely innate;
2. Contagious;
3. Can produce physiological and psychosocial benefits;

4 Can beneficially occur alone;
5 Can be involuntary/spontaneous or voluntary/purposeful;
6 Passive listening is beneficial;
7 Able to be self-induced;
8 Trainable;
9 Associated with cheerfulness and playfulness;
10 Associated with smiling and able to induce the Duchenne smile, a mark of genuine pleasure;
11 Can occur due to pathology, be harmful, and pose a risk;
12 Able to be drug-induced;
13 Influenced by and adaptable to context and location;
14 Influenced by individual differences; and
15 Influenced by cultural differences.

Perhaps the most significant output from this research is the multi-faceted Humour-laughter-affect (HuLA) model, which brings in the four humour styles we saw in Chapter 2, reproduced in Figure 6.2.

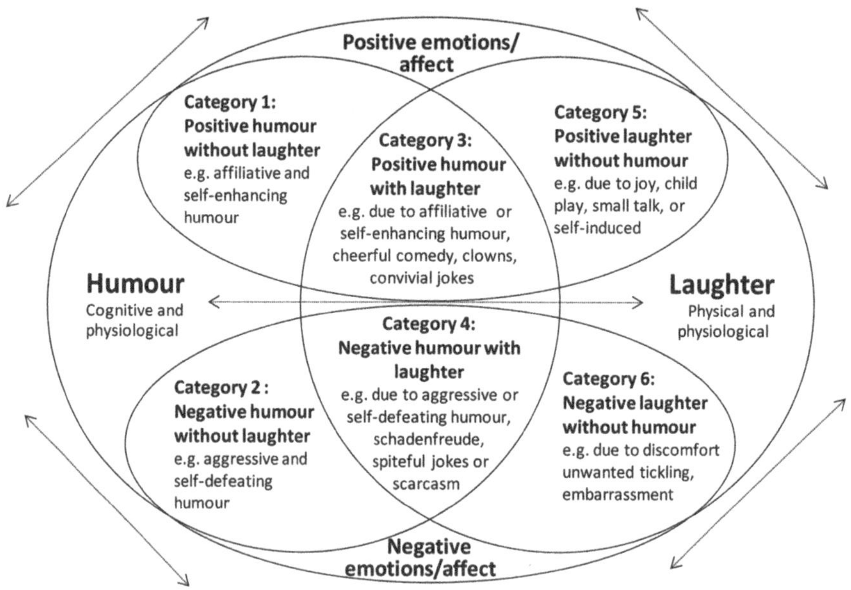

Figure 6.2 Humour-laughter-affect (HuLA) model (Gonot-Schoupinsky et al., 2020).

Key. Arrows show given or potential bi-directional cause and effect relationships, for example, happy people have positive and unhappy people have negative humour styles.

The application of the HuLA model is examined further in research by Gonot-Schoupinsky et al. (2024) into the therapeutic benefits of a new laughter therapy, the "Laughie", where the individual is prescribed with the (at least once) daily task of recording laughter lasting one minute. The therapy aims to enable individuals and their health providers to assess improvements and/or changes.

As these two studies show, there are several challenges with undertaking a systematic review, the main one being the lack of homogeneity in the studies that fall within the scope of the review. An important study may, as a result, be omitted simply because its approach differs too radically from that of the reviewers. The quality – and therefore reliability – of the underlying studies poses a challenge if we are trying to arrive at a generalisable conclusion. Thirdly, the languages used in reporting studies remain an issue, hindering the sharing of English-language and non-English-language studies. Hopefully, technological advances will eradicate this barrier soon.

So, the question remains: if both these systematic reviews rely on data that may be flawed by study design, cultural or other unidentified bias, as well as the scope of the reviews themselves, how conclusively can we conclude that humour and laughter are (a) good for us and (b) helpful in the therapeutic setting?

Pause for thought

What further evidence might we need before we conclude on the question posed at the start of the chapter: Do we know if humour and laughter positively impact therapeutic outcomes?

Can a phenomenon as emotional, idiosyncratic, enigmatic and ephemeral as humour be categorised and measured and then distilled and prescribed as if it were a medication?

If not, how do we test its contribution in the therapy space?

Summing up

Humour and laughter in therapy have been researched extensively since the turn of the century, though very little of the research has focused on person-centred therapy.

Qualitative research into the experiences of therapists and clients paints a richly detailed picture of *complex, beneficial therapeutic relationships* built with the help of humour and contrasts that with descriptions of what happens *when the humour misfires*. Quantitative research offers additional evidence on the benefits of introducing humour into a wide range of therapeutic settings, but *shortcomings in study quality* undermine the reliability of findings. Perhaps, most revealing of all, analyses of *Carl Rogers'* work show that he was not averse to allowing humour into the therapy space.

References

Briggs, E., & Owen, A. (2022). Funny, right? How do trainee and qualified therapists experience laughter in their practice with clients? *Counselling and Psychotherapy Research, 2022*(22), 827–838. https://doi.org/10.1002/capr.12525

Chang, C., Tsai. G. & Hsieh, C.-J. (2013) Psychological, immunological and physiological effects of a Laughing Qigong Program (LQP) on adolescents, *Complementary Therapies in Medicine, 21*, 660–668. http://dx.doi.org/10.1016/j.ctim.2013.09.004

Cooper, M., & Knox, R. (2018). Therapists' self-reported chronic strategies of disconnection in everyday life and in counselling and psychotherapy: An exploratory study. *British Journal of Guidance & Counselling, 46*(2), 185–200. https://doi.org/10.1080/03069885.2017.1343457

Dionigi, A., & Canestrari, C. (2018). The use of humour by therapists and clients in cognitive therapy. *European Journal of Humour Research, 6*(3), 50–67. https://doi.org/10.7592/EJHR2018.6.3.dionigi

Gibson, N. (2014). The best medicine? Psychotherapists' experience of the impact of humour on the process of psychotherapy. [DProf thesis, Middlesex University / New School of Psychotherapy and Counselling]. https://eprints.mdx.ac.uk/15730/

Gonot-Schoupinsky, F., Neal, M., & Carson, J. (2024). *The positive psychology of laughter and humour*. Emerald Publishing.

Gonot-Schoupinsky, F. N., Garip, G., & Sheffield, D. (2020). Laughter and humour for personal development: A systematic scoping review of the evidence. *European Journal of Integrative Medicine, 37*. https://doi.org/10.1016/j.eujim.2020.101144

Hsieh, C.-J., Hsiao, Y.-L., Liu, S.-J. & Chang, C. (2005). Positive psychological measure: constructing and evaluating the reliability and validity of a Chinese humor scale applicable to professional nursing. *The Journal of Nursing Research, 13*(3), 206–215. https://doi.org/10.1097/01.JNR.0000387542.91254.42

Hussong, D. K., & Micucci, J. A. (2021). The use of humor in psychotherapy: Views of practicing psychotherapists. *Journal of Creativity in Mental Health, 16*(1), 77–94. https://doi.org/10.1080/15401383.2020.1760989

Kneisel, K., Smith, L., & Capundan, K. (2022). Humor and laughter in counseling: A content analysis of 39 videorecorded counseling sessions. *Journal of Creativity in Mental Health*. https://doi.org/10.1080/15401383.2022.2074590

Longe, O. (2018). Can I laugh now? Understanding humour within psychotherapy from the client's perspective [Master's dissertation, Dublin Business School]. https://esource.dbs.ie/handle/10788/3968

Lorish, C.D. & Maisiak, R. (1986). The face scale: A brief, nonverbal method for assessing patient mood. *Arthritis & Rheumatism, 29*, 906–909. https://doi.org/10.1002/art.1780290714

Malchevska, O. (2023, August 2). "It's like playing with death" – Ukraine's female front line soldiers. *BBC News*. https://www.bbc.co.uk/news/world-europe-66254964

Talens, P. (2020). When working in a youth service, how do therapists experience humour with their clients? *European Journal of Psychotherapy & Counselling*, *22*(*1–2*), 80–96. https://doi.org/10.1080/13642537.2020.1766526

van der Wal, C. N., & Kok, R. N. (2019). Laughter-inducing therapies: Systematic review and meta-analysis. *Social Science & Medicine*, *232*, 473–488. https://doi.org/10.1016/j.socscimed.2019.02.018

Velasquez, P. A. E., & Montiel, C. J. (2018). Reapproaching Rogers: A discursive examination of client-centered therapy. *Person-Centered & Experiential Psychotherapies*, *17*(3), 253–269. https://doi.org/10.1080/14779757.2018.1527243

Yonatan-Leus, R., Tishby, O., Shefler, G., & Wiseman, H. (2018). Therapists' honesty, humor styles, playfulness, and creativity as outcome predictors: A retrospective study of the therapist effect. *Psychotherapy Research*, *28*(5), 793–802. https://doi.org/10.1080/10503307.2017.1292067

Part III

Humour and the person-centred approach

Chapter 7

Carl Rogers and humour

Introduction

The problem – the reason this book was written and probably the reason you're reading it – is that, despite all the research evidence we have seen, Rogers never actually wrote – or, it seems, said – anything about humour in therapy. Consequently, we can only infer what Rogers might have thought, drawing on the recollections of people who knew him and on transcripts and recordings of sessions with clients, interviews and public debates.

DOI: 10.4324/9781003638773-11

In this age of Google, Wikipedia and even GenAI, it is easy to assume that all knowledge is accessible at the click of a virtual button. So much is already known about Rogers' theories – through his writings and those who followed – but his personal life is less widely known. What follows is indebted to Howard Kirschenbaum's exhaustive 2007 biography. It provides much of the material in this brief archaeological exercise in detecting what, if anything at all, Rogers thought of humour's place in the therapy room.

Pause for thought

We might hypothesise that, if Rogers was comfortable with humour *per se*, and he worked as congruently as he could, then perhaps humour was not banned from the therapy room but was welcomed into the relationship between therapist and client.

Early life

Born on 8 January 1902 in Illinois, in midwestern America, Carl Rogers was the fourth of six children: four brothers and a sister. The suburban district of Oak Park, described by its residents as "the place where the saloons end and the churches begin" (Kirschenbaum, 2007), was ideally suited to Rogers' parents. His father, Walter, a civil engineer and successful businessman, came from a Congregational family and his mother, Julia, was a strict Baptist who, during Rogers' childhood, grew "increasingly fundamentalist".

Exceptionally bright, Rogers had already become proficient at reading by the time he started school. He was also "a rather sickly child – slight, shy, prone to tears, often the target of jokes and teasing by his older brothers". Nonetheless, he seemed ever ready to take on his brothers when they teased and taunted him. Fighting inside the house was forbidden, however, so the boys were told, "Go outdoors and beat your brains out if you want, but don't come screaming to me when you get hurt".

When Rogers was 12, the family moved away from the dubious influences of the suburbs, where they had counted the Hemingways among their neighbours, to a 300-acre farm outside Chicago. The move was significant for him in several ways. Rural life brought a sense of isolation, which did not help his social awkwardness, but he developed a passion for the natural world and farming in particular. From observing growth processes in plants and animals, he developed a deep appreciation for natural development that would later translate into his belief in the human organism's innate tendency towards growth and self-actualisation.

He found solace from the isolation in reading, acquiring a taste for "Dickens, with his humor and his indignation at oppression of any kind, and his wonderful characters... Mark Twain with his chuckles can always knock out my homesickness", he wrote while working and residing at a lumber yard owned by an uncle in North Dakota.

Rogers later described his childhood as lonely and emotionally restrictive; Kirschenbaum notes that, to his knowledge, Rogers did not speak or write about his parents with fondness or affection. Their emphasis on moral superiority and intellectual achievement created an environment where emotional expression was discouraged and unconditional acceptance was notably absent. This personal experience of conditional love – where acceptance was contingent upon meeting parental expectations – was another influence that would later inform his concept of unconditional positive regard as essential for psychological health. Another source of youthful confusion is noted in his ambivalence about intimacy, emotional or physical. "Anything that was important was private and concerned things nobody else could understand", he wrote, and, on observing a young newlywed couple, "I think perhaps it was... the first time in my life I realized that loving someone could be *fun*" (emphasis in original).

Following in the family footsteps, Rogers went to university at Wisconsin in 1919, and initially took up studying agriculture. Liberated from the rural isolation of his younger years, Rogers seems to have flourished, engaging in numerous extracurricular activities. He notes poignantly in his journal that "I have made the first friend I ever had and hosts and hosts of fine acquaintances". But his initial enthusiasm for agriculture studies was supplanted (excuse the pun) a year later at a Young Men's Christian Association event by a new mission (excuse the pun): "During Eddy's morning speech I almost made up my mind to go into Christian work and during his afternoon speech I made my final decision. God help me keep it!".

But perhaps the most transformational of Rogers' university experiences was his taking part in the World Student Christian Federation's conference in Beijing – then Peking – in China in April 1922, which over six months took him across South East Asia, Japan and Hawaii. Rogers combined making acquaintances with Christians from numerous other cultures with visiting as many sites as time allowed, including one nighttime hike to the summit of Mount Fuji from where he witnessed sunrise. The experiences had mixed impacts on him, according to Kirschenbaum, who observes that while Rogers came to respect individuals from other cultures and races, he showed "a lack of interest and respect for the cultures themselves beyond that of the superficial tourist". However, he did not return home entirely unchanged: increasing doubts about the religious doctrines practised by his parents emerged, along with a new sense of personal autonomy. We see, perhaps, in this growing maturity and tendency towards intellectual and emotional freedom, the theme of clients being freed to discover their own authentic paths rather than conforming to external expectations.

Rogers' gravitation to a more humanistic approach to Christianity continued when, despite his father's attempts at bribing him to attend the "outstanding Fundamentalist seminary" Princeton, he and Helen, his new wife, moved to New York. There, he studied at Union Theological Seminary, a progressive institution that promoted social justice and where Rogers found "there was no pressure of an orthodoxy of any kind". During his studies, the newlyweds spent several months in 1925 at a rural community in southern Vermont where Rogers worked as a pastor. At the time, a hotly contested trial – the first to be broadcast on national radio – was taking place in Tennessee, in which a schoolteacher, John Thomas Scopes, was found guilty of violating state law prohibiting the teaching of human evolution in public schools. Rogers gave sermons on this and other examples of disputed Biblical inerrancy, but, aware that his audience might not have been on the same page, he wrily noted: "I found it absolutely impossible to make my sermons longer than twenty minutes, a fact which disturbed me but for which my congregation was doubtless thankful".

Psychologist, psychiatrist, psychotherapist

A growing interest in psychology led Rogers to transfer to Teachers College at Columbia University, a private research university in New York. In the 1920s, psychology was still a young science, and Rogers soon found himself engaged in the then-favoured activity of "testing" (see earlier chapters), which combined his childhood interest in scientific observation with a burning desire to understand what makes people tick.

In need of a salary to support his young family, Rogers took up his first professional position at the Rochester Society for the Prevention of Cruelty to Children, where he would work as a clinical psychologist until 1939. Many ascribe the development of Rogers' theories as stemming from his time in California, not always admiringly. But it was here, on the Eastern Seaboard, that Rogers' radical ideas took their shape.

The work brought him into close contact with troubled children and families, and much of it combined psychology with psychiatry, social work and psychotherapy. He questioned the limitations of the traditional diagnostic and interpretive approaches being used. The experience greatly influenced his theoretical development, which we see in his 1939 book, *The Clinical Treatment of the Problem Child.* In it, he documents his efforts at applying the various therapy modalities in vogue at the time, including psychoanalysis and interpretative therapy, and why he found them inadequate. Rogers was quick to acknowledge that the approach took its inspiration from concepts developed by Otto Rank. A psychoanalyst and close collaborator of Sigmund Freud, Rank came to challenge the concept of the Oedipal complex with his own theories about separation traumas arising from the birth process. Freud's ostracising of Rank led to the latter's emigration to the United States, where his ideas – including the importance of the therapeutic relationship, time-limited therapy and the focus on present experience rather than historical reconstruction – found a friendlier reception.

In his book, Rogers describes four characteristics of relationship theory derived from his clinical observations of the parents he had worked with. First, the parents must want to receive help with their children. Second, the "worker" must provide

> an atmosphere in which the parent can come freely to experience and realize his own attitudes. The worker creates this atmosphere by her acceptance of the parent, by her failure to criticize, by her refusal to impose on the parent any program or recommendations, and by her refusal to answer questions except when the parent genuinely desires an answer and is unable to answer for himself.
>
> (1939)

Thirdly, provided the parents receive the acceptance of the worker, they may come to accept themselves and their limitations, achieved less through instruction or advice and more through the ability to express their feelings freely. Finally, and again as a result of the previous characteristics, the autonomy of the parents is respected and they are trusted to make their own judgements about how to treat their child. The worker avoids intervening even when they seem about to make a decision the worker believes would be inadvisable, because "there is the feeling that even mistaken decisions, independently made, make for growth".

Here then, we see the nascent concepts of unconditional positive regard, empathy and non-directivity. Rogers goes on to formulate the concept of the actualising tendency: "most children, if given a reasonably normal environment which meets their own emotional, intellectual, and social needs, have within themselves sufficient drive toward health to respond and make a comfortable adjustment to life". Already well-known in New York state, the publication of *The Clinical Treatment of the Problem Child* saw Rogers' reputation extend far beyond, and in 1940 the family moved to Columbus, Ohio, where Rogers took up a professorship at Ohio State University. Here, he further formulated the concepts of client-centred non-directive therapy and began undertaking research into the approach that included the recording of sessions, unheard of at the time. His second book, *Counseling and Psychotherapy: Newer Concepts in Practice* (1942a), was a bestseller.

During World War II, Rogers was asked to lead several governmental research projects, including a project during 1944–1945 to give intensive counselling training to workers engaged with helping returning military personnel adjust to civilian life. The day-long workshops were held most weeks, and Kirschenbaum estimated that in total around 5,000 volunteer workers were trained. It was during the parties that concluded these workshops that Rogers was obliged to sit through repeated skits parodying the non-directive approach they had spent the day studying and role-playing: a volunteer "counsellor" parrots the desperate words of a serviceman "client" who, threatening suicide, walks to the open window and jumps to his death (Kirschenbaum, 2007). It was time to drop the label *non-directive*.

A husband and father

We step back from the professional and academic life and wonder, given his theories on actualising tendency, conditions of worth, unconditional positive regard and so on, as well as his own upbringing, what kind of husband and father Rogers turned out to be.

Helen and Carl had, in fact, met during their early school years when the Rogers family lived in Illinois. They lost touch when the family moved away and were reunited at university, where Helen was studying art. Carl proposed to her before he left on his trip to the Far East, but she did not accept until he returned. Their marriage, in August 1924, did not meet with approval from Rogers' parents because he had not completed his education and could not support Helen. The newlywed couple also moved to New York, which must have met with greater disapproval.

We see some aspects of the relationship between husband and wife shedding light on Carl's evolving humanist and therapeutic ideas. For example, realising that neither he nor Helen was experienced or otherwise prepared for the act of sex, Carl set about remedying Helen's lack of satisfaction through dialogue. Taking part in research on the subject – a "more personalized forerunner of the Kinsey researches" (Rogers, 1972) – he noted the attitude of the interviewer as being calm and at ease – qualities we see when we view tapes of Rogers' practice. The experience bolstered his own determination to talk to Helen:

> It was frightening because every question and every answer made one or the other of us so vulnerable – to attack, to criticism, to ridicule, to rejection… we seem to have realized that the thing which cannot *possibly* be revealed to the other *can* be revealed, the problem which you *must keep* to yourself can be shared.
>
> (emphasis in original)

Helen, too, wrote about their sex life:

> What I feel was most fortunate for me was Carl's ability to be open and frank and truthful in facing all our problems, including our sex life. We were able to establish a free communication with each other, never allowing misunderstandings or hurts to fester. It gave us a basis for growth and closeness which has lasted through the years. His ability to listen and be empathic was there in the very first years of our marriage.
>
> (H. Rogers, 1965)

A surprising reminiscence about married life reveals a leaning towards the negative humour styles that we discussed in earlier chapters. Growing up, Rogers and his siblings seemed to have thrived on sarcasm and teasing in their interactions with each other. Rogers was often a target of the gibes but not the only one, as he recalls:

> The brothers mercilessly teased their shy sister on one of her rare dates and just about destroyed "any interest she had in boys"... probably one of the reasons she never got married.
>
> (Kirschenbaum, 2007)

One wonders what their parents thought about this distinctly unchristian, sibling rivalry. The pain stayed with Rogers, as did the behaviour:

> I learned, early in our marriage, that the sarcasm which was so much a part of my family life, where we were continually throwing verbal barbs at one another, was something which hurt her [Helen] deeply and which she would not tolerate.
>
> (Rogers, 1972)

In addition, Rogers mentions an "annoying behavior which we have both exhibited at times", namely public humiliation: "When one spouse, in a social or public situation, ridicules or humilitates or puts down the other, almost always as a 'joke'". An example is given, though tellingly, he recalls another couple's exchange instead of something he or Helen had said. He does see it for what it is:

> ...a cowardly copout. If I have some negative feeling about something she [Helen] has done, I would much prefer to take the more courageous step of voicing it to her when we are alone, rather than 'jokingly' needling her in a social situation.

The roles that Carl and Helen played in their relationship were distinctly conventional: the husband as breadwinner, the wife as nest-builder and nurturer. More than once, Helen expressed her satisfaction with the arrangement, including:

> I am essentially a homemaker and have always felt that to make the wheels run smoothly and have an attractive home in which to bring our friends has contributed very substantially to the success and prominence to which Carl has risen.
>
> (1965)

It was while living in New York that the couple bore their son David in March 1926. Natalie was born in October 1928 in Rochester. The recollections of both children revealed some surprising disparities between their experiences and the views Rogers espoused on parenting. Writing on developments in approaches to parenting, Rogers was emphatic about:

> the growing weight of evidence regarding the vital importance of deep emotional security and affection for the infant… No longer do we find stress on rigid schedules, on the importance of definite rules, on the hospital-like method of caring for infants. Instead there is a wholesome stress on the infant's need of affection and cuddling, on the fact that such emotional security is as important as cod-liver oil.
>
> (1942b)

Yet, both David and Natalie observed his remoteness from them, which they ascribed to his shyness and his devotion to his work. David described his father as a "comfortable comrade" (D. Rogers, 1995):

> Thus, it is "doing things" with him, rather than conversations, that I recall. We would wash the dishes together, mow the lawn, and the like. I remember him as being shy, outdoorsy, gentle, but not around very often. I don't really remember many conversations with him.

He did speak often and fondly of his father's "unconditional regard", though Kirschenbaum cites an occasion when he annoyed Rogers so much that he said something that

> I remember was very crushing. He said, 'You just never know when to quit, and I hope you never take a drink because if you do you'll be a drunkard.' It was about the harshest thing he ever said to me.
>
> (2007)

Natalie's relationship with her parents was more conflicted; her recollections contradict her father's rejection of "definite rules" in favour of "the infant's need of affection and cuddling" (Rogers, 1942b):

> Although Carl had rebelled against his very strict Congregational upbringing, some of that cloak still hung over his dealings with us. Parents were definitely the authority. Rules were rules, and 'No' meant *no*. We were to "Do as you are told, with no monkey business!'
>
> (N. Rogers, 1995, emphasis in original)

She spoke of his remoteness in no uncertain terms: "I never felt close to my father until I was about thirteen". Ironically, she also criticised what she saw as shortcomings in his core conditions:

> I am embarrassed to say that I often thought of him as naive and frequently dense when it came to understanding interpersonal relationships. Hindsight can be illuminating. I now understand that he was not dense, only uncommunicative. He was a master of listening and letting you know you were understood. However, in my relationship with him, he often lacked the willingness or ability to say what he was thinking and feeling at the moment.

By contrast, Natalie felt that her mother's creative nurturing brought out her own creative instincts: "Mother's love, warmth, and genuine caring for us was good medicine for self-esteem, which is one of the foundation blocks for creativity". As she matured, she found herself coming closer to her father, however:

> On several visits home, when I was in torment about my life, I asked to talk to my father, alone. I knew that he would let me come to my own decisions whereas Mother would overwhelm me with her opinions.
>
> (N. Rogers, 1980)

Natalie married in 1950 and began adopting a life of the dutiful wife and devoted mother (to three daughters), much as her mother had done: "Becoming a mother was the highest priority in my life" (N. Rogers, 1995). Her later years saw an awakening to more potentialities, however, starting with taking up psychology studies. Encouraged by no less a figure than Abraham Maslow, who mentored her through her master's thesis, her studies brought together her interests in person-centred therapy and artistic creativity. She went on to lecture on artistic therapy, but with greater life fulfilment came tensions in the marriage. However, having never seen her parents fight, or even argue, she felt ill-equipped to deal with marital conflict:

> I never had any models for how to deal with anger… As kids we were sent to our rooms to deal with our feelings… There was no facilitation of open feelings in the family by anybody.
>
> (Kirschenbaum, 2007)

Depression and suicide ideation followed until, in 1970, they divorced. Natalie was able to shake off the stigma of single-motherhood and moved with her children to California. Here she essentially reinvented herself: an arts therapist, a single mother, a feminist. The upheaval brought about new, updated reflections on her upbringing, which she mused upon in the redemptive memoir *Emerging Woman: A Decade of Midlife Transitions* (1980). In it, she expresses conflicted views on what she came to see as Helen playing down her own artistic talents and aspirations in order to keep house and husband: anger at how poorly she felt she had been prepared for married life and motherhood, despair at Helen's oxymoronic self-deprecating pride and also tender awe at her unfailing love for all the family. Natalie's reinvention also brought her closer to her father, to whom she suggested, in 1974, that they work together. His response was instantaneous, asking simply what she thought they might do (N. Rogers, 1995). Over a period of six years, the two of them, together with five colleagues, delivered a residential summer workshop called "The Person-Centered Approach". The programme was developed largely by Natalie. The group came from different backgrounds and had differing professional interests but shared humanistic values. She writes:

> We laughed and cried together. We got angry at each other and found ways to appreciate and use our anger constructively. We played and laughed and did rather foolish things together. We shared our dreams as well as our visions of the future. We were all learners, and we made collective decisions.

She went on to develop her own enormously successful practice, blending person-centred therapy with expressive arts, though she often struggled with what she perceived as standing in her father's shadow.

David became a much-respected medical doctor with a reputation for public service. He married and had three children, with much of their care seen to by their mother:

> It's my bet that my children felt (as I now do) that I was too busy professionally to give them enough attention.
>
> (D. Rogers, 1995)

It seems that, in the domestic sphere at least, Rogers did not entirely shake off the attitudes with which he had grown up. And it was Helen who parented more person-centredly. Many parents assess their children's progression by measuring their height each birthday, marked with fondness and pride on a door frame somewhere. Rogers went further, subjecting both Natalie and David to IQ tests annually for 12 years (Kirschenbaum, 2007). Was this idle scientific curiosity? Or did he fear they might embarrass him? He must have expected the experience of the testing would leave an introjection or two – the need to impress, to excel, perhaps – and concluded that some conditions of worth were tolerable, if not welcome.

A recollection of Helen's suggests that although Rogers may not have been the most fun father in the world, he did not banish mirth and levity from the family home:

> We were all dead tired from having driven for two days through blizzards and ice to reach Columbus. Carl was stretched out on the floor of our new house, our teenage son [David] was helping unload. He came through the livingroom carrying a large article on his shoulders - walked through the unfurnished dining room and crashed into the low hanging chandelier. It splintered into a thousand pieces with a shattering clatter. Carl, lying on the floor in a near comatose state, turned his head, opened one eye, and said in a soft voice, "Son, you learn the hard way." It brought roars of laughter and has been a byword in our family ever since.
>
> (H. Rogers, 1965)

Increasing stature

Rogers' most productive years followed the end of the war, initially with a move to Chicago where he set up the University's first counselling centre alongside his continuing educational work. Some of the students at Ohio came with him, notably Victoria Axline, herself already a well-known play therapy practitioner. His research continued, focused on sessions with seven to ten clients whom he often saw more than once a week. The work brought an increasing awareness that therapy was most effective not when the therapist relied on a technique but when the therapist adopted and conveyed to the client the attitudes of authenticity, acceptance and understanding. These ideas, together with the Theory of Personality and Behavior – 19 "Propositions" that set out his thinking on the actualising tendency, were set out in his 1951 book *Client-Centered Therapy*. He described the process of actualising as an almost evolutionary impulse in all living things to strive for optimum growth and satisfaction, however they may be construed. The actualising tendency's end goal – if this term can be used – is eloquently described by Christine Brown:

> ...the more I accept and value my experiences and myself, purely as I am in relation to those experiences, the greater my capacity to self-direct internal change and development becomes, and the greater trust I build in my own perceptions and values, the more I can accept and connect to others without the need to seek to change them.
>
> (Brown, 2015)

In 1957, Rogers broke more ground with the article *The Necessary and Sufficient Conditions of Therapeutic Personality Change* – a distillation of research into effective therapy that Rogers warned "may be disproved" but which remains the guiding North Star for person-centred therapists. That same year, he and

Helen moved to Wisconsin, where, in 1961, he published *On Becoming a Person* (2004), a synthesis of his work and theories to date. In 1964, they moved to La Jolla, on the coastal outskirts of San Diego, California and Rogers joined the Western Behavioral Sciences Institute, where he engaged in group work and encounter groups. Personality clashes led to a splinter group, including Rogers, leaving the Institute (which became defunct in 1991) to establish the Center for Studies of the Person (CSP). The CSP continues to this day, promoting person-centred thinking and research.

One side of Rogers that isn't immediately obvious from reading his works and watching the recordings is the emotional impact of the opposition he met at various points in his career. Helen Rogers recounts that:

> Chicago also was to be a time of trouble for us, a time when the pressures became so great, in his counseling of disturbed people, that my husband began to lose confidence in his own ability to help others, and to be on the brink of psychosis himself. One morning he started out for work and in ten minutes came back to the apartment saying, "I can't do it! I can't go on – let's get out of here *right now*." And we did. Within the hour we were packed and in the car driving away - south and east - no destination in mind. He calls this his "escape period." It lasted a number of months. We finally came to roost at our hideaway on Seneca Lake and spent a month of roughing it in our cabin in the cold temperatures of May in New York State. There were periods of real despair which we weathered together. It never occurred to me that he could not or would not recover. We roamed the hills and I taught him all I could about painting. We both spent many hours enjoying and exploring and painting the countryside.
>
> (1965, emphasis in original)

She also noted how Rogers found the time at Wisconsin less satisfying, despite the prestige of the professorship, because he felt "'hemmed in' and not allowed to be of influence on his students" (1965).

It is tempting to assume that Rogers naturally enjoyed the stature – the fame – that his work brought him. My first contact with his work came through reading *On Becoming a Person*. I found the wisdom it contained frighteningly obvious: obvious because why wouldn't someone want to be treated with acceptance, with empathy and with authenticity? And frighteningly obvious because it seemed to me that the book should be read by everyone, that it should be taught in schools as part of the National Curriculum. And yet it wasn't, so was I missing something or is the world just mad? Pondering on what kind of person writes such a book, I grew acutely aware of Rogers' humility. But there was something more. In the autobiographical first chapter, *This is me*, he talks about the criticism his ideas have attracted over the years. Given their radicality, he must have anticipated resistance. But what seems to have wearied him just as much is the clamour of what he ironically calls his "uncritical and unquestioning 'disciples'". This was not a man, it seemed, who craved adulation, the limelight. He found his "most fruitful periods of work are the times when I have been able to get completely away from what others think, from professional expectations and daily demands". The observations conclude with the mournful, "I prize the privilege of being alone" (Kirschenbaum, 2007). It should come as no surprise that we find no humorous anecdotes along the lines of "A Funny Thing Happened To Me In Therapy" tucked away in this book.

Reflection

During the 1980s, my father worked on the periphery of the music business, and through him, I met a number of pop stars. I won't drop any names, because that would be vain of me. I was in my mid-teens, an age when I was easily impressed and readily overawed by these musical giants. But I recall that whether it was Marc Almond, Ian Dury, Andrew Eldritch, Laurie Anderson or (I could go on) David Bowie, one thing stands out – their distance, a combination of shyness, aloofness, diffidence, reticence and wariness. It is, of course, unlikely that they were overawed by the experience of meeting me, but perhaps, like Rogers, they found the constant adulation overwhelming and longed for quieter moments when they could retreat, re-energise and return to their work.

How did others see Rogers?

Does this mean Rogers had no sense of humour? Contemporaries and family alike described him as "very hard-headed", "disciplined", "cool, collected, competitive... intellectually tough" and "certainly not 'cuddly'" (Kirschenbaum, 2007). Writing on the years in California, Kirschenbaum cites instances of Rogers' growing fatigue with critics and opponents, which revealed itself in "his acerbic wit".

His shyness was taken by some as aloofness, particularly in large gatherings where he was billed as the star of the show, something he dreaded. On paper, however, he could be sharp-witted and sarcastic, as when corresponding with the accounting department at the University of Chicago, or the University's Chancellor to whom he sent a memo in 1956 answering what he considered to be ill-founded criticism from a hospital: "I submit that we may be an outstanding organization in the field of mental health, or we may be a group working illegally, unethically and dangerously. I do not believe it possible that we are *both*..." (emphasis in original).

Recollections of a lighter-hearted nature come from Maria Villas-Boas Bowen, who worked with Rogers at the CSP, La Jolla: "I remember sharing fantasies, our dabbling with psychic phenomena, our search for spirituality, the laughter and tears" (1987). And:

> I'll never forget a trip we made to Europe in 1983. He was in Stuttgard [sic], answering questions before an audience of over 800 people after having given a talk on peace, when someone asked him from the floor whether he wasn't being too naive. His answer was, "I've been accused of that all my life." I had to chuckle at the irony of it all.

Another colleague who worked with Rogers on the Peace projects, Deborah Brink, recalls a 1972 workshop where Rogers was invited to speak:

> His was a magnetic presence: trustingly open in a roomful of strangers, connecting easily with individuals, responding forthrightly to their questions, some very personal, at times with a gentle, twinkling humor, the entire time fully there. It was an inspiring experience to see an abstract concept (full-functioning) come to life before my eyes.
>
> (1987)

Norman Demb trained at the University of Chicago Counseling Center, where Rogers was Director (or perhaps one should say nondirector). He observed:

> In our necessary naivete of inexperience, we thought all we needed to do therapy was a good heart, a sense of humor, and to copy Rogers's style and technique. Of course that did not work…
>
> (1987)

All of Rogers' associates speak of him as having been as much a friend as a colleague. Shirley Shochot, a South African, met Rogers at a seminar in La Jolla in 1981. Straightaway, they seemed to have bonded, and Shochot facilitated Rogers' visits to what was still Apartheid South Africa:

> For me, and for all South Africans who share my deep sense of humility and privilege to have experienced him, his essence, always tinged with his inimitable humor, will be here always. He will continue to touch our lives and make a difference, and like a pebble in a pond, the ripples are moving in widening circles, touching the lives of more and more people.
>
> (1987)

Reflection

The question remains: why, if Rogers believed that humour had a place in the therapeutic relationship, did he not write about it? Is it because humour is as elemental and as familiar to us as the early morning sun (S. Haugh, personal communication), there is no real need? Rogers didn't write that the therapist should remember to breathe during the session or to visit the toilet before it begins.

So much of what Rogers wrote was revolutionary at the time, a direct confrontation with the medicating, pathologising tendencies of psychoanalysts and doctors towards their patients. His theories were criticised and, at times, ridiculed. And so, I wonder if he was compelled to pick his battles carefully, and that to raise the possibility that the journey towards healing can be joyful was one battle too many.

Coda

Taking the many recollections and vignettes together, it seems obvious that Carl Rogers was no stand-up comedian. Indeed, his diaries from the mid-1970s suggest a man not always at ease with himself, particularly in his relationship with Helen. By this time, they had been married for 50 years; he writes with some bitterness that Helen resented his being "a sober person to live with – no lightness, no humor, a lousy conversationalist", and also with self-reproach:

> I wish I could learn to *play*, just for *fun*... I've never been much good at that and I'm much worse now... I need to appreciate and like myself more.
>
> (Kirschenbaum, 2007, emphasis in original)

After his death, Peggy Natiello poignantly recalled:

> Many people told you what you and your work had meant in their lives. There was an outpouring of caring for you. As usual, you didn't take it in very well. You said several times, "If you meet the Buddha, kill the Buddha." You were so afraid of adulation that sometimes you failed to hear the simple, unadulterated love and appreciation. I always felt sorry about that. So many of us love you.
>
> (Natiello, 1987)

But as we will see in Chapter 8, humour and laughter were not banished from Rogers' therapeutic relationships. Far from it. Rogers worked with humour, congruently, of course. So why wouldn't we?

Summing up

Carl Rogers wrote on most challenges and issues to do with therapy; however, his writings make *no mention of humour or laughter*. By his own account, and those of the people who lived or worked with him, he was rather shy and certainly not the soul of the party. He was uncomfortable with the attention – positive as well as negative – that his revolutionary ideas brought him. But *he was not humourless*. Family, friends and associates all recall moments of laughter, joy and humour in his company.

References

Brink, D. C. (1987). Tributes and memories. *Person-Centred Review*, *2*(3), 375–377.

Brown, C. (2015). *Understanding person-centred counselling: A personal journey*. SAGE.

Demb, N. (1987). Tributes and memories. *Person-Centered Review*, *2*(3), 385–386. Sage.

Kirschenbaum, H. (2007). *The life and work of Carl Rogers*. PCCS Books.

Natiello, P. (1987). Letter to Carl. *Person-Centred Review*, *2*(3), 340–343.

Rogers, C. R. (1939). *The clinical treatment of the problem child*. Houghton.

Rogers, C. R. (1942a). *Counseling and psychotherapy: Newer concepts in practice*. Houghton Mifflin.

Rogers, C. R. (1942b). The psychologist's contributions to parent, child, and community problems. *Journal of Consulting Psychology*, *6*, 8–18. https://doi.org/10.1037/h0059896

Rogers, C. R. (1951/1999). *Client-centered therapy: Its current practice, implications and theory*. Constable.

Rogers, C. R. (1957). The necessary and sufficient conditions of therapeutic personality change. *Journal of Consulting Psychology*, *21*(2), 95–103. https://doi.org/10.1037/h0045357

Rogers, C. R. (1972). *Becoming partners: Marriage and its alternatives*. Delacorte.

Rogers, C. R. (2004). *On becoming a person: A therapist's view of psychotherapy*. Constable & Robinson.

Rogers, D. (1995). A ripple in the pond. In M. Suhd (Ed.), *Positive regard: Carl Rogers and other notables he influenced*. Science and Behavior Books, Inc.

Rogers, H. (1965). A wife's-eye view of Carl Rogers. *Voices*, *1*, 1–8.

Rogers, N. (1980). *Emerging woman: A decade of midlife transitions*. Personal Press.

Rogers, N. (1995). A creative journey. In M. Suhd (Ed.), *Positive regard: Carl Rogers and other notables he influenced*. Science and Behavior Books, Inc.

Shochot, S. R. (1987). Tributes and memories. *Person-Centred Review*, *2*(3), 426–428. Sage.

Villas-Boas Bowen, M. C. (1987). In memory of Carl Rogers. *Person-Centered Review*, *2*(3), 307–310.

Chapter 8

Is there a place for humour in the person-centred therapy room?

Introduction

We have so far examined theories of humour and what they tell us about the transmitters and receivers of humour. We have reviewed the therapeutic modalities that apply humorous interventions or are themselves humour-based modalities and asked why they have not entered the mainstream of humanistic counselling. In Chapter 7, we took the archaeologist's brush to Carl Rogers' writings for clues about his views on humour and therapy, together with recollections of those who lived and worked with him. Here we attempt a further step, looking at the principal theories underlying the person-centred approach through the bifocal lens of humour – bifocal because the perspectives of both the client and the practitioner will be considered.

Reflection

It might perhaps have been appropriate to open this chapter with an apology. There are person-centred practitioners who view Rogers' theories – as written – as something akin to the Bible's Ten Commandments. *We shall not be in the least bit directive. We shall not ask questions of any kind. There shall be only six conditions necessary for therapeutic change to occur, no more, no less. We shall not give clients any impression that we possess any kind of expertise.* And so on. All this, despite the fact that Rogers put his theories forward as hypotheses and was content enough to adjust them as experience and research required, the facts being, he said, friendly. Rogers also spoke out vociferously against dogma, and this is evidenced by his willingness to experience new approaches, variants of his core approach. We think here of the encounter groups he "hosted" in California, his work in South Africa, Moscow and Northern Ireland, the work in art therapy he explored with his daughter Natalie.

DOI: 10.4324/9781003638773-12

The convergence of therapy and personal fulfilment

Frank Prerost (who gave us the Humorous Imagery Situation Technique (HIST) – see Chapter 5) claimed that Rogers maintained the view that fully functioning folks had a sense of humour (1994). As we saw in Chapter 7, this isn't strictly true, but it is easy to see where Prerost was coming from. So, perhaps, we might start at the end of the therapy road, with the fully functioning person (1951/1999, 1963). The concept follows on from Abraham Maslow's characterisation of "basically satisfied" people (1943, 1970), and the two models of personal fulfilment share many similarities. In particular, both assume that man is essentially good.

Rogers' fully functioning person is open to experiencing whatever there is to experience, both internally and in the environment, positive and negative. This is the opposite of defensiveness, where experiences are distorted or ignored in order to reduce the incongruity created by those experiences. Freed from this defensiveness, the individual would live presently, from moment to moment. This is a state similar to what is nowadays understood as mindfulness: we adapt to the experiences we experience rather than attempting to control what comes next (and fretting over the impossibility of that!). The third attribute of the fully functioning person is the ability to trust our senses to reliably inform us of what we are experiencing and to be able to respond in a healthy way. Rogers argues that – in this fully functioning state – if we make a mistake because we missed some aspect of the experiencing, we are open to correcting the mistake and moving on. He analogises this to a "giant electronic computing machine" which takes in data from "sense impressions, from his memory [early computers were conceived as male, imagine!], from previous learning, from his visceral and internal states…" Once all the data is fed in, the fully functioning (male) giant electronic computing machine "quickly computes the course of action which would be the most economical vector of need satisfaction in this existential situation. This is the behavior of our hypothetical person" (1963).

Maslow's conception of the "self-actualised individual" (1970) concerns the whole of the person, who is motivated by a need similar to Rogers' actualising tendency to strive for self-actualisation psychically, physiologically and socially.

Reflection

I encountered Maslow's model numerous times in the corporate sphere, where it is used in training to help managers figure out how to motivate their staff. The hierarchy is depicted as a pyramid, with all the basic needs such as nutrition, clothes, shelter, sleep and so on at the bottom level. Once these physiological needs are met, people can begin aspiring to and/or working towards safety and security – health, employment, property, family and social stability. The next level of needs promises friendship, intimacy and a sense of connection and belonging. Next come "higher" psychological needs such as confidence, achievement, respect and individualism, while at the pyramid's apex are found the benefits of self-actualisation: purpose, meaning, inner potential, creativity, acceptance, morality and spontaneity.

The model is popular thanks to its apparent simplicity, aided perhaps by the pyramid-shaped graphic used to illustrate the hierarchy, which one imagines could have been designed with the specific purpose of motivating low-ranking managers to strive for loftier positions.

Maslow's vision of the self-actualised person encompasses the attributes discussed above in Rogers' fully functioning person and, in addition, he/she possesses a "philosophical, unhostile sense of humor" (1970). This distinguishes our self-actualised individual from the "ordinary" and "average man" who will be more inclined to laugh at others' hurt or inferiority, at "the unfunny, Oedipal, or smutty joke" or at "punning, joking, witty remarks, gay repartee, persiflage of the ordinary sort". Instead, the self-actualised sense of humour tends towards the philosophical, by "poking fun" at people (including themselves) who are foolishly self-aggrandising and raises a smile rather than laughter. For this reason, the average man will find the self-actualised person "to be rather on the sober and serious side".

There are other points of digression between the fully functioning and self-actualised persons, primarily resulting from Maslow's emphasis on the individual as a whole. We might question if it is possible to transpose Maslow's self-actualised sense of humour to Rogers' fully functioning person, but perhaps there is no need, because if *fully functioning* means *open to experience*, we would therefore have to be also open to humour, to seeing the funny side of things and to laughing at them and/or ourselves. Might we even – on realising that we have succeeded in decluttering the conditions of worth accumulated over the years and relocated our locus of evaluation to where it belongs – be rather pleased, if not cock-a-hoop? Might we allow ourselves a smile, a chuckle, a full-on belly laugh?

But back to reality…

The "necessary and sufficient conditions of therapeutic personality change"

If we accept that the fully functioning person can allow without distortion the experiencing of humour, the question then is whether such an experiencing fits with Rogers' concept of therapy? To explore this, we turn to the revolutionary

"Necessary and Sufficient Conditions of Therapeutic Personality Change", first published in 1957.

In summary, the conditions are:

1 The therapist and client meet at a psychological level;
2 The client is in distress;
3 The therapist is (mostly) congruent;
4 The therapist experiences "unconditional positive regard" towards the client;
5 The therapist experiences empathic understanding of the client's world; and
6 The client perceives the therapist's unconditional positive regard and empathy (and congruence)

Rogers believed:

(a) that if these conditions were present in the relationship over a period of time, then constructive personality change would follow; and
(b) that no other conditions were necessary.

It must be emphasised that although Rogers derived these conditions from extensive research and practice, he was adamant that they represented his thinking at the time of writing and that he would welcome any evidence that cast doubt on their validity and required a revision. He observed that psychotherapists "steadily refused to make any scientific investigation of their therapy or permit others to do this. I can understand this reaction because I have felt it" (2004). He nonetheless consistently asserted that "the facts are friendly" and that the theory "is useful only if it can be put to test". This means that the six "conditions, and the theory of conditions, need to be tested in every therapeutic encounter" (Tudor, 2010).

In that same spirit, the following attempts to test the necessary and sufficient conditions through the lens of humour.

Our first challenge is to determine an appropriate approach: should each condition be examined separately or as a whole? There is a strong argument for taking the latter approach, at least to some extent: the three conditions of congruence, unconditional positive regard and empathy became known by academics and practitioners as the "core" conditions, largely because they are the conditions that therapists *do*. They are what training institutions focus on when educating students in the belief and/or hope that it is possible to learn *how to do* them. Peggy Natiello, for example, provides insightful guidance on how therapists might personify the attitudes of these three conditions, which she "viewed as a trinity" (2001).

These three conditions emanate from the therapist to varying degrees as the session progresses, with the therapist observing the client's responses and adjusting the emphasis as appropriate. Maintaining this attitude could be compared to a footballer preparing to take a penalty shot: a relatively straightforward task which challenges the penalty taker to kick a stationary ball into the net, bypassing the goalkeeper along the way. The task may seem straightforward enough, and it will have been practised many times before. But its execution requires the footballer to make a number of judgements concerning – among other things – the ball, the goalkeeper, the crowd, the weather conditions and her own energy, confidence and stress. Too many to keep in conscious awareness at the same time, the majority of these micro-judgements are made at a preverbal level in the footballer's brain. In those brief moments before the shot is taken, innumerable muscles are called to action simultaneously, although not one of them is foremost in the footballer's mind. Instead, concepts such as "muscle memory" and "eye-foot coordination" come into play, and whether the penalty is scored or not depends on the footballer's ability to shoot the ball on target and, if she succeeds, whether the goalkeeper is up to the task of intercepting the ball. The therapist, too, applies a kind of core-condition-muscle-memory in the therapy room, and she does this on top of managing her awareness of any number of other potentially intrusive sensations and impulses, from a hunger pang or needing the toilet to a nagging fear that the parcel she ordered has been delivered to the recycling bin or left out in the rain. And because those core conditions are rehearsed in training and honed in practice, much of the work is done automatically, even when a greater emphasis on one of them might be called for in any given moment during the session.

There is much less said in the literature about the other three conditions. Keith Tudor concludes that these "ubiquitous references to the so-called core conditions have led to an over-emphasis on the therapist's part in the therapeutic relationship" (2010). This is perhaps unfortunate because, in requiring "the client's active participation in therapy", they encapsulate how the therapist and client are connected (their "relationality") and how their individual subjectivities are shared (their "intersubjectivity").

Since there are so many factors to consider, perhaps it will make for a clearer examination to consider each of the Necessary and Sufficient Conditions separately. In doing so, it is hoped that the relative importance of any one condition is not distorted. Some overlap is, however, inevitable.

Condition 1: The therapist and client meet at a psychological level

That there should exist a relationship between the therapist and the client was described by Rogers as so obvious and straightforward that it might be taken as an assumption rather than the result of an activity (1957). Unlike the other five conditions, which Rogers considered to "exist on continua" (1959), that is, to a lesser or greater extent, this condition was conceived as a binary phenomenon, which has been likened to electrical contact:

> All parts of a circuit need to be connected before electricity can flow, and the switch that connects is either on or off. Once the switch is on, electricity is flowing, and we can harness its power for all manner of tasks. Likewise, once we are in psychological contact the relationship is, so to speak, current, and all manner of things are possible.
>
> (Tudor & Worrall, 2006)

If we view this condition as being a prerequisite to the functioning of the other conditions, it follows that it arises – or should arise – at the outset of the therapeutic process, when a client and therapist encounter each other for the first time. During these opening minutes, the two attempt (to use an analogue analogy) to tune into each other. The client, understandably, will be preoccupied with whatever the distress might be. At the same time, there will be questions: is this stranger in front of me the right person to be speaking to? Was reaching out to a stranger such a good idea in the first place? Distractions such as domestic duties, financial concerns, career prospects, the weather and whether or not England's men will ever again win the World Cup might also be preying on the client's mind. The counsellor may well be similarly distracted, but will hopefully be most concerned by the quality of the relationship about to be offered to the client, for it is this that will have the greatest impact:

> Clinical experience and research evidence underscore that the relationship accounts for as much of the outcome as particular treatment methods.
>
> (Norcross, 2002)

Achieving psychological contact may be a minimum requirement, like closing an electrical circuit, but the quality of that contact is critical. First impressions count. A great deal hinges on the opening minutes of that first encounter at a time when both parties may be more than a little nervous. It is also worth highlighting the contact that is made before the counsellor and client meet: the first enquiring telephone call or email, or even WhatsApp message, all convey impressions to clients-to-be. Whether we are working from a room at an organisation's offices or a doctor's surgery, a room at home or a summerhouse at the bottom of the garden or online, we are mindful of the impression the venue gives. And so, we take steps to make the space welcoming, perhaps calming, certainly as unclinical as possible. The statement we make is: "Whatever distress you are experiencing, being here should not add to it". Thus, before we have met our clients, we have made interventions, intentionally or not.

Reflection

Sigmund Freud's house in Vienna is now home to a museum. In it is a waiting room staged to appear how it must have appeared back in the day: velvet-upholstered furniture that is comfortable but not too inviting; on the walls are prints of paintings from the Romantic School. Curiously, for someone famously averse to self-disclosure, there are also various framed credentials, including one from the British Psychological Society granting Freud honorary membership.

Given that we know he liked a joke or two, I can't help thinking Freud would have liked one of those engraved wooden plaques on the wall that says: *Man muss nicht verrückt sein, um hier zu arbeiten, aber es hilft.*

Counsellors speak of being conscious of the imbalance of power at the beginning of the relationship: clients are in distress (see condition 2), and they expect or at least hope that the counsellor will be in a position to help. Ann Shearer notes, remarkably, that some psychotherapists are reluctant even to "greet a patient with a smile" (2016). Many counsellors will, however, offer light-hearted comments or questions to "break the ice" to help put their client at some ease, for example:

- "The traffic's so bad today it would have been quicker to walk here"
- (working in a doctor's consulting room) "Sit wherever you like, but maybe not on the examination table".
- (working over the internet) "Whoever put men on the moon could come and fix my Wi-Fi".
- And, of course, virtually any comment or observation concerning the weather.

A little humour both reassures the client that the counsellor is "also human" but sets the tone for a meeting of equal persons. Starting off with a little humour and setting that tone also eases fears that clients might have of when it would be safe to allow their own humour to emerge (Longe, 2018). If both the therapist and the client wait for the other to introduce humour, it is unlikely to emerge, unless something funny intrudes on the session, say, for example, someone's mobile phone ringing with the Looney Tunes ringtone.

Certain institutional settings bring additional challenges for client and counsellor alike at the start of the relationship. Often the client is required to attend counselling as a sanction or a condition for avoiding sanction, for example, anger management for someone convicted of assault, a parent or guardian trying to regain custody of a child and addicts wanting to avoid custodial sentences. They are in effect forced into counselling because to refuse it could mean losing a job or not staying out of prison. They have little or no choice about the nature of the counselling, who provides it, where or for how long. Perhaps, most challenging, they have to "pass" the counselling programme in order to meet the conditions set for them. Clients in such situations have no power at all; they may feel they have to "play along" and have no confidence in the helping potential of the therapy they have been assigned. Addicts must additionally go through an assessment process before treatment begins. These settings are therapeutic "hoops" (Miller et al., 1997) the client must jump through, a very different experience to the client who attends out of choice and who might find the first encounter provides a much-needed boost in optimism or self-esteem. The counsellors then must work harder to build a rapport with clients and gain their trust and confidence. A smile would be the bare minimum a counsellor could offer to help ease the client's tension and mistrust, but humour of the affiliative kind (see Chapter 2), for example, a wry comment about the paperwork, can convey a sense of counsellor and client being "in it together" and thus coming together at a psychological level.

Pause for thought

Take a moment to consider the occasions when you arranged to meet someone – anyone – for the first time. A date, perhaps, a job interview, your therapist or supervisor…

What emotions and thoughts were coming up for you?
Were you excited? Apprehensive?
Do you feel you came across as warm or aloof?
How – if at all – was the ice broken?
And was humour present? If so, do you feel it helped?

Condition 2: The client is in distress

Rogers' second necessary and sufficient condition captures the reason the client needs the help of the therapist, that is, he is feeling "vulnerable or anxious", or in other words, "incongruent" (1957).

The "Seven Stages of Process" (1959) describes clients who are initially resistant to the idea of therapy, wary of the therapeutic set-up and sceptical of the therapist's character, motives and competence – clients who either don't want to be clients or don't think they need to be clients. Such people are not just defensive in the clinical sense, but:

> ...reacting or perceiving in an intensional fashion... [tending] to see experience in absolute and unconditional terms, to overgeneralise, to be dominated by concept or belief, to fail to anchor [their] reactions in space and time, to confuse fact and evaluation, to rely upon abstractions rather than upon reality-testing.

One might assume, then, that any humour coming from the therapist at this stage of the relationship could be a misjudgement of the client's state of mind. Therapists might, therefore, be wary of allowing humour into their interaction if they feel there is a risk that the client perceives it as proof that their problems are not being taken seriously or even that they are being laughed at.

Reflection

We need to be aware of the potential gap between humorous intent and perception. A client – a partner in a local firm of solicitors – came to see me following the breakdown of her marriage. Her third. I could hear myself saying, "A third breakdown? That's got to be getting expensive. I hope you managed to find good legal advice". But I stayed silent. Outside the therapy room, my impulse on hearing bad news is often to (attempt to) say something funny. It's a way of expressing empathy, and for reasons I've yet to comprehend it sounds more genuine to me than mere sympathising. Inside the therapy room, however, I am aware that this impulse of mine serves my own nerve-soothing purposes and isn't necessarily what the client wants or needs to hear. Somewhere out in a parallel universe, however, I am bold/reckless enough to convey greater transparency, and the client responds with a smile of recognition: I have heard the desperation in her voice and accurately, empathically reflected it.

Paradoxically, the client might perceive that the therapist *is* taking the pain seriously, that she *gets it*. Clients are seen as people, not as problems needing to be fixed (Berg et al., 2009).

Although it is safe to say that the client does not "come into therapy full of joy" (K. Christie, personal correspondence), it may actually be the client who introduces the humour. The motives for doing so vary, and warnings about our clients' use of humour abound in the literature. Shearer suggests a number of reasons a client might use humour as a form of defence:

> Everyone knows that children learn through play, but might we here do well to suspect a manic defence? The strategy might be an attempt at manipulation, an invitation to collude. It might be an act of aggression, a ploy to control the therapy and even destroy the therapist.
>
> (2016)

The seductive pleasure of humour can cause "a rupture intrapsychically and/or interpsychically", and a client may be wishing humiliation upon themselves through the therapist's laughter (Gibson & Tantam, 2017).

Reflection

We will explore how we as therapists might respond to our clients' defensive humour in detail in Chapter 9. One experience with a client some time ago highlighted how challenging it can be to stay with the client who is in this frame of mind.

Client: I'm trying to figure out why I can't leave my boyfriend. He's such a leech. Always wanting money. "Lend me a tenner, I'll pay you back." Never does. I've got three jobs, 'cause I'm terrified of being broke. He's supposed to be out getting himself a job but then I get home and I'm dead on my feet and there he is answering the *Call of Duty* on the

	Playstation. My Playstation, mind. And that's if he's at home at all.
Counsellor:	You're being taken for a ride.
Client:	Well, yeah. [laughs scornfully] Only I'm not. Every other woman in town is getting a ride. Just not me. I'm Billy-No-Mate, me.
Counsellor:	Poor choice of words.
Client:	Not your fault. I'm being shafted. It's true. [laughs] Just not like I'd like to be.
Counsellor:	And you can't leave him.
Client:	Yeah. [tearful] No. It's my house, so it would have to be him who leaves.

The client expressed her distress using intense self-deprecating humour which, as I came to learn, was a characteristic of her communication style. I recall the exchange felt like a fencing match: she parried each of my attempts at conveying my empathic understanding with a humorous retort.

Counsellor:	You want him to leave, but you can't picture sitting on that sofa by yourself.
Client:	[singing] "All by myself". Yeah. Failed again.

The client may use humour as a form of semiotic armour against the pain of exploring distress, deflecting both self and therapist from doing precisely that. A client laughing at himself, dismissing his feelings as indulgent, pitiful, idiotic or out of character, disguises the depth of feeling. According to much of the literature, the therapist's laughter colludes with (i.e. "encourages") this avoidance (e.g. Gibson & Tantam, 2017; Hussong & Micucci, 2021). This admonition risks glossing over the nuances of the humour expressed by the client; it may well be the case that the client is fearful of addressing the distress. Suggesting that we "collude" with our client while he is in this state by laughing along with him would seem to be bypassing the person-centred aim to be as non-directive as possible. If the client is not ready to dig deeper, the therapist cannot force him to, but instead goes alongside, continuing to facilitate the conditions in which the client can feel secure enough to confront the pain.

In summary, the client comes to us in distress, struggling to cope and needing help, and so the client's use of humour can provide us with clues as to the nature and intensity of the distress as we begin the process of gaining empathic understanding.

Condition 3: The therapist is congruent

The concept of congruence seems straightforward at first glance, but it can be challenging to apply in practice. In the 1957 and 1959 discussions of congruence, Rogers explored two aspects of what he called "The therapist's genuineness in the relationship" (1957). The first is the therapist's free and deep awareness of the emotions that come to the fore during the therapy session. Rogers illustrated this aspect with a hypothetical situation in which the therapist feels afraid of the client: the therapist is congruent if those feelings of fear are not suppressed or ignored but acknowledged; otherwise, the therapist is being incongruent.

That fear could distract the therapist from attending to the client's process – a state that a layperson might call *incongruence*; however, if we are aware of that distraction, we are, in fact, person-centredly congruent. The key here would seem to be that if we are aware of what we're feeling, we are being congruent.

Pause for thought

Consider a comment made by a client that ran counter to your beliefs.

What was your experiencing?
Were you aware of the feelings that the client's comment provoked?
Did you ignore the comment – and the feelings that it provoked?
Were you able to reflect on the experience and how it affected your empathy and unconditional positive regard?
Did you feel it necessary to take the experience to supervision?

The second aspect of congruence concerns the extent to which we communicate our congruence/incongruence to our client. Expanding on the idea that congruence "is the opposite of presenting a façade, either knowingly or unknowingly" (1957), Rogers asked of the therapist:

> Should he also express or communicate to the client the accurate symbolization of his own experience? The answer to this question is still in an uncertain state. At present we would say that such feelings should be expressed, if the therapist finds himself persistently focused on his own feelings rather than those of the client, thus greatly reducing or eliminating any experience of empathic understanding, or if he finds himself persistently experiencing some feeling other than unconditional positive regard.
>
> (1959)

Unfortunately for the student counsellor, Rogers stopped short of fully exploring when and how the therapist's genuineness in the relationship might – or might not – be communicated to the client. In later writings, he spoke of the client being able to discern the therapist's "genuineness, realness, or congruence", which are "transparent" because there is "no holding back on the part of the therapist". The tension between the therapist being completely transparent and also deciding on which "feelings and attitudes" to communicate was still not resolved, other than to suggest that they should be communicated "if appropriate" (1980). We might argue that "if appropriate" could be translated as "being helpful to the client", and perhaps that commonsense might tell us that if we are suddenly, mid-session, seized by the nagging apprehension that we may have forgotten to arrange with our partner who was to pick the children up from school, we need not share this with the client. And yet, if that apprehension prevents us from focusing on our client, or indeed if we suppress that apprehension so that it doesn't prevent us from focusing on our client, then we have failed to be congruent and, therefore, helpful to our client.

Pause for thought

Again considering a comment made by a client that ran counter to your beliefs.

What was your experiencing?
How did you judge whether or not to share that experiencing with the client?
How did the client respond?
To what extent did that sharing / non-sharing affect the relationship with your client?

A number of later writers have examined the conceptual difficulties of this aspect of the theory. Sheila Haugh highlighted the challenges of applying a Cartesian-Newtonian approach to Freudian theoretical formulations, for example, the idea that if X happens to a young child, Y will result (probably unconsciously) and suggested that other paradigms are needed to better understand Rogers' theories (2001). Marvin Frankel and Lisbeth Sommerbeck highlight conceptual difficulties in the evolution of Rogers' theories. They argue that when Rogers wrote in 1951 that "To be of assistance to you. [the client] I will put aside myself – the self of ordinary interaction – and enter your world of perception as completely as I am able" (1951/1999):

> Rogers is informing the client that he is going to be introduced to Rogers the therapist and that Rogers the therapist is rather different from Rogers in other contexts.
>
> (Frankel & Sommerbeck, 2007)

In 1957, Rogers revised the depiction to what we have already discussed, going so far as to say that the therapist is "accurately himself in this hour of this relationship… this includes being himself in ways which are not regarded as ideal for psychotherapy" (1957). The issue raised by Frankel and Sommerbeck isn't so much that Rogers' thinking evolved, but that the congruence defined in 1957 undermined the other two core conditions, empathy and unconditional positive regard. Citing the recording of the session with Gloria, in which Rogers tells her what a fine daughter he thinks she is an interjection that Rogers justifies "not by citing his therapeutic aim but on the basis of possessing that strong feeling" (Frankel & Sommerbeck, 2007), they highlight the conditionality of the positive regard and the resulting impact on the non-directive foundation of the relationship. Jerold Bozarth raises a similar point, namely how Rogers reconciled congruence and non-directivity in his later years:

> I might tell a client, "I'm really bored by what you're saying." It doesn't guide him. It does provide him with some rather jolting data which he must handle in some way or other. But I'm not telling him what he should do to avoid boring me. Maybe he would just as soon bore me; that's up to him.
>
> (Bozarth, 2012)

And so, finally, we come to the question of what to do about humour. If we accept Frankel and Sommerbeck's interpretation of the 1951-Rogers-The-Therapist and attempt to enter our client's world of perception, then we might well encounter humour in that world. If we sense something humorous in what the client says – an irony, perhaps, in a recounting of a recent event that repeats an earlier one, of lightning striking the same place twice – and consider the sensation to be an accurate perception, we might then consider its effect. Does it make us want to express that sensation, perhaps to smile, giggle or laugh out loud? If so, would that be appropriate? How would the client most likely react? Janet Tolan proposes that the therapist might respond with a "gentle teasing of the client when we have already identified something. Like a client who is very task-focused making a task of relaxing more!" (personal communication).

Reflection

During training, I found that clients expressed themselves humorously when I least expected it.

One client, who lost her mother to cancer and felt unable to express her own grief while supporting other grieving family members, talked about neglecting her usual routine of housework. She began comparing her domestic laxity with her failure to attend to her own feelings until, at one point, she joked about needing to "keep her drawers tidy". She stopped suddenly and laughed heartily. I laughed with her. I couldn't have imagined not joining her laughter. In our final session, she observed that she was feeling better able to confront her feelings.

Another client told me that to make living with fibromyalgia bearable, she watched films. "Name a film I haven't seen", she challenged me. My brain froze. What kind of film should I pick? An arthouse film from my student days? A horror flick? *One Flew Over the Cuckoo's Nest* sprang to mind, and in my desperation to dismiss it, I said, "The Evil Dead?" There was a brief pause, and then she laughed. "Sam Raimi. I love zombie films". She laughed again and added, "In a zombie apocalypse, I know I would be the first to go". We talked about another film where the zombies only killed and consumed perfectly healthy people. "So, you'd be fine", I said. "Yeah. And I'd have Brad Pitt saving me, too". This exchange came towards the end of a particularly tough session. When we signed off, she said, "Thanks. I really needed a giggle today".

If we then accept the later Rogers-The-Person variation presented by Frankel and Sommerbeck, where whatever bubbles up inside us is there to share, transparently, with the client, it would seem a corollary that humour would be included. We would not be attempting to suppress a humorous impulse; instead, we would share it, potentially even if not "helpful to the client" (though this presumes we can accurately anticipate whether our sharing humour will benefit the client).

Christine Brown recounts an experience with a client who had previously been in an abusive relationship and who started screaming and ranting at her as if she were her current partner:

> I wasn't frightened because it wasn't directed at me, but it knocked me back. When she paused, I said, "I feel like I'm facing the she-bitch from hell," and she stopped in her tracks, burst out laughing. And then she went very

> reflective and said, "Chris, do you think I've become the abuser?" And I said, "Well, what do you think?" And she said, "Yes." And I said, "Well, it seems that way to me, too."
>
> (personal communication)

Arguably, Brown's comment was not the most classically empathic, but it was certainly congruent. In this instance, the client's laughter revealed the shock of her recognition.

Pause for thought

Do you have a "poker face"? Can people always tell what you're feeling and thinking? How do you cope in those moments when you know you should be serious or solemn but some bizarre, inappropriate and ominously irrepressible mirth suddenly begins to bubble up inside you?

It has been argued that humour brings with it risks that potentially outweigh the benefits. Yet, the client not receiving the communication of the therapist's mirthful congruence in the way in which the latter intended is not unique to its humorous character. Any intervention by the therapist – a reflection, a tentative checking, even a silence – has the potential to distract, belittle or offend the client. Indeed, suggesting to a client that he is boring us might be compared with the kinds of aggressive humour Farrelly promoted in Provocative Therapy (see Chapter 5), which justified responses of the "pull yourself together, if you can reach" variety on the grounds of transparency and genuineness.

Rogers assured us that it is impossible to be completely congruent (1957) that instead we should strive for "a close matching, or congruence, between what is being experienced at the gut level, what is present in awareness, and what is expressed to the client" (1980). In other words, the therapist, not being entirely congruent but more congruent at least than the client, chooses what to share with him, including humorous content.

Steven Sultanoff, examining how the necessary and sufficient conditions accommodate the therapist's humour, finds that the humour must be genuine to be "effective" and that if the humour is somehow "incongruent", then it will be experienced by the client as "fake, insincere, clumsy, or out of context" (2013). Similarly, Haugh looks for humour that is "authentic and genuine, and [comes] from a place of compassion and caring" (personal communication). The assumption here is that the client will receive the humour concomitantly with the way it is expressed by the therapist, which, as has been shown, cannot be taken for granted.

The person-centred therapist's transparency, or authenticity, is as much a hallmark of person-centred therapy as the psychoanalyst's self-presentation as detached and neutral, where the analyst is seated out of the sight-line of the client who is reclining on a couch. Originating with Freud, the "rule of anonymity" requires therapists to abandon "naturalistic attitudes and conventional social modes of interaction" (Smith, 1990) and, in particular, forbids any self-disclosure by the therapist. Shearer fears that in this situation the client may suffer echoes of "emotional absence and rejection" that were suffered at the hands of the client's parents or other care-providers (2016). It seems that there may well be some leakage from psychodynamic orthodoxy into person-centred teaching regarding how the therapist ought to react to the emergence of humour in a session. Shearer additionally suspects some therapists may be disinclined to indulge in therapeutic humour if they "long to find satisfaction in deepening relationships, but want to keep these as far as they can under their own control". Conversely, however, therapists might be more inclined to use humour to deflect their reactions to the issues raised by the client, for example, where the therapist has in the past suffered a similar trauma to the client. Therapists' desire for safety in relationships formed in the therapy room might therefore not necessarily exclude laughter or mirth, as Shearer seems to suggest, but it is certainly a factor for the therapist to consider.

Condition 4: The therapist experiences "unconditional positive regard" towards the client

The therapist's unconditional positive regard is characterised as a warm, positive and acceptant attitude towards what is in the client (Rogers, 2004); it sees the therapist as caring for the client without wanting control over – or judging – the client. In many respects, it is antonymous with another of Rogers' concepts, conditions of worth (1959), in that the client reclaims the freedom to think, to do and to speak without fearing others' judgements. Germain Lietaer considered unconditional positive regard and congruence to be closely related:

> they are parts of a more basic attitude of "openness": openness toward myself (congruence) and openness toward the other (unconditional acceptance).
>
> (1984)

Thus, unconditional positive regard is very much an attitude, a respect for the other's autonomy. Perhaps, as such, it is easier to identify the therapist's unconditional positive regard when it is hardest for her to offer it, as when Paul Wilkins (2002) describes his work with an extremely challenging client who was openly racist and misogynist. Perhaps, if we were to meet such a person in a social setting, we'd avoid them like the Severe Acute Respiratory Syndrome Coronavirus 2. Wilkins, however, did not have that option, and so:

> Between sessions, I read about prejudice and how it might arise. Almost without noticing, I slipped from being challenged by my client's way of being to an appreciation of the person of worth behind the views. As this happened, there was a softening in him, sessions began to include humour and a sense of companionship in the counselling enterprise. It was as if, as he accepted himself more, he became more accepting of the world.
>
> (2002)

Pause for thought

The attitudes of our clients can affect our congruence and our unconditional positive regard. And as we saw in Chapter 2, humour comes in many forms. The client may use humour aggressively, for example, in the form of derogatory comments directed at the therapist, sarcasm being the most obvious example (Dionigi & Canestrari, 2018).

Supposing a client used derogatory humour: how would you react? Perhaps this has already happened to you. Did you challenge the client in any way? If so, did that undermine your unconditional positive regard for your client?

As Wilkins suggests, the client's use of aggressive or offensive humour tells us something about the client's emotional state and, at the very least, that he has a long way to go on the journey of therapeutic growth. The therapist's challenge might not so much be to remain po-faced when confronted with the client's humour but to be congruent with any feelings of defensiveness sparked by the humour, be aware of the potential threats to her unconditional positive regard towards the client and seek to understand what underlies the humour.

As we also saw earlier, the research suggests that when clients perceive the humour of their therapist, they respond positively, feeling safer in the relationship and better understood and accepted.

Reflection

For some weeks, I had been counselling a trans-male following the break-up of a long-term relationship. Although their father was aware of and approved of their relationship, they had not yet "plucked up the courage" to tell him about their plans for gender reassignment surgery. They had not been able to afford the cost of private treatment and so joined the NHS waiting list, knowing that the wait would be around three years. They told me the waiting meant they did not have to face the prospect of speaking to their father straight away, something they had hoped to be able to do with the support of their now ex-partner. I sensed there were several sources of anxiety at play in that moment: their pain at the breakdown of the relationship, the anticipation of how their father might react to their decision to undergo gender reassignment surgery and the prospect of having to wait three years to start the process they dearly desired. After a few moments' reflection, I spoke, "That's the first time I've heard a good news story about NHS waiting lists". A couple of seconds passed, and then they burst out laughing. "I hadn't thought of that", they said, "Maybe we should tell the health secretary", I added, "That'll cheer him up".

I had not planned to say something amusing; it came from somewhere inside me. I might instead have continued the reflective silence or made a verbal reflection of the feelings that were going on for them: the frustration, the powerlessness and the loneliness, all of which I felt too in that moment. The gallows-type humour summed up all of that empathic understanding, without judgement and consistent with my personality and my own feelings (including about the state of the NHS). On reflection, I was relieved by their reaction. We were working by telephone, and it occurred to me momentarily that I had breached the telephonic safety screen and perhaps spoken out of turn. So, the response confirmed that I had not misjudged my gut feeling. I felt also that the shared humour brought us closer together, consolidating the trust they were offering me and going some way to making the safety screen redundant.

We might therefore conclude that humour eases at least some of the client's distress. But this is not always the case. The assertion that "certain clients lack a sense of humor" (Gladding, 1995) might strike some as simplistic or dismissive, as well as falling short in unconditional positive regard. It does, however, point to the more likely situation where the client is not able to appreciate the humorous intent of the therapist, due perhaps to defensiveness, distress or a narrowing of thinking. This could, in turn, prevent the detection of the incongruity or absurdity contained within the humorous intervention (Sultanoff, 2013). In such situations, the humour will be missed and so not realise its therapeutic potential; it could indeed halt or even reverse any therapeutic improvement.

Another possibility is that the client perceives the therapist's humour as an expression of *conditional* rather than *unconditional* positive regard (Gibson, 2014; Hussong & Micucci, 2021; Mann, 1991). There are, however, subtleties that are worth noting. Sophie Scott, a researcher of the cognitive neuroscience of voices, speech and laughter at University College London, has shown that the client's "nervous laughter" stops being "nervous" when the therapist laughs, too: "such laughter may be a plea to the other not to be upset, inviting a reciprocal laugh which reassures that together they will be able to manage this" (cited in Shearer, 2016). As therapists, we do not want the client to depend on us for approval. It places us in an untenable position of superiority. Perhaps, then, a more compassionate response is sometimes warranted, such as is portrayed in Stephen Grosz's account of his work with Lily, a woman straining under the weight of her relationship with her parents, whom she does not feel strong enough to confront. In their sessions, she talks about her anger, adding a humorous "punchline" that acts as a release but leaves her too deflated to explore what she feels. Grosz wonders if Lily wants him to laugh at the punchlines so that she won't feel bad about mocking her parents, but the opposite is true: Lily recalls how, suffering a breakdown at boarding school; she phoned and begged her parents to come and take her home. "When you laugh", she told him, "I know that you see things exactly the way I do – that you wouldn't have said no, you'd have let me come home" (2014).

Perhaps there is something more in Lily's desperate humour: an attempt to make the exploration of emotional pain more bearable. Humour here takes on the symbolic role of protector, like a deep-sea diving suit. It is akin to gallows humour, a stress-relieving reaction to an unbearably stressful situation. In some cases, it could also signify a realisation that the worst is over, that healing is about to begin: "when you do go there, you realise this chasm that you thought had no bottom has a bottom and you can come up. You can climb up from it" (C. Brown, personal communication).

Condition 5: Empathic understanding

The third of the core conditions, empathic understanding, often shortened to just empathy, is not to be conflated with sympathy. Sympathy is when we feel sorry for someone's plight and when we make suppositions about that person's feelings. "I know just how awful you must feel", we might say to someone who has just been made redundant, not supposing that the individual might be glad to be released from a mind-numbingly tedious routine or an overbearing ogre of a boss. Sympathy may be shown to someone with or without congruence, hardly ever without judgement of some kind. For this reason, empathy is closely bound together with the other two core conditions: it is achieved when the therapist sees the world through the client's eyes.

As we saw earlier, the empathic content in humour can bring the client towards deeper self-exploration and provide a release for the anguish (Yonatan-Leus et al., 2018; Talens, 2020). Sultanoff further highlights that the communication of the therapist's empathy will be demonstrated by the creation of humour (2013).

Perhaps the most significant benefit of empathy comes from a sense of mutual understanding, which Haugh suggests is essential to the question of whether humour is shared:

> there won't be a lot of humour coming from me unless the other person is being funny. And at that point I also need to make sure I am fully in their world so I can "hear" any other feelings that are being expressed too and not get distracted by humour.
>
> (personal communication)

This sense of "being in it together" is also captured by Janet Tolan, who suggests that, appropriately timed, "some empathic light-heartedness with depressed clients is important so we don't sink together" (personal communication).

Pause for thought

In an earlier chapter, we considered the concept of "gallows humour", the kind of expression we might make in the face of a desperate situation. A classic portrayal of this comes at the end of *The Life of Brian* (Chapman et al., 1979) when the eponymous anti-hero, having been mistaken for Jesus, is crucified. His death is a pointless humiliation: his comrades in the People's Front of Judea congratulate him on "the occasion of your martyrdom", his mother berates him for abandoning her, and on top of all of that, he is cajoled into looking on the "bright side of life". The closing song, *Always Look on the Bright Side of Life*, is still a popular choice at funerals in the UK.

What do you think? Does gallows humour remind us that things are bad, but *not that bad*, not yet? Does it comfort us? Or is it a means of suppressing and denying our pain?

Recent neurological research suggests that our brains are hard-wired to respond to interpersonal interactions, governed mostly by the right hemisphere, which is linked to unconscious implicit communication and relational phenomena such as attachment. Lisa Valentine and Glen Gabbard observed that "Mutual emotional knowing between therapist and patient... involves a right brain-to-right brain communication from one relational mind to another, without conscious processing or understanding" (2014). Alan Schore (2011) maintains that the two hemispheres of the brain process information differently and, unlike the left brain's verbal and logical processing, the right brain handles emotions, nonverbal communication and stress regulation, and it does so largely outside conscious awareness and certainly at a quicker rate: we feel before we can comprehend what we feel. In other words, this is significant for therapy, he argued; lasting therapeutic change requires engaging the right brain's implicit emotional systems, not just the left brain's verbal understanding. This challenges the supposition that therapy relies primarily on insight and interpretation, suggesting instead that emotional attunement – that is, empathy – and regulation are the key mechanisms of healing.

Vittorio Gallese (2009) and Gallese et al. (2004) further propose a link between shared intuitive understanding and special brain cells called mirror neurons, which fire both when an individual performs an action and when they observe another person performing the same action. First discovered in the 1990s by Italian neuroscientist Giacomo Rizzolatti et al. (1995) while studying macaque monkeys, these neurons were later identified in humans using neuroimaging techniques.

The discovery has an important implication for counsellors. Because mirror neurons respond to goal-directed actions rather than simple movements, they help us understand not just what others are doing, but why they're doing it. They therefore provide a neurobiological basis for our ability to "put ourselves in someone else's shoes" – to be empathic, in other words – by internally simulating observed actions and emotions. Mirror neurons might also explain how counsellors and clients unconsciously mirror each other's postures and expressions.

How does this apply to humour? Valentine and Gabbard put forward a compelling argument that our mirroring reflex does not start when the client says something amusing but "in the preceding split second in which the therapist intuitively senses the patient's receptiveness" (2014). Thus, our empathic occupying of the client's frame of reference tells us how open the client might be to any intervention, including humour. Valentine and Gabbard go on to suggest that the laughter shared by the therapist and client as a result of the humour makes a significant contribution to change in the client:

> Such moments take both members of the dyad by surprise. While an intellectual understanding of a joke may be necessary to "get it," a major part of the therapeutic value probably lies in the relational connection that is beyond cognitive understanding.
>
> (2014)

Gabbard also notes that clients often recall the humorous exchanges with the therapist that "departed from the usual format of the therapy" (2010).

Pause for thought

Do medics have to switch off their empathy when they are working with their patients? Would a surgeon, for example, be able to amputate a person's limb if her brain were wired to intuit the pain the patient would be feeling? Instead, she would perhaps have to rationalise the procedure – tell herself that it will bring an end to the patient's suffering?

The intuitive, embodied imagining that our brains appear to be capable of perhaps also fosters greater creativity in our thinking. As we saw in earlier chapters, our brains love making connections and figuring stuff out. Our innate inventiveness and imagination are stimulated by puzzles, metaphors (and, of course, jokes), and so humour, it has been suggested, can enable the client to see things differently, from a different perspective and gain new insights.

Condition 6: The client's reception of the therapist's unconditional positive regard and empathy (and congruence)

We know that the second necessary and sufficient condition of therapeutic change requires that the client is in distress, defensive and not open to experience, and so on (Rogers, 2004). Yet, for the sixth and final necessary condition to be met, the client must be able to perceive – to a "minimal degree" – the therapist's empathic understanding of and unconditional positive regard for the client (1957; 1959).

In later writing, Rogers added the therapist's congruence (1980), and many people do the same (e.g. Mearns & Thorne, 1988/1996). The co-opting of congruence into the sixth condition might have been a corollary of Rogers' later thinking that the therapist's congruent feeling was "transparent" to the client, and/or it reflected the growing influence of the shorthand term "core conditions", attributed to Robert Carkhuff and Bernard Berenson (1967).

Taking into account the discussion earlier in the chapter about the therapist's transparency, even if such transparency might not be therapeutically helpful, one might conclude that, of course, the appearance of humour in the therapy room should not be ignored, distorted or blocked. This conclusion resonates with the definition of therapeutic humour offered by Louis Franzini (2001, see chapter 4), which allows for the possibility that the therapist's humour may not have an impact on the client's therapeutic process. We may take the view that we need not be 100% transparent with our client, particularly if we feel our feelings might not be of relevance or beneficial to the client. Thus, the question arises of whether the therapist's mirthful feeling should be shared or not, as well as whether the client will perceive the humorous content as it was intended. This may often be the justification given for not allowing humour into the therapy space, but it is, at the same time, a justification for doing just that because the same rationalisation applies to *any* intervention the therapist makes. The client may not perceive an intervention from the therapist, humorous or otherwise, in the way the therapist intended. Where the relationship is strong enough, however, the client should be able to "forgive" the therapist if an intervention misfires in some way (Sultanoff, 2013).

Necessary and sufficient?

A further condition of the six necessary and sufficient conditions – the seventh perhaps – is that these six alone suffice to facilitate therapeutic change in the client. The statement was revolutionary for two key reasons. The first was that it precluded the therapist from directing the client's process or taking responsibility for the client's therapeutic change. This fundamental principle of non-directivity was antithetical to the medical and psychoanalytic profession Rogers had trained with. As we saw in Chapter 7, non-directivity was mocked for being passive and superficial, but as any person-centred therapist knows, not jumping in and trying to rescue our client or even to point out where the client is *obviously going wrong*, is really hard to do.

Non-directivity can be considered akin to empathic understanding because it requires us as therapists to see the world from the client's perspective – or frame of reference. The second reason is that any direction from us will inevitably come from our frame of reference rather than the client's, and to impose our perspective on the client would imply we believe we have expertise in the client's experience:

> Without the guiding and the limiting role of the nondirective attitude, for example, congruence can be construed as self-disclosure, unconditional positive regard can be construed as praise of the client and empathic understanding can be construed as the therapist's imaginings about the client.
>
> (Brodley, 1997)

And yet, despite asserting the completeness of this septet of conditions, Rogers also envisaged that other approaches, elements, would come into play, and always emphasised the primacy of the therapist-client relationship over the mechanical application of techniques. For example, as we saw in Chapter 7, he actively took part in Natalie Rogers' art-based therapeutic work. And as his long-time colleague Natiello concluded: "after 15 years of research… the person of the therapist is the most important ingredient of therapy" (2001).

Inevitably then, the original theories have been re-visited, challenged and adapted. Some writers take a "pluralistic" view, arguing that if it works for the client, then it must be "client-centred" and therefore good enough. Others suggest that Rogers' own thinking continually evolved and would have continued to do so had he lived (even) longer. An example is his ponderings on other dimensions to human relationships, which were taken up and developed by Dave Mearns and Mick Cooper (2005/2018) and which we know now as "relational depth".

> **Reflection**
>
> An in-depth review of "post-classical" person-centred thinking is beyond the scope of this volume and the competence of this author. It is however noteworthy, I think, that humour – or indeed humour-based therapeutic modalities – continues to be absent from the main body of contemporary "person-centred" literature.

Summing up

Humour has the potential to be congruous with the key principles underlying the person-centred approach.

First, the *fully functioning* person is as open to humour, mirth and laughter as to other feelings and experiences. The therapist who acts *congruently* in the relationship recognises when humour arises in the therapeutic space and makes the same choice regarding whether to share that experiencing with the client as for other emotions and thoughts. Humour can affirm the therapist's *unconditional positive regard* for the client even when the latter's humour is defensive or aggressive. The therapist can consider the client's expressions of humour and mirth as lenses through which the client's world can be better – more *empathically* – understood. Finally, humour, mirth and laughter can bring the client and the therapist closer together in the *relationship*, reducing power imbalances, forging the healing alliance or simply reminding them of the goal of therapy.

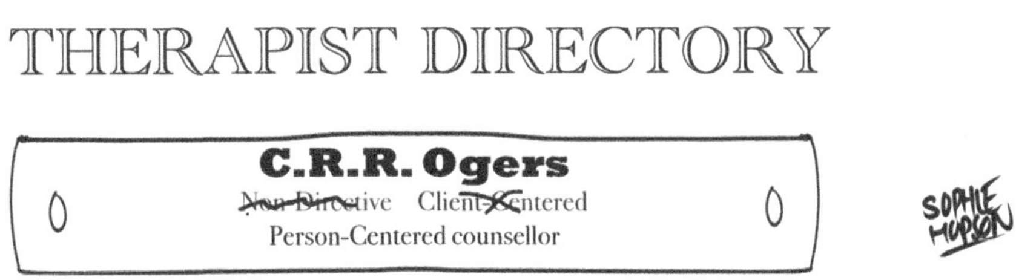

References

Berg, R., Parr, G., Bradley, L., & Berry, J. (2009). Humor: A therapeutic intervention for child counseling. *Journal of Creativity in Mental Health*, *4*(3), 225–236. https://doi.org/10.1080/15401380903192705

Bozarth, J. (2012). "Nondirectivity" in the theory of Carl R. Rogers: An unprecedented premise. *Person-Centered & Experiential Psychotherapies*, *11*(4), 262–276. https://doi.org/10.1080/14779757.2012.740317

Brodley, B. T. (1997). The nondirective attitude in client-centered therapy. *The Person-Centered Journal*, *4*(1), 18–30.

Carkhuff, R. R., & Berenson, B. G. (1967). *Beyond counseling and therapy*. Holt, Rinehart & Winston.

Chapman, G., Cleese, J., Gilliam, T., Idle, E., Jones, T. & Palin, M. (1979) *Monty python's life of Brian* (directed T. Jones). Handmade Films.

Dionigi, A., & Canestrari, C. (2018). The use of humour by therapists and clients in cognitive therapy. *European Journal of Humour Research*, *6*(3), 50–67. https://doi.org/10.7592/EJHR2018.6.3.dionigi

Frankel, M., & Sommerbeck, L. (2007). Two Rogers: Congruence and the change from client-centered therapy to we-centered therapy. *Person-Centered & Experiential Psychotherapies*, *6*(4), 286–295. https://doi.org/10.1080/14779757.2007.9688448

Franzini, L. R. (2001). Humor in therapy: The case for training therapists in its uses and risks. *The Journal of General Psychology*, *128*(2), 170–193. https://doi.org/10.1080/00221300109598906

Gabbard, G. O. (2010). *Long-term psychodynamic psychotherapy: A basic text* (2nd ed.) American Psychiatric Publishing.

Gallese, V. (2009). Mirror neurons, embodied simulation, and the neural basis of social identification. *Psychoanalytic Dialogues*, *19*(5), 519–536. https://doi.org/10.1080/10481880903231910

Gallese, V., Keysers, C., & Rizzolatti, G. (2004). A unifying view of the basis of social cognition. *Trends in Cognitive Sciences*, *8*(9), 396–403. https://doi.org/10.1016/j.tics.2004.07.002

Gibson, N. (2014) The best medicine? Psychotherapists' experience of the impact of humour on the process of psychotherapy. [DProf thesis, Middlesex University/New School of Psychotherapy and Counselling]. https://eprints.mdx.ac.uk/15730/

Gibson, N., & Tantam, D. (2017). The best medicine? The nature of humour and its significance for the process of psychotherapy. *Existential Analysis*, *28*(2), 272.

Gladding, S. (1995). Humor in counseling: Using a natural resource. *Journal of Humanistic Education & Development*, *34*(1), 3–12. https://doi.org/10.1002/j.2164-4683.1995.tb00106.x

Grosz, S. (2014). *The examined life*. Vintage.

Haugh, S. (2001). The difficulties in the conceptualisation of congruence: A way forward with complexity theory? In G. Wyatt (Ed.), *Rogers' therapeutic conditions: Evolution, theory and practice volume 1: Congruence* (pp. 116–130). PCCS Books.

Hussong, D. K., & Micucci, J. A. (2021). The use of humor in psychotherapy: Views of practicing psychotherapists. *Journal of Creativity in Mental Health*, *16*(1), 77–94. https://doi.org/10.1080/15401383.2020.1760989

Lietaer, G. (1984). Unconditional positive regard: A controversial basic attitude in client-centered therapy. In R. E. Levant & J. M. Shlien (Eds.), *Client-Centered therapy and the person-Centered approach: New directions in theory, research and practice*. Praeger.

Longe, O. (2018). *Can I laugh now? Understanding humour within psychotherapy from the client's perspective* [Master's dissertation, Dublin Business School]. https://esource.dbs.ie/handle/10788/3968

Mann, D. (1991). Humour in psychotherapy. *Psychoanalytic Psychotherapy*, *5*(2),161–170. https://doi.org/10.1080/02668739100700211

Maslow, A. H. (1943). A theory of human motivation. *Psychological Review*, *50*, 370–396.

Maslow, A. H. (1970). *Motivation and personality* (2nd ed.). Harper and Brothers.
Mearns, D., & Cooper, M. (2005/2018). *Working at relational depth in counselling and psychotherapy* (2nd ed.). Sage.
Mearns, D., & Thorne, B. (1988/1996). *Person-centred counselling in action*. SAGE Publications.
Miller, S. D., Duncan, B. L., & Hubble, M. A. (1997). *Escape from babel: Toward a unifying language of psychotherapy practice*. Norton and Company.
Natiello, P. (2001). *The person-centred approach: A passionate presence*. PCCS Books.
Norcross, J. C. (2002). *Psychotherapy relationships that work: Therapist contributions and responsiveness to patients*. Oxford University Press.
Prerost, F. J. (1994). Humor as an intervention strategy. In H. S. Strean (Ed.), *The use of humor in psychotherapy* (pp. 139–147). Jason Aronson.
Rizzolatti, G., Fadiga, L., Gallese, V., & Fogassi, L. (1995). Premotor cortex and the recognition of motor actions. *Cognitive Brain Research*, *3*, 131–141.
Rogers, C. R. (1951/1999). *Client-centered therapy: Its current practice, implications and theory*. Constable.
Rogers, C. R. (1957). The necessary and sufficient conditions of therapeutic personality change. *Journal of Consulting Psychology*, *21*(2), 95–103. https://doi.org/10.1037/h0045357
Rogers, C. R. (1959). A theory of therapy, personality, and interpersonal relationships, as developed in the client-centered framework. In S. Koch (Ed.), *Psychology: A study of a science, study 1, volume 3: Formulations of the person and the social context* (pp. 184–256). McGraw-Hill.
Rogers, C. R. (1963). The concept of the fully functioning person. *Psychotherapy (Chicago, Ill.)*, *1*(1), 17–26. https://doi.org/10.1037/h0088567
Rogers, C. R. (1980). *A way of being*. Houghton Mifflin.
Rogers, C. R. (2004). *On becoming a person: A therapist's view of psychotherapy*. Constable & Robinson.
Schore, A. N. (2011). The right brain implicit self lies at the core of psychoanalysis. *Psychoanalitic Dialogues*, *21*(1), 75–100. https://doi.org/10.1080/10481885.2011.545329
Shearer, A. (2016). *Why don't psychotherapists laugh?* Routledge.
Smith, D. (1990). Psychodynamic therapy: The Freudian approach. In W. Dryden (Ed.), *(1990). Individual therapy* (pp. 18–38). Open University Press.
Sultanoff, S. (2013). Integrating humor into psychotherapy: Research, theory, and the necessary conditions for the presence of therapeutic humor in helping relationships. *The Humanistic Psychologist*, *41*, 388–399. https://doi.org/10.1080/08873267.2013.796953
Talens, P. (2020). When working in a youth service, how do therapists experience humour with their clients? *European Journal of Psychotherapy & Counselling*, *22(1–2)*, 80–96. https://doi.org/10.1080/13642537.2020.1766526
Tudor, K. (2010). Person-centered relational therapy: An organismic perspective. *Person-Centered & Experiential Psychotherapies*, *9*(1), 52–68.
Tudor, K., & Worrall, M. (2006). *Person-centred therapy: A clinical philosophy*. Taylor & Francis Group.
Valentine, L., & Gabbard, G. O. (2014). Can the use of humor in psychotherapy be taught? *Academic Psychiatry*, *38*(1), 75–81. https://doi.org/10.1007/s40596-013-0018-2
Wilkins, P. (2002). Unconditional positive regard reconsidered. In J. D. Bozarth & P. Wilkins (Eds.), *Unconditional positive regard*. PCCS Books.
Yonatan-Leus, R., Tishby, O., Shefler, G., & Wiseman, H. (2018). Therapists' honesty, humor styles, playfulness, and creativity as outcome predictors: A retrospective study of the therapist effect. *Psychotherapy Research*, *28*(5), 793–802. https://doi.org/10.1080/10503307.2017.1292067

Part IV

Working with humour

Chapter 9

Practical considerations

Introduction

Previous chapters took us through the theories of what humour is, and what it means, to the question of whether person-centred thinking naturally accommodates the presence of humour in the therapy space.

This chapter proposes a broad framework for working with humour in person-centred therapy rooms. It is closely aligned with the core conditions and emphasises the critical importance of the relationship between therapist and client.

Working with humour

The framework proposed here is grounded in the therapeutic objective of *working with humour*. This contrasts with the various methodologies discussed in earlier chapters that *use humour* as a tool or a technique (Figure 9.1), something that is deployed to further the therapy goals, for example:

> therapeutic humor is created when a health practitioner consciously and purposefully chooses humor based on specific behavioral skills (including the ability to create funny interventions)… Therapeutic humor can be added to a skilled clinician's repertoire of clinical interventions…
>
> (Sultanoff, 2013)

It is proposed in this chapter that we can:

- Work with humour authentically, neither forcing nor suppressing it;
- Work with the client's humour, accepting it as an elemental part of our client's experiencing; and
- Work with humour to gain empathic understanding of our client's world.

DOI: 10.4324/9781003638773-14

Figure 9.1 Using humour as a tool is not without risk...

Working authentically with humour

Working authentically with humour means neither forcing it into our interactions with the client nor suppressing it if it does materialise. In Chapter 8, we explored how the therapist's congruence might be conveyed through humour and mirth. Experience shows that this looks easier on paper than it is to achieve in practice: we need always to be aware of what we are feeling in the moment and why, and we must also decide whether or not to share this experiencing with the client. Our awareness of humour can tell us a great deal about the mood and personality of our client, and how we react to it can also shed light on ourselves.

Reflection

In my second session with a client at a bereavement service, she began by saying she had had "an ok week", and then promptly burst into tears. When she stopped, she said she didn't know what had caused the tears, whether it was seeing our therapy room again or seeing me. She looked at me and laughed and, sensing that her momentary incongruence wasn't dissimilar to my own slight nervousness at being in a new relationship, I laughed, too.

We can start by reminding ourselves that humour comes in various guises. Humour that is aggressive, sarcastic or demeaning is likely to be unhelpful (though, as we saw in Chapter 5, Frank Farrelly would *provocatively* disagree). So, it is worth checking in with ourselves why we feel the impulse to allow humour into the therapy space. It might, for example, be that we are attempting to mask our mocking of the client. Suppose the client were to say something that we found offensive: we may feel unable or unwilling to challenge the client, and so we might – in our frustration – find ourselves resorting instead to humour that demeans the client. While this might placate our natural indignation it is unlikely to come across as authentic or acceptant. Another motivation that could undermine the therapeutic alliance is an urge to use humour to come across as clever or to ingratiate ourselves with our client. Here, it would seem that we are only likely to reveal our own need for external validation.

Pause for thought

What are our barriers to allowing humour into the therapy room?

Perhaps we sense humour or mirth bubbling to the surface in a session: what if it offends the client in some way?

If we get it wrong, we risk disrupting the process and undermining the therapeutic endeavour, so is it perhaps better to avoid humour altogether?

A technique?

We saw in Chapter 4 a number of humour-based methods and techniques used by therapists and other care-sector practitioners for the benefit of their clients and patients. In Chapter 5, we also reviewed entire methodologies premised on the therapist's use of humour. Among person-centred practitioners (those who believe humour does have a place in therapy) there is disagreement about whether humour should be consciously *used* in the therapy room or allowed to emerge organically and spontaneously. The latter position aligns closely with the concept of therapists' non-directivity. Introducing humour into the dialogue might intrude on the client's processing. Also, the decision to use humour and the humour itself emanates from the counsellor's frame of reference at a time when she would normally be striving to attain empathic understanding of the client's frame of reference.

Both these objections suppose the counsellor first gains awareness of something humorous or mirthful, stops listening to the client – albeit for the briefest of moments – to decide whether to share it or not, and then formulates how the intervention should be expressed. Such an interlude might last a fraction of a second, such that the client does not notice the counsellor's fleeting absence, or it might preoccupy the counsellor to such an extent that she risks losing touch with her client. The objections also differentiate an intervention with humorous content from other interventions. But is a non-humorous reflection of what the client has been processing during a session so much different from one that does contain humour?

The humour need not result in belly laughs. Or any laughs at all. Our own authentic chuckle may indeed be enough to signal to the client that we are present in the relationship. We offer our interventions tentatively to our clients, and if they are worded with gentle humour they can help set aside blockages and resistance. They can be the key that unlocks the door.

Reflection

Working over the phone with a client who had survived a childhood mired in emotional abuse from his father, we talked at length in a number of sessions about the "brainwashing" that resulted from the abuse. He was somehow blocked and unable to comprehend how profound the effect on him had been.

"He would tell me black is white and I believed him", he said, "and I don't know the difference anymore".

Earlier in the session, he had shared his experience volunteering at a dementia service, when one of the patients stuck a blob of clay on his nose. The nurses had wanted to scold him, but the client had laughed it off because, he told me, the patient didn't mean any harm and anyway wouldn't have understood the reprimand.

So I suggested, "You say you don't know the difference between black and white. But you know that laughing when someone with dementia pops a blob of clay on your nose is a better response than telling them off".

There was silence.

After about 30 seconds, I said, "I can almost hear the resistance on the phone line".

He laughed then.

"It's uncanny".

He laughed again and said, "I know what you're getting at. I just wish I could feel it".

What if we aren't funny?

A reservation about working with humour might be that we feel we simply don't have the capacity to be funny. We can't remember jokes, let alone tell them with confidence. And we worry that our humour will come out wrong and fall flat. That can be about as amusing as having to try to explain a joke. Counsellors may hold back their humorous impulses for fear of coming across as "unprofessional" to clients, colleagues and peers. This can be an issue for inexperienced counsellors, too, who worry that they will be judged as not taking their new career seriously enough. Conversely, a counsellor lacking in confidence may latch on to humour to avoid going deep with their client, for fear of finding themselves out of their depth.

We are, of course, a world away from stand-up comedy. Nonetheless, it does pay to "read the audience". Keith Christie talks of his first time leading a group session at a men's prison, when, in order to calm his nerves and perhaps ingratiate himself with his group, he opened the session with a joke. No one laughed. Afterwards, his supervisor suggested to him that he had succeeded only in reminding the prisoners that after the session he would be going home while they would not (personal communication). He recognised he had been guilty of putting on a front and hoping his joke would disguise his nervousness.

Being confident working with humour is harder for some than others. And no one wants to come across as if they were the Chancellor of the Exchequer presenting the Budget. For those who feel less confident about letting their humour be seen, there are training organisations that can help improve their humorous attitudes, for example, the clowning and expressive arts workshops offered by Ugly Bucket (see Chapter 3). The primary aim here, however, is for us not to be afraid of the humour that emerges. These moments are spontaneous and for the most part lie outside the planned technical interventions of the therapist, and they may be something as simple as a "shared belly laugh" (Valentine & Gabbard, 2014).

Germinating the seeds of the relationship

We have seen that the counsellor can help the client see his issues more clearly with or without the introduction of humour. How might humour contribute to forging the alliance between counsellor and client?

Reflection

In some respects, it has never been easier to find a therapist. Not only are there numerous "general" therapist directories on the Web, but there are also many more that specialise in offering counselling for specific issues and/or to specific groups of people. Even if one assumes that therapists list themselves on more than one directory, it must seem to people in distress as if there are enough therapists in England to populate a small town.

Scrolling down the lists, a client once told me, is like searching for a date on an app (though, thankfully, without the swiping – *Tender* rather than *Tinder*?). These listings reflect how we have as a society adapted to finding connection in the digital age. Add to that the multifarious therapeutic modalities of therapy on offer (or "brands" as the aforementioned client suggested to me) and the cost of a session, and it is a brave individual indeed who takes the plunge and seeks out help.

This brings up an important question: how should person-centred counsellors project themselves in these digital spaces? When it comes to profile photos – often the first impression potential clients have – the conventional wisdom is clear: aim for warmth, professionalism, approachability and trustworthiness, ideally with a gentle, natural smile. I always say that if you look like your passport photo, you're not well enough to travel. Yet browsing through listings reveals a startling range of expressions, from "undertaker" to "Mona Lisa". Many photos are obviously selfies, with some hastily taken in the driving seat of (presumably) their car, or shots grabbed at a social gathering where someone's shoulder remains in frame despite cropping efforts. People say they don't like their photos taken – not many people do – but looking as if you don't want your photo taken might make persuading folks you're empathic, professional, approachable, etc. more of a challenge than it needs to be.

"Also", my client said, "The age of some of those photos! They need carbon-dating! How's that going to build trust?"

The first session is typically nerve-wracking for clients; it can also be stressful for practitioners. In addition to personal factors (shyness, for example), those working within an organisation might be challenged by the conflicting desire to be authentic and the obligation to meet the organisation's priorities. For counsellors working in private practice, the challenge might be yet more personal; even though we believe our work is governed by the needs of our clients, our income suffers if, for whatever reason, they do not return. Regardless, all practitioners must hope their clients benefit in some way from meeting them. So if we feel that our stress – and that of our clients – would be reduced if we could allow some lightness into our interaction, we might be tempted to go beyond a welcoming smile with some ice-breaking remarks. The weather, traffic, wi-fi, coffee machine – the possibilities are endless. I invariably see clients visibly relax when they hear that I am human, or at least not as scary as a dentist, solicitor or their old headmaster. Martha Straus and Kevin McKenzie additionally suggest that a little levity at the outset allows the therapist to assess the client's "metacognitive capacity" – how ready they are to experience therapeutic change. "Can they take their foot off the gas long enough to smile? It bodes well for the therapy if they can" (2022).

Steven Sultanoff recounts his experience with a client who knew she needed help but had left three previous therapists after the second session out of fear of the pain she anticipated she would have to confront. Sultanoff seems to have intuited that the client would respond well to a re-framing of the client's avoidant behaviour, and so started their second session with the words, "Since this will be our last session…" (2013). He reports that the client recognised the incongruent absurdity of her behaviour and laughed. She continued seeing him until she moved away from the area a year later.

Reflection

The contracting at the opening of the relationship is an opportune moment to introduce a little levity. I am always conscious of how much power resides in the counselling contract, much as I may try to make it a consensual process. So, I might make reference to those epic terms and conditions we are expected to read and sign off before we can use a product from the likes of Apple and Microsoft and which, of course, are non-negotiable. A dear friend of mine recently gave me a tip about addressing the possibility that she and a client might encounter each other outside the therapy room. "When we're talking about how I'll acknowledge them only if they acknowledge me first I say they've no need to worry about seeing me waving and hollering at them in the middle of Aldi" (Duffy-Booth, personal communication).

It is true that a good part of my motivation for introducing humour at this point is for my benefit: like a lot of people who think they're funny, I'm actually rather shy. Mainly, though, I feel uncomfortable with the weight of the power that the contracting places on me, even if it is entirely necessary for the client's protection. Nonetheless, I nearly always perceive the client growing a little less apprehensive, beginning to open up, together with a sense almost that we're in this together.

Working acceptantly with the client's humour

As we have seen, humour can shield and shelter us, it can render the unbearable bearable, we can use it to birch our backs, it can let us catch our breath. And, of course, it can affirm our pleasure, our joy and, in the therapy room, it can signal our recovery. When humour is introduced by the client, it can help the practitioner to understand – empathically – where that humour is coming from. Our first step is to accept it. It is as much an elemental part of the client's experiencing as anything non-humorous he may say. And what he says may be funny or it may not; it may be positive and self-reinforcing or negative and self-defeating. In Chapter 2, we explored how psychologists have assessed and categorised humour in its various forms, and awareness of those theories can help us understand our client better.

Pause for thought

How often does laughter occur during your sessions with clients?

Carl Marci et al. (2004) studied the frequency of laughter in ten psychodynamic therapy sessions at the Psychiatry Outpatient Department of Massachusetts General Hospital. Each session saw ten different therapists meet different patients; that is, no one participated more than once.

In total, they recorded 145 laughter episodes – where one of the interlocutors said something that gave rise to immediate laughter – during a total of seven hours and 30 minutes, giving an average of one laughter episode every three minutes and ten seconds, or 14 and a half times each session. Although laughter patterns varied considerably between sessions, patients laughed on average 11.9 times per session, while therapists laughed much less often: 4.8 times on average. Patients laughed at their own comments on average 7.1 times, and at the therapist's comments 2.3 times. The therapists – psychodynamic, let's not forget – laughed just 2.6 times at their patient's comments and 0.3 times at their own comments.

The defensive humour shield

Humour can be used by the client to deflect or evade the curiosity of the therapist, though the client might not realise what is being said until after it has been said.

A classic example of this is "self-defeating" humour (Martin et al., 1993). Here, the speaker humorously puts himself down (not in a veterinary sense):

> I'm late, *surprise, surprise*. I'll probably be late for my own funeral.
> I'm such a bad cook I use the smoke alarm as a timer.

As we see here, there is nearly always what Patricia Talens refers to as a "dual meaning" (2020), an observation about oneself which is expressed in intentionally humorous terms. The duality of the semantic meaning may also lie in the messages themselves. The speaker is, on the face of it, being modest: always late, a terrible cook. But perhaps another message is being conveyed. It might be that the modesty is in fact false, that the speaker doesn't really believe she is habitually tardy, or that he considers himself to be a gourmet chef. Perhaps, more commonly, the humour may be intended as a decoy.

> I'm late not because I can't keep to my commitments but because it took me two hours to build up the confidence to leave the house.
>
> I'm not just a terrible cook, I'm a terrible father, too.

It follows that this type of humour is often prompted by a sense of shame that is felt too deeply to be expressed directly. The humour invites the listener to think worse of the speaker.

> I'm the world's worst father. I can't even cook. In fact, I'm such a bad cook I use the smoke alarm as a timer.

Reflection

Cyn, a retired postal worker, sought help to eliminate her anxiety and low self-esteem, two issues that are frequently encountered in therapy but which, of course, manifest themselves in unique ways. As she talked about herself, she would laugh, very, very loudly. She explained that she was renowned for her laugh. "If anyone at the sorting office ever asked where I was, they would say, 'Just follow the laugh'", she told me, followed by another loud laugh. Cyn repeated this line at the next session, word for word. It quickly became clear that her laughter expressed, not joy or mirth or even gallows-facing stoicism, but a formidable defence shield. It seemed to say, "I need to be heard but I do not want to be seen".

After some more sessions, I came to understand that she trusted neither herself nor me. Her low self-esteem told her she was worthless; it also warned her that others would see her in the same way. She said to me, "I am walking across a frozen sea and every step I take I can hear the ice cracking beneath my feet". Her laughter came from the fear that the ice would give way and swallow her whole.

For reasons I still have not fathomed, Cyn and I could not build a successful partnership, and so we agreed to terminate our work before it had really got started. Certainly, she did not feel she could trust me. Perhaps she thought she was ready for therapeutic change, but wasn't. In any case, I regret not having been able to work with her to dismantle her defensive shield.

As they say, sometimes "the best form of defence is attack". And in this way, we experience humour that is not self-deprecating but demeaning and aggressive. Sarcasm and ridicule might imply the speaker feels superior:

Therapist: What brings you here?
Client: Well I thought I was coming to see an expert, but I can see I've failed there, too.

It might be a smoke screen deployed by the client which says, "I'm not really here", or a decoy that says, "Better look over there". This militaristic imagery is deliberate: the client feels under fire and wants to be somewhere other than the therapy room.

Of course, we are not in the business of diagnosing our clients. However, humour reveals so much information about our characters and how we relate to people, as in this scene from the popular film *Bridget Jones's Diary*, when Bridget meets Darcy and, glass of wine in one hand and cigarette in the other, she lapses into "verbal diarrhoea":

> I was in London at a party last night, so I'm afraid I'm a bit hungover. [nervous laugh] Wish I could be lying with my head in the toilet like all normal people. New Year's resolution: drink less. Oh, and quit smoking. Hmm. [laughs] And keep New Year's resolutions. [laughs] And... [laughs] stop talking total nonsense to strangers. In fact, stop talking full stop.
>
> (Maguire, 2001)

Humour intended to deflect may act for the client as a protective shield against threats – physical or verbal, real or imagined – from family, intimate partners, classmates, colleagues. The shield provides relief and makes the person feel safer. It helps preserve an inner sense of self. In the therapy room, we might understand the humour as saying, "I do not trust you". It may, however, say, "I do not trust myself". It is the client's way of warding off powerful, painful emotions, thoughts and memories. A note to self: *I do not know if I can go there*. We may have just about managed to achieve psychological contact with the client, but the client is some way off perceiving our core conditions.

Whatever the underlying motivations, none of our clients' attempts at defensive or deflective humour should deter or diminish our aim of offering them unconditional positive regard. However, Marie Adams (2001) warns against humour and laughter that represents "collusion rather than holding of the therapeutic boundary". This warning will resonate with many graduates of counsellor training courses (Briggs & Owen, 2022; Buşu & Buşu, 2021), who will have been admonished for doing that very thing they're supposed to do, namely going alongside their client without forcing the direction of the process. The client is not ready to dive in: are we really supposed to push him in? Perhaps the expectation is that the client, seeing the trainee counsellor's deadpan response, will drop the deflective attitude (and we're assuming here that the attitude is feigned) and get down to the Serious Business Of Therapy. I think it's worth emphasising here that this received wisdom does not originate with Carl Rogers.

If the therapist perceives the humour as persistently deflective and becoming a barrier to the therapeutic process, she might choose to address the defensiveness directly. This could well be an appropriate response where the client's humour comes across as particularly self-deprecatory or aggressive. However, the act of addressing the client's humour requires some directiveness on the part of the practitioner: the client will necessarily break the flow, such as it is, and potentially cause the process to take a new direction.

The psychotherapists interviewed by Elizabeth Briggs and Alison Owen (2022) described clients wanting to avoid painful topics, denying things that were happening or holding the therapist at bay. One participant described an occasion when a client was using humour to be deflective, and she realised that she herself often behaved in a similar way. She continued:

> I went "Hold up, I know what you're doing, let's double back here and I'm repeating that because you just laughed it off but I'm not having it."
>
> (2022)

By making such an intervention, the practitioner's shared congruence can open the client's eyes to the inconsistencies in his behaviour and forge a path towards deeper emotional exploration, which might otherwise have taken much longer to reach. Other, perhaps gentler, challenges might include:

> I wonder if by making fun of this makes it easier to handle?
>
> or
>
> I notice we get so far and then we seem to stop when the humour comes in – why do you think that is?

Such interventions are not very different to other challenges a practitioner might make to a client. For example, "I notice we're talking a lot about what happened to you and not so much about how it made you feel..." The difference with deflective humour is that the practitioner's intervention conveys a very powerful message: "Your attempts at deflection/avoidance are not necessary, so let's not bother with them?" A client might use such humour with friends and family as a means of keeping them at bay; here, the practitioner is letting the client know that his deflective shield is not needed, that he is safe.

It is important to note that the client's humour is not always defensive or avoidant. Indeed, a client's laughter may indicate that they are receiving our unconditional positive regard and empathic understanding that they feel safe enough to bring their authentic self to the relationship:

> ...even though we're talking about something very serious and traumatic, we can still have a shared giggle over something.
>
> (Briggs & Owen, 2022)

Reflection

A while ago, it became clear to me – after more than one visit to the vet – that owning cacti was incompatible with owning three cats. The sharp-spined and the sharp-clawed housemates were going to have to be separated, so my wife suggested using my newly refurbished therapy room at the end of the garden. The room is quite small and wouldn't have suited the cats, so it was that the cacti were relocated. All 13 of them. Problem solved.

Several times, clients have commented on them, often on their first visits when I assume they are taking in the new surroundings, settling in. And I felt a little pride that the plants gave the room a more homely, less clinical air.

Until one day, a client was talking about her recently deceased father: "He wasn't a bastard. He wasn't... He was... he was as prickly as your fucking cactuses!"

We were deep in the moment, and I was about to let the comment go unremarked. But I said, "They remind you of your dad? That wasn't the aesthetic I was aiming for". She laughed.

"You know, I love them? They remind me of that story you told me, you know, about the potato plant or whatever it was. And so when I come here and I see them, I think, fuck it, if those cactuses can survive, so can I."

Working with humour to gain an empathic understanding of our client's world

As with any non-humorous expression, our curiosity about how our clients use humour can inform us about the kind of person they are, what they are feeling and what they are allowing into experience – or not. The client may use humour, for example, to alleviate the unbearable intensity of his feelings, as a means of coping and self-soothing. This might arise, for example, with topics that are taboo, or deeply shaming for the client. And so, it is important – as with other forms of expression the client uses – for the counsellor to judge what is going on for the client in that moment by what I call *listening between the lines*.

Metaphor to the fore

One of the richest forms of semantic expression is metaphor. It infuses our literature as well as our everyday conversation with resonance, depth and emotion. *It's raining cats and dogs. I am over the moon.* While we don't know how much Rogers thought humour would aid the therapeutic process, we do know he liked a metaphor: all living organisms, even potatoes abandoned in a cellar, will strive to reach their potential, such is the universality of the actualising tendency.

Giorgio Nardone and Claudette Portelli suggest that metaphor:

> …does not simply arouse our emotions or allow their expression. The experience of metaphor is of itself an emotion or sensation. This tool offers a emotionally corrective experience that touches us.
>
> (2007)

Clients use humorous metaphors in many ways, perhaps delighting in the playfulness of the words, and this may be a signal that healing is underway.

Reflection

Periodically, I invite clients to review our work. It provides me with useful feedback and allows clients to explore how they feel they are progressing. There is often some levity in these conversations. For example, one client compared our sessions to the scariest rollercoaster at Alton Towers, a popular theme park in the Midlands. Another client, whose long-term partner ended their relationship, told me she was enjoying her newly imposed freedom by reverting to living like a tramp. The bedroom they had shared was now, she said, her "floordrobe". Another client sent me a text message when her long-awaited diagnosis for bipolar disorder had come through. In it she wrote:

> Finally I'm officially :):

Clients may also use metaphors to paraphrase how they're feeling, avoiding speaking directly because the subject matter is painful or shameful. Briggs and Owen cite an occasion when a client said, "I feel like a rich tea and I want to be a hobnob". The counsellor took up the metaphor as she worked towards empathic understanding by reflecting that it sounded like he felt weak and wanted to be stronger, to which he replied, "Yeah, I think you saved me having to say that" (2022).

Guillaume Chaloult and Claude Blondeau report a client who has been responding for so long with hostility to the counsellor's attempts at understanding her that eventually he "thanks" her for having helped him discover a second vocation, that of a customs officer. He explains:

> I have the impression that your experience of our sessions must be similar to that of going through customs. I sometimes imagine I am a border agent… and you are a tourist subjected to intense interrogation on a weekly basis.
>
> (2017)

The client reportedly smiled at the "submissive analogy", recognising how the dynamic between them had evolved; from then on, there was less inhibition preventing her from confiding fully in her therapist.

Reflection

A client who was grieving the death of her partner from Covid-19 was struggling with anxiety about her own mortality. Her "self-medication" comprised a diet of malt whisky and repeated viewings of dystopian and post-apocalyptic films and shows.

"It's no wonder I wake up in the mornings exhausted. It's like I'm not really there", she told me, "I can barely get out of my bed to go to work, you know? And I spend all day as if… I don't know…"

My first thought was to say, "…in a fog". Instead, I said, "Like one of those zombies on tv". It seemed more appropriate, it felt somehow more empathic.

At first she didn't respond, and I thought I must have misspoken. So I back-pedalled and added, "Like in a fog".

She looked at me and grinned. "Yeah", she replied bitterly. Then she chuckled. "Yeah. Like a zombie in the effing fog."

Metaphors invite the listener momentarily to see themselves through the speaker's eyes, gaining distance that might allow for a new perspective. And we see that humour and metaphor go together like – sorry – horses and carriages. Our *attitude* of congruence, acceptance and empathy, deploying the creative network of a billion or so mirror neurons (see Chapter 8), creates the fertile conditions in which the therapist co-creates meaning with the client.

Working with different humour

The question is often asked: how does all this apply in contexts where the practitioner is *different* to the client? We live in a world that is often unjust, where the majority's voice drowns out that of minorities. Correcting those many and various injustices occurs at different paces, and new injustices arise or are brought to light. How we as practitioners negotiate these shifting paradigms is beyond the scope of this book. Our challenge is always how to work in the moment with the client in front of us. Take, for example, the trope that people living with autism have no sense of humour: we saw in Chapter 2 that this is unfounded, but we did see that neurodivergent people's sense of what is funny can diverge from what we think is funny – or, more precisely, what we think *most people* think is funny.

In some respects, humour is something of a litmus test when it comes to sensitivity to each other's differences. If we assume that the world as we see it is the same for everyone, we are quickly going to alienate our clients. Conversely, we run the risk of perpetuating stereotypical perceptions if we assume that everyone with a certain difference feels, thinks and behaves in the same way. Take, as an example, this advice for counsellors working in the United States:

> Although they may appear restrained and disciplined due to dictating cultural norms, Asian Americans have a playful and endearing sense of humor that is very much a part of their culture under certain circumstances.
> (Maples et al., 2001)

How helpful advice such as this is to counsellors is unclear.

If we say something that we intend to be perceived as humorous and it is not received as such, there could be any number of reasons for the missed connection. Our task as therapists is to explore what is preventing the connection from being made, and to adjust our attitude accordingly, and this applies to humour as much as any other interaction.

Pause for thought

What are your feelings about these concerns? Do they resonate with your experience, either as a practitioner or a client?

The relationship

Deepening the bond

One aspect of the therapeutic relationship that has attracted much discussion is that of the reciprocity of the relationship itself, which Rogers proposed in his "tentative law of interpersonal relationships":

> Assuming a minimal mutual willingness to be in *contact* and to receive communications, we may say that the greater the communicated *congruence* of *experience*, *awareness*, and behavior on the part of one individual, the more the ensuing relationship will involve a tendency toward reciprocal communication with the same qualities, mutually accurate understanding of the communications, improved *psychological adjustment* and functioning in both parties, and mutual satisfaction in the relationship.
> (1959, emphasis in original)

The proposition here expands on the six necessary and sufficient conditions that the client and therapist be in psychological contact and that the client perceives the therapist's empathy and acceptance. The proposition has been expanded on, too, with the development of the concepts of relational depth (Mearns, 1997) and mutuality (Murphy et al., 2012).

For Dave Mearns, meeting at relational depth involves both client and therapist coming together and relating to each other at a deeply trusting, vulnerable and transparent level, often at a non-verbal level. These moments – often fleeting – are characterised by the intense convergence of the three core conditions, including a "highly somatic" empathy, feeling changed by the client, also losing track of time, being free of distractions and feeling entirely immersed in the relationship (Cooper, 2005).

Reflection

While working with a bereaved client, I found that our thoughts seemed to be occurring in some kind of matched sequence: she would be talking about her grief and then pause, as if to take a breath. In that fleeting moment, it felt to me as if the storm clouds were parting and a ray of sunshine were breaking through. And the client would then say something amusing, we would laugh, and then her processing continued. This briefest of connections brings to mind the concept of relational depth.

A somewhat more mechanical, process-outcome perspective (arguably more closely aligned with Rogers' affinity with empirically observed research) comes from David Murphy and colleagues:

> The term mutuality refers to the bi-directional, reciprocal experience of empathy, unconditional positive regard, and congruence of each person within the dyadic relationship.
>
> (Murphy & Cramer, 2014)

The principle underlying mutuality, as defined here, is the back and forth between the client and therapist of those core conditions. For example, if the therapist perceives that the client is perceiving her acceptance, she will herself feel accepted in the relationship. In this respect, the therapist benefits from the experience of therapy, satisfying her own need for positive regard.

Much research into the efficacy of therapy has been carried out through the lens of this relational feature, notably in a wide-ranging study by Jeffrey Cornelius-White et al. (2018), which concluded there was a strong relationship between mutuality and the quality of the therapeutic session. In studies into humour (see Chapter 6), humour has been found to help to forge what Adams calls "the real relationship" (2001), while Aakriti Malik refers to "a significant moment of bonding" (2021). In their study of psychotherapeutic practice, all six of the therapists interviewed by Briggs and Owen mentioned that humour made it possible to meet each other on a deeply connected level, with one therapist stating, "Having that laugh together just feels like you are meeting at that point in that relational depth because there is something so palpably shared" (2022).

What we find then are significant intersections between perceptions around mutuality and relational depth with the presence of humour, laughter and mirth, for example, the self-disclosure inherent in humour, the willingness to be seen, to take risks in the communication and the desire to eliminate the power imbalance.

Briggs and Owen talk of humour as a place in the relationship where the therapist and client are "really meeting each other on a deeply connected level" (2022). Elizabeth Briggs finds humour even in her work with clients living with histories of trauma and abuse. She tells of how a "running gag" – something of a light-hearted nature that is shared and repeated in subsequent sessions – shows the client that the therapist "cared enough" to remember the in-joke (personal communication).

Reflection

Pete, a former footballer, came to see me after surviving a horrific car crash in which his wife had died. In the early sessions, he said very little and cried a lot. He told me he saw no future for himself that he wished he had died instead of his wife or that he had died with her. He rarely left his house. I began to wonder how much our sessions were really helping.

Then, one week, he told me that his sister, who lived overseas, had bought him a ticket to see his football team at the weekend. I asked what team he supported.

"Spurs".

"Tottenham Hotspur?"

He nodded. I spied a twinkle in his eye.

"Seeing Spurs play is supposed to cheer you up?"

We both laughed. Really loudly. It felt as if a pressure valve had been released.

The next time we met, towards the end of the session, when he was gathering himself to face the outside world again, I asked him how the match had been (confident in knowing that Spurs had lost). We laughed again and chatted about the team's many shortcomings, and I shared that I supported their arch-rivals Arsenal. Curiously, a kind of routine then crept into our sessions, where we would often finish off talking about football. It seemed to help him prepare to leave, and I think he was grateful that we were able to allow into the therapy room something to ease the pain (though not for Spurs, obviously).

What happens if things go wrong? If the humour misfires for some reason, the practitioner might encounter a rebuff and/or unintentionally provoke more or greater defensiveness on the part of the client. As noted previously, any intervention or reflection has the potential to be misconstrued. In such circumstances, the practitioner apologises and returns to the matter at hand. If the relationship is robust enough, the client will not be likely to be so defensive or take umbrage for long.

Couples and groups

We saw in Chapter 6 that humour also has an important role to play in group therapy settings. Do the considerations discussed in this chapter extend to group and couple work? Because communication takes place between clients in addition to the exchanges between therapist and client(s), it might seem that the therapist has more work to do. But the counsellor who allows himself to be seen, who is authentic, acceptant and curious, can do so equally when there is more than one client in the room, or indeed if there is another counsellor present.

Reflection

After a number of sessions with a couple in their 30s during which they had communicated largely by bickering and tossing grenade-like put-downs at each other, one of them asked me what I thought about their situation. I felt torn between stock reticence (e.g. I'm hearing that you're concerned about how your relationship looks to others) and self-disclosure (congruence and transparency!). I pictured them for a second. They had talked about how much they loved the theatre, visiting it almost every other week, and all I could think of was Samuel Beckett's Vladimir and Estragon. I said, "I'm wondering if you're waiting for Godot". It wasn't meant to be funny, and for a moment nothing was said. Then one of them said, "You must be Estragon", to which the other retorted, "Are you serious? You're Estragon. I'm Vladimir". The two of them then laughed. We talked about the play, which they were much more familiar with than I was. "We are like two drunks", one (Estragon, I think) said finally, "two drunks propping each other up. When one wobbles the other falls".

To a couple seeking help in making sense of a relationship that has become chronically mired in resentment and miscommunication, a touch of humour from the therapist can defuse some of the tension and may also help the couple see a way towards reconciliation.

> **Pause for thought**
>
> "I know if I walk past a therapy room and I hear laughter, then healing is happening" (C. Brown, personal communication).
>
> Do you agree?

Summing up

A person-centred framework is proposed, grounded in the therapeutic objective of *working with humour* such that we can:

- work with humour authentically, neither forcing nor suppressing it;
- work with the client's humour, accepting it as an elemental part of our client's experiencing; and
- work with humour to gain empathic understanding of our client's world.

References

Adams, M. (2001). Humour in the psychotherapeutic relationship: Not to be trifled with. In P. Milner & S. Palmer (Eds.), *Counselling: The BACP counselling reader, volume 2* (pp. 437–441). SAGE Publications.

Briggs, E., & Owen, A. (2022). Funny, right? How do trainee and qualified therapists experience laughter in their practice with clients? *Counselling and Psychotherapy Research, 2022*(22), 827–838. https://doi.org/10.1002/capr.12525

Buşu, O.-V., & Buşu, A.-D. (2021). The use of humour as communication skill in counselling and psychotherapy. *Annals of the University of Craiova Seria Psihologie, Pedagogie, 43*(2), 205–216.

Chaloult, G., & Blondeau, C. (2017). Perspectives sur l'usage de l'humour en psychothérapie. *Santé Mentale au Québec, 42*(1), 425–443. https://doi.org/10.7202/1040263ar

Cooper, M. (2005). Therapists' experiences of relational depth: A qualitative interview study. *Counselling and Psychotherapy Research, 5*(2), 87–95. https://doi.org/10.1080/17441690500211130

Cornelius-White, J. H. D., Kanamori, Y., Tickle, D. M. & Tickle, E. (2018). Mutuality in psychotherapy: A meta-analysis and meta-synthesis. *Journal of Psychotherapy Integration*, *28*(4), 489–504.

Maguire, S., Director. (2001). *Bridget Jones's diary* [film]. Miramax Films: Working Title Films.

Malik, A. (2021). Working with humour in psychotherapy. In E. Vanderheiden & C.-H. Mayer (Eds.), *The Palgrave handbook of humour research*. https://doi.org/10.1007/978-3-030-78280-1_25

Maples, M. F., Dupey, P., Torres-Rivera, E., Phan, L. T., Vereen, L., & Garrett, M. T. (2001). Ethnic diversity and the use of humor in counseling: Appropriate or inappropriate? *Journal of Counseling and Development*, *79*(1), 53–60. https://doi.org/10.1002/j.1556-6676.2001.tb01943.x

Marci, C. D., Moran, E. K., & Orr, S. P. (2004). Physiologic evidence for the interpersonal role of laughter during psychotherapy. *Journal of Nervous & Mental Disease*, *192*(10), 689–695. https://doi.org/10.1097/01.nmd.0000142032.04196.63

Martin, R. A., Kuiper, N. A., Olinger, L. J., & Dance, K. (1993). Humor, coping with stress, self-concept, and psychological well-being. *HUMOR: International Journal of Humor Research*, *6*(1), 89–104.

Mearns, D. (1997). *Person-centered counselling training*. SAGE Publications.

Murphy, D., & Cramer, D. (2014). Mutuality of Rogers's therapeutic conditions and treatment progress in the first three psychotherapy sessions. *Psychotherapy Research*, *24*(6), 651–661. https://doi.org/10.1080/10503307.2013.874051

Murphy, D., Cramer, D., & Joseph, S. (2012). Mutuality in person-centered therapy: A new agenda for research and practice. *Person-Centered & Experiential Psychotherapies*, *11*(2), 109–123. https://doi.org/10.1080/14779757.2012.668496

Nardone, G., & Portelli, C. (2007). L'usage de l'humour et d'autres actes créatifs comme véhicule de changement en thérapie stratégique brève. *Cahiers critiques de thérapie familiale et de pratiques de réseaux*, *2*(39), 83–92. https://doi.org/10.3917/ctf.039.0083

Rogers, C. R. (1959). A theory of therapy, personality, and interpersonal relationships, as developed in the client-centered framework. In S. Koch (Ed.), *Psychology: A study of a science, study 1, volume 3: Formulations of the person and the social context* (pp. 184–256). McGraw-Hill.

Straus, M., & McKenzie, K. (2022). You've GOT TO BE kidding. *Psychotherapy Networker*, *46*(3), 23–27.

Sultanoff, S. (2013). Integrating humor into psychotherapy: Research, theory, and the necessary conditions for the presence of therapeutic humor in helping relationships. *The Humanistic Psychologist*, *41*, 388–399. https://doi.org/10.1080/08873267.2013.796953

Talens, P. (2020). When working in a youth service, how do therapists experience humour with their clients? *European Journal of Psychotherapy & Counselling*, *22*(1–2), 80–96. https://doi.org/10.1080/13642537.2020.1766526

Valentine, L., & Gabbard, G. O. (2014). Can the use of humor in psychotherapy be taught? *Academic Psychiatry*, *38*, 75–81. https://doi.org/10.1007/s40596-013-0018-2

Chapter 10

Training to work with humour

Introduction

In Chapter 9, we reviewed approaches to working with humour in the person-centred therapy room. We conclude this book with the question of how we might go about training counsellors how to do just that, beginning with a review of the current education landscape and some initiatives and research into humour training, including developing one's own sense of humour. We propose an approach that might be applied in counsellor training courses and for supervision.

Trainees want and need training

Trainees both want and need training in how to work with humour (Banmen, 1982; Briggs & Owen, 2022; Buşu & Buşu, 2021). Research suggests their effectiveness and satisfaction suffer from a lack of confidence when they experience "unsystematic exposure to humor" (Ruch et al., 2018). In supervision, too, the need for humour is significant. As far back as 1988, humour was the criterion most frequently cited by therapists when assessing the competence of their supervisors: "not only do they use humour in the supervision relationship, but they also guide trainees in how best to work with humour" (Liddle et al., 1988).

In 1995, Daniel Shapiro proposed a new disorder for inclusion in the DSM-IV, namely the Fledgling Therapist Disorder (FTD). A number of symptoms of FTD are described, including "a fear of looking at one's watch during sessions without seeming to be uninterested in the client", a fear of "being exposed for the fraud he or she is", an inability to tolerate silence during sessions, a "fierce desire" to self-disclose, or to rush in and cure the client in the first session, a need for props such as a clipboard or a beard, a "fear of charging clients for services rendered" and "Hyper-Rogerianisms (the overuse of reflections)" (1995).

Of course, the proposal did not make it into the DSM. Shapiro observed that therapists outgrow symptoms of FTD after four to five years of practice, though some never recover.

DOI: 10.4324/9781003638773-15

The issue is far from new: as far back as 1982, John Banmen advocated for training programmes to "include lectures and workshops on the use of humour to assure that those using humour in a therapeutic process are able to feel comfortable with it". Steven Sultanoff emphasised the risks of sending therapists out to work without being trained in how to "avoid negative humour… it is essential for the helping professional to learn how to differentiate between potentially therapeutic humor and potentially harmful humor" (1994).

The ethical implications have not been recognised hitherto. The British Association for Counselling and Psychotherapy's (BACP) Ethical Framework from 2018 (and the revised Framework, in draft at the time of writing) requires a commitment by the counsellor to do no harm to the client, which is in part assured by ensuring our work adheres to professional standards of competence, including "listening out for how clients experience our working together".

Some might argue that such frameworks stifle flexibility, creativity and improvement. For example, would the BACP approve of using exaggerated humour to mock a client's obsessive behaviours, as was promoted by Frank Farrelly (see Chapter 5)?

But it isn't taught

Readers who have undergone counsellor training will recognise Joseph Richman's lament for the lack of opportunities for training in the use of humour (1996). Some specialised courses do exist (see previous chapters). Sophia Dziegielewski et al. (2003) pointed to a growing number of courses and workshops in the United States on how to develop or improve one's sense of humour, and even specialist therapy training programmes for counselling children and HIV/AIDS clients where humour was incorporated as a "key" component.

But humour continues to be "overlooked in psychotherapy training in general"; Oprea-Valentin Buşu and Andreea-Denisa Buşu observed:

> …a culture of silence regarding humour while training in a traditionally psychodynamic context. Psychotherapists were very much depicted as sober, ready to analyse the client's content and self-disclosure in general, and by correlation through the use of humour as well was frowned upon.
>
> (2021)

In research, trainee therapists spoke about being "extremely hesitant" to use humour. They felt the topic was "taboo" and not considered serious by their training institutions, even though they all felt they would benefit from at least a discussion of it during their training programmes (Longe, 2018).

As a consequence, therapists who have not been trained on the use of humour in the therapeutic context are unlikely to use it in practice (Eberhardt, 2018).

At this point, it feels appropriate – if not inevitable – that we should mention a notorious article from 1971 that turns up in the majority of research papers and articles on the topic, mainly for critical balance and its catchy title. *The destructive potential of humour in psychotherapy* is an opinion piece by Lawrence Kubie published in the *American Journal of Psychiatry*. Sometimes cited as a call for the banning of humour altogether from the therapy room, it is, in reality, not quite so emphatic. Nonetheless, it stands alone as by far the most outspoken counter-argument to the consensus view. The article draws on Kubie's extensive experience as a Freudian psychoanalyst (his clients included Tennessee Williams and other celebrities of the day) and is one of a considerable number of equally eye-catching articles, including *A Psychiatrist contemplates* The Cocktail Party, *To prevent the hi-jacking of planes* and *Protection for those who charter small yachts*. At the time he wrote his piece, he worked as a Consultant on Research and Training at a psychiatric hospital in Baltimore and as Clinical Professor at the University of Maryland; so, his influence must have been considerable. He opens with the caveat that he does not believe humour in therapy is always destructive (Kubie, 1971) and – having taken something of a side-swipe at the "echolalia technique of Carl Rogers" – ends boldly with:

> Humor has its place in life. Let us keep it there by acknowledging that one place where it had a very limited role, if any, is in psychotherapy.

The article is more informative in highlighting the types of humour that are more likely to harm than help, and in this respect, it is consistent with the academic literature previously discussed. However, trainee therapists would have shuddered at his portentous conviction:

> It is especially to the beginner that humor seems to be easier than any other way of introducing topics that are painful both to the patient and the therapist. In fact, it is during the learning period that humor is most alluring and its use most dangerous. Unless he is psychologically callous and unfit, the young psychiatrist, new to the therapeutic situation, takes up his responsibilities with a tense combination of masked terror and anger, from which humor is an escape and against which it is a defense.

Louis Franzini highlighted in 2001 the chicken-and-egg conundrum of not training therapists in using humour until the use of humour (by untrained therapists, presumably) has been shown to be effective. He noted a parallel with the then novel and still untested Eye Movement Desensitisation technique. Francine Shapiro, the technique's founder, had begun issuing certifications in the use of the technique to attendees at her "expensive" workshops, despite widespread ethical and scientific concerns at the time. "With humor skills", Franzini observed, "the cost of training would be far less – at least until the invention of a certification program" (2001).

> **Pause for thought**
>
> What were your experiences – if any – of training to work with humour?

Can it be taught?

Historically, the question of whether "effective" humour can be taught attracted hypothetical rather than empirical responses. Writers such as Margot Tallmer and Joseph Richman argued that although humour as a therapeutic tool could be learned, its effectiveness depended on the therapist's "artistic and stylistic talents" (1994). They might have been referring to Albert Ellis, Frank Farrelly and Walter O'Connell (see Chapter 5), whose personalities must surely have underpinned much of their theories (and which might indeed explain the absence of much continued interest following their deaths).

Sultanoff firmly believed that therapists "who want to expand their comic vision" can learn to work with humour, and likened the skill of humour to that of empathy in the sense that both require a modicum of aptitude in the trainee therapist as well as practice in order for the therapist to be effective (2003).

Based on his research during the 1980s, Waleed Salameh concluded that "Like biofeedback, psychodrama, hypnosis, or any other therapeutic technique, humor is a skill that can be taught, learned and practiced" (1987). His Humor Immersion Training workshop was developed specifically with therapists in mind based on his *Integrative Short-term Psychotherapy* (ISTP, see Chapter 4). Although the philosophical underpinnings of Salameh's workshop will strike person-centred counsellors as heterodox, the components would, in principle, be of interest and worthy of consideration. In summary, the components – or "facets" – cover:

- The advantages of humour including emotional well-being, mental processing, physical health, financial gains, improved interpersonal interactions and stress reduction.
- Removing mental barriers that hinder us from discovering and expressing our comedic nature.
- Making humour, exploring individual comedic memories using guided imagery techniques, using humour to spark creative thought through playing with ideas, challenging assumptions, altering concepts, overcoming mental blocks and boosting creative expression.
- Distinguishing therapeutic humour from harmful humour using the Humor Rating Scale (developed by Salameh).
- Membership of the Laughers Anonymous organisation (founded by Salameh), with newsletters and resources access.

(Salameh, 1987)

Franzini, too, proposed that a "formal course in humor training" be developed, comprising lectures, seminars, workshops, demonstrations and humour-related exercises for therapists, "regardless of their specific theoretical orientation: psychodynamic, behavioral, cognitive, or the most frequently endorsed orientation, eclectic therapy" (2001), though notably not humanistic or person-centred therapists.

More recently, studies have explored the efficacy of programmes designed to *improve* a person's sense of humour based on research such as Barbara Fredrickson's work at the University of North Carolina leading to the Broaden-and-Build Theory (1998), which proposed that someone with a positive frame of mind (or frame of reference) would be more able to "reframe" adverse events. The concept is less about using humour to cope with adversity – which we saw in the Coping Humor Scale in Chapter 2 – and more about adopting a mentality that is essentially optimistic. This is one of the tenets of Positive Psychology (see also Chapter 4), a discipline which has roots in the works of Jung, Maslow and Frankl as well as in Eastern mysticism and which has come to prominence through the research of Martin Seligman and Mihaly Csikszentmihalyi (Gonot-Schoupinsky et al., 2024).

Another approach to refining a person's sense of humour is the American psychologist Paul McGhee's 7 Humor Habits Program developed originally in the 1990s as the 8-Step Humor Skills Training Program. McGhee also devised a humour measurement method similar to the psychometric tools we reviewed in Chapter 2. The Sense of Humor Scale assessed "playful attitude, positive/negative mood, and sense of humor" (Goldstein & Ruch, 2018) and has been used in a number of studies since its first publication in 1996. The seven "habits" and how they are cultivated in training sessions and in "home play" are very briefly outlined below:

1. "Surround yourself with humor (and think about the nature of your sense of humor)" – Theory study, exploration of humour preferences.
2. "Cultivate a playful attitude" – Exercises to develop sense of playfulness.
3. "Laugh more often and more heartily" – Studying how jokes are told, laughing louder and longer, even when one would not normally laugh.
4. "Create your own verbal humor" – Humour-building skills.
5. "Look for humor in daily life" – Exercises to imbue everyday life with humour.
6. "Take yourself lightly. Laugh at yourself" – Exercises to promote the use of humour (especially self-deprecating humour) to cope with stress.
7. "Find humor in the midst of stress" – Exercises to embed humour-related habits in daily routines, further enhancing emotional resilience.

(Ruch et al., 2018)

Pause for thought

What do you think about the 7 Humor Habits? Do you feel any of them would help raise your spirits – or your clients' spirits – in times of adversity?

Positive results have generally been reported by research studies into the training of humour based on McGhee's Humor Habits conducted around the world, for example, in Australia (Crawford & Caltabiano, 2011), Germany (Falkenberg et al., 2011), Austria (Tagalidou et al., 2018), Iran (Momtaz et al., 2020) and Spain (León-Pérez et al., 2021). While the research continues, McGhee's *7 Humor Habits* has been published as a self-help book.

A large-scale longitudinal study of humour undertaken by Laura Korock and Tabea Scheel at the Europa-Universität, Flensburg, Germany, in conjunction with the Deutsches Institut für Humor (2025), drew on techniques typically associated with workplace-oriented skills training. A two-day humour skills course was devised and delivered 29 times over nearly five years to a total of 166 participants from various occupational backgrounds. Focusing on how humour skills can improve people's efficacy and satisfaction in the working environment, the course comprised three elements:

- Humour basics and communication techniques (such as exaggeration and humorous mirroring);
- Exploring humour as a technique for managing stress at work; and
- Examining humour as a mindset, understanding obstacles such as perfectionism and taking oneself too seriously and identifying best practices.

Regarding skills acquisition, temporary increases in affiliative, self-enhancing and self-defeating humour were observed, but significant long-term effects on humour styles were not sustained. Participants' perceptions that using humour is risky were found to have reduced, but beliefs regarding humour's unlearnability or social inappropriateness were unchanged over time, possibly due to attitudes rooted in established social norms and personal experiences. Humour usage did appear to improve perceptions of self-efficacy, coping, ability to manage stress and improve self-esteem. However, irritation levels remained unchanged, suggesting participants could still not "switch off" from work-related stressors.

Undoubtedly, the research in this area will continue and improve in sophistication. We can point to two potential trends in how training programmes might be developed and assessed. Firstly, the Korock et al. (2025) programme signals a shift away from the approach embodied in McGhee's 7 Humor

Habits Program where participants are encouraged to open themselves up to the healing power of humour in ways that at times resemble a Revivalist service. Instead, a format informed by modern but well-established didactic approaches is relied upon by Korock et al., specifically the three-stage model for acquiring skills proposed by Phillip Ackerman (1988). According to the theory, different mental abilities come to the fore at different stages of learning new skills:

> Employees progress from a cognitive stage (understanding humour concepts), to an associative stage (practice and feedback refine humour use, potentially reducing negative humour), and finally to an autonomous stage (applying humour intuitively and naturally in workplace interactions).
>
> (Korock et al., 2025)

Another important factor in how humour training might best be delivered is seen in the impact of the growing body of neurological research. As we saw in Chapter 8, the brain's left hemisphere is ideally suited to processing the largely cognitive learning that is called upon in the workshops described previously. The intuitive, in-the-moment and reactive functioning of the brain's right side, however, plays a fundamental role in how humour originates and is received. This could be taken to mean that training humour does not, in fact, achieve any meaningful or durable change. So, perhaps a different approach is required, one that eschews the study of humour styles and measures and how to be amusing in favour of "mentalising" in the therapeutic relationship. Mentalising is derived from the "theory of mind" concept, originating with a study of chimpanzees in the 1970s (Premack & Woodruff, 1978). It involves the parts of the brain that aid us in understanding others' differing perspectives, inferring others' thoughts and feelings based on their non-verbal behaviour and expressions, predicting how others might act and understanding that others' actions are driven by their beliefs, including their false beliefs. Lisa Valentine and Glen Gabbard (2014) identified three benefits to trainees of enhancing their understanding of mentalisation: in "reading" their clients in the therapy room and anticipating their receptivity to humour (or, indeed, any other intervention!), reflecting after the session on how accurate the anticipation of the client's responses was, and:

> Teaching trainees how humor operates at multiple levels serves to demystify the therapeutic process, providing an explanation for these "now" moments complete with thoughts about how to potentially harness them in the service of the patient.
>
> (Valentine & Gabbard, 2014)

A way forward?

How do we teach working with humour to student person-centred counsellors? How do we teach them *anything*?

> It seems to me that anything that can be taught to another is relatively inconsequential, and has little or no significant influence on behaviour.
>
> (Rogers, 2004)

The following is a proposed framework of learning objectives aimed at enhancing trainees' confidence and competence in working with humour. It is assumed that training programmes that are accredited for the purposes of obtaining a recognised qualification, such as that granted by the BACP, will not be facilitated in the student-centred ethos envisaged by Rogers (2004), but will be characterised by a certain quantity of directive lecturing and assessment.

Humour and person-centred therapy learning objectives

A. Humour and relationships

A.1. Theories and humour styles

Background reading of the theories and humour styles and discussion of how they can help us obtain greater empathic understanding of our clients – how and why they introduce humour into the therapy space – and to gain insights into what our humour preferences say about us.

A.2. Humour and person-centred thinking

An understanding of how humour theories and styles intersect with person-centred thinking and can be used to enhance the therapeutic alliance in the framework of Rogers' Necessary and Sufficient Conditions of Therapeutic Personality Change (1957).

A.3. Working with different humour

People living with neurodivergence can have different preferences for humour to what we might expect (assuming we are not ourselves neurodivergent). Similarly, people from different cultures from our own may experience humour differently. While it is paramount that we, as person-centred counsellors, engage with our clients as individuals and recognise that we all have different humour preferences, it will be helpful to understand how to respond and adapt to those differences when they arise.

B. Working with humour

B.1. Studying recorded therapy sessions (either of experienced therapists or of trainees' own work) for insights into moments when humour arose or did not arise but might have, and examining the thoughts and feelings in the moment:

- Pausing and wondering about what's happening in the moment. Specifically, what is your understanding of what was going on in the client's mind at that moment and how do you imagine the client was feeling just before you made that humorous comment?
- Asking about feelings and thoughts rather than just behaviours;
- Exploring different perspectives on the same situation; and
- Noting ruptures in the therapeutic relationship and exploring them collaboratively.

This work can also be carried out in supervision discussions of placement work.

B.2. Experiential practice that focuses on attuning the trainee therapist's empathic understanding, that is:

- Genuine curiosity and "not-knowing";
- Humility about understanding others' minds;
- Comfort with uncertainty and different/differing perspectives; and
- Willingness to acknowledge mistakes and misunderstandings.

C. Humour skills

An exploration of ways in which we can learn to become comfortable and confident with certain expressions of humour.

D. Self-care

An understanding of the benefits humour, mirth and laughter can bring in the counsellor's routine of self-care.

Reflection (or, Finding the FUN in fully FUNctioning)

The job is tough. Embodying the person-centred attitude is a tall order for anyone – as we saw in Chapter 9, the man himself (by his own admission) did not always succeed.

I think of the Necessary and Sufficient Conditions as the counsellor's fuel. Unleaded, of course, and in need of replenishment on a regular basis. Self-care comes in countless different forms. Some of us can meditate and contort our bodies into implausible postures, others of us will find reinvigoration through fasting, or sky-diving, running a marathon or crocheting a falafel. Others of us "offset the heaviness and distress that we hold with a visit to a comedy club" (S. Chisholm, personal communication), where we can poke fun at the absurdity of it all and laugh until we pull a muscle.

Supervision

Not all jurisdictions mandate the mentoring – or *supervision*, as the jargon goes – of a counsellor's work by a more experienced counsellor. Although Rogers referred to the practice of mentorship and apprenticeship, he had little to say on the subject (1951, 1957). Indeed, he is cited by Keith Tudor as objecting to "very direct evaluation" and portraying learning in a student-centred environment as essentially self-directed and self-evaluated even in the presence of a facilitator (Tudor, 2024). The BACP's view, set out in the Ethical Framework, is that supervision is "essential to how practitioners sustain good practice" and:

> provides practitioners with regular and ongoing opportunities to reflect in depth about all aspects of their practice in order to work as effectively, safely and ethically as possible. Supervision also sustains the personal resourcefulness required to undertake the work.
>
> (2018)

In the BACP's Framework, supervision is required for trainee and qualified counsellors, and also counsellors who act as supervisors.

Pause for thought

Supervision requires not just experience, but additional skills and training (BACP, 2018). So, if supervision requires the input of a more experienced practitioner, one must be forgiven for wondering who it is that supervises the supervisors and who it is, in turn, who supervises the supervisors' supervisors, and so on. Spare a thought then, for the ÜberSupervisor, the Godparent of Supervision, without whom the whole pyramid of supervision would surely collapse.

Figure 10.1 The supervisors' supervisor.

Supervision, then, functions as a mentoring relationship where the supervisee can seek guidance on, for example, working with a client from a different cultural background. It is also a form of self-care, where practitioners can explore feelings that are provoked by their client relationships. In this respect, the relationship is likened to the therapeutic relationship between the counsellor and client. For Rogers, supervision and counselling occupied a continuum within which the supervisor should follow the supervisee's lead as in any other person-centred relationship.

Finally, for all practitioners but especially trainees and the newly qualified, the supervisor might be perceived as something of a model, someone whose practice – good and bad! – the supervisee learns from. These inter-relationships are depicted in the innovative and immediately comprehensible diagram (Figure 10.2).

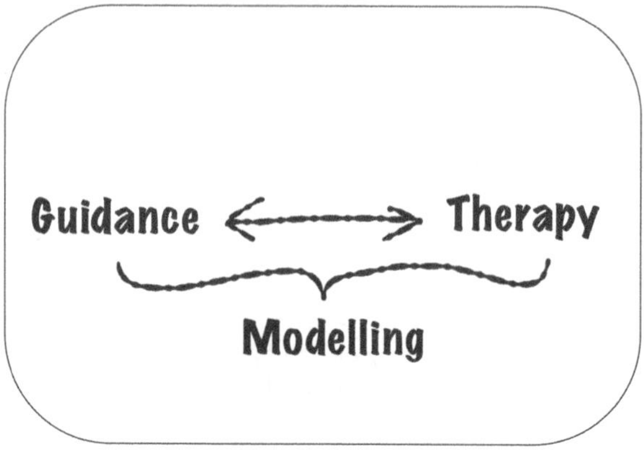

Figure 10.2 The supervisory spectrum

Where the supervision session nears the therapeutic end of the spectrum, the considerations applying to any other therapeutic relationship might also apply, as in the following exchange:

Supervisee: I'm just juggling so much, and I don't know how I can keep all these balls in the air.
Supervisor: You might drop one.
Supervisee: [laughs] I just pictured one of my balls dropping! Sorry, that's rude, isn't it?
Supervisor: [laughs] Maybe we should talk about spinning plates!

The unintentional levity here brings about shared humour, which might lead to a sense of relief for the supervisee and greater confidence going forward.

Towards the opposite end of the spectrum, humour might facilitate the development of the relationship in similar ways. William Fry and Waleed Salameh suggest that

> The supervisor's humor signals to the student that he or she is interacting with a compassionate, malleable, and tolerant individual, therefore encouraging genuine student self-disclosure and honest expression of problematic issues in a freer atmosphere.
>
> (1987)

They go on to stress that the humour does not suggest supervisees should make light of, or dismiss, the distress of their clients, but that it might be better understood if viewed from a different – presumably less heavily loaded – angle.

In addition, the supervisor might be asked to comment on the supervisee's experience of humour in working with a client. If the supervisor is trained and experienced in humour in therapy, the guidance can be invaluable to helping supervisees approach their work with greater confidence and competence.

The humour does not, however, always come from the best of places. One instance is where practitioners (including trainees) in an institutional setting make derogatory references to their clients or make fun of their experiences with them. As we saw in earlier chapters, humour can be used as a coping mechanism in stressful environments, as the case example from a clinical setting offered by Julie Aultman and Emily Meyers shows:

> Given the recent pandemic and panic buying of toilet paper in the United States, a physician, after his patient died from COVID-19 respiratory failure, was overheard by the medical team saying, "at least there will be more toilet paper for the rest of us."
>
> (Aultman & Meyers, 2020)

Gallows humour of this nature will be familiar to most, if not all, psychotherapists. It can help relieve tension, recover from compassion fatigue and can also encourage greater cohesion in the team. But Aultman and Meyers reported that it also carried ethical risks, not least if the patient's family happened to be within earshot of the physician. In addition, it may mask resentments or prejudices on the part of the speaker, for example, if the patient and physician came from different cultures or if the physician felt the patient was partly responsible for being ill in the first place. The physician might be suffering from compassion fatigue and in need of self-care, and/or the humour might offend colleagues and therefore be detrimental to the team's togetherness. In a setting such as a clinic, the supervisor may not be present, in which case the "supervision" needs to be initiated from within the team, in other words, by peers. This might be challenging for those colleagues, they concluded, particularly if the source of the undesirable humour occupies a senior role. Here, perhaps, humour of a more affiliative nature might keep tension levels low and reduce resistance.

Pause for thought

If you are a supervisor, how do you work with humour in your relationships with your supervisees?
To what extent do you feel comfortable with modelling humour in your relationships?

Summing up

The institutions training person-centred counsellors do not address working with humour. Consequently, new counsellors are unprepared for the challenge of working with their clients' humour and lack confidence in their own capacity to bring humour into the therapy relationship. This deficiency raises ethical questions about the competence of counsellors and their supervisors.

Drawing on the research, a set of learning objectives is proposed to be included in the curricula of training institutions, which includes humour theories, humour and person-centred thinking, humour differences, working practically with humour, humour skills and self-care. The role of supervisors in helping counsellors gain competence and confidence is also explored.

References

Ackerman, P. L. (1988). Determinants of individual differences during skill acquisition: Cognitive abilities and information processing. *Journal of Experimental Psychology. General, 117*(3), 288–318. https://doi.org/10.1037/0096-3445.117.3.288

Aultman, J., & Meyers, E. (2020). Case and commentary: Does using humor to cope with stress justify making fun of patients? *AMA Journal of Ethics, 22*(7), E576–E582.

Banmen, J. (1982). The use of humour in psychotherapy. *International Journal for the Advancement of Counselling, 5*(2), 81–86. https://doi.org/10.1007/BF00119088

Briggs, E., & Owen, A. (2022). Funny, right? How do trainee and qualified therapists experience laughter in their practice with clients? *Counselling and Psychotherapy Research, 2022*(22), 827–838. https://doi.org/10.1002/capr.12525

British Association for Counselling and Psychotherapy (BACP). (2018). *Ethical framework for the counselling professions*. BACP.

Bușu, O.-V., & Bușu, A.-D. (2021). The use of humour as communication skill in counselling and psychotherapy. *Annals of the University of Craiova: Seria Psihologie, Pedagogie, 43*(2), 205–216.

Crawford, S. A., & Caltabiano, N. J. (2011). Promoting emotional well-being through the use of humour. *The Journal of Positive Psychology, 6*(3), 237–252. https://doi.org/10.1080/17439760.2011.577087

Dziegielewski, S. F., Jacinto, G. A., Laudadio, A., & Legg-Rodriguez, L. (2003). Humor: An essential communication tool in therapy. *International Journal of Mental Health, 32*(3), 74–90. https://doi.org/10.1080/00207411.2003.11449592

Eberhardt, S. (2018). *Counselor perspectives on humor in addiction counseling: Implications for practice and training*. [Doctorate dissertation, Capella University]. Proquest 10289837.

Falkenberg, I., Buchkremer, G., Bartels, M., & Wild, B. (2011). Implementation of a manual-based training of humor abilities in patients with depression: A pilot study. *Psychiatry Research, 186*, 454–457. https://doi.org/10.1016/j.psychres.2010.10.009

Franzini, L. R. (2001). Humor in therapy: The case for training therapists in its uses and risks. *The Journal of General Psychology, 128*(2), 170–193. https://doi.org/10.1080/00221300109598906

Fredrickson, B. L. (1998). What good are positive emotions? *Review of General Psychology, 2*, 3. https://doi.org/10.1037/1089-2680.2.3.300

Fry, W., & Salameh, W. (Eds.). (1987). *Handbook of humor and psychotherapy: Advances in the clinical use of humor*. Professional Resource Exchange.
Goldstein, J., & Ruch, W. (2018). Paul McGhee and humor research. *Humor*, *31*(2), 169–181. https://doi.org/10.1515/humor-2018-0031
Gonot-Schoupinsky, F., Neal, M., & Carson, J. (2024). *The positive psychology of laughter and humour*. Emerald Publishing.
Korock, L., Ullmann, E., & Scheel, T. (2025). Effectiveness of work-related humour trainings: Humour use, humour styles and well-being. *Human Resource Development International*, 1–29. https://doi.org/10.1080/13678868.2025.2535292
Kubie, L. (1971). The destructive potential of humor in psychotherapy. *The American Journal of Psychiatry*, *127*(7), 861–866.
León-Pérez, J. M., Cantero-Sánchez, F. J., Fernández-Canseco, Á., & León-Rubio, J. M. (2021). Effectiveness of a humor-based training for feducing employees' distress. *International Journal of Environmental Research and Public Health*, *18*(21), 11177. https://doi.org/10.3390/ijerph182111177
Liddle, H. A., Davidson, G. S., & Barrett, M. J. (1988). Outcomes of live supervision: Trainee perspectives. In H. A. Liddle, D. C. Breunlin, & R. C. Schwartz (Eds.), *Handbook of family therapy training and supervision* (pp. 386–398). Guilford Press.
Longe, O. (2018). *Can I laugh now? Understanding humour within psychotherapy from the client's perspective* [Master's dissertation, Dublin Business School]. https://esource.dbs.ie/handle/10788/3968
Momtaz, Y. A., Ansari, M., & Foroughan, M. (2020). Humor training program on sense of humor among older adults: A randomized controlled trial. *The Open Psychology Journal*, *13*(1), 333–340. https://doi.org/10.2174/1874350102013010333
Premack, D., & Woodruff, G. (1978). Does the chimpanzee have a theory of mind? *The Behavioral and Brain Sciences*, *1*(4), 515–526. https://doi.org/10.1017/S0140525X00076512
Richman, J. (1996). Points of correspondence between humor and psychotherapy. *Psychotherapy: Theory, Research, Practice, Training*, *33*(4), 560–566. https://doi.org/10.1037/0033-3204.33.4.560
Rogers, C. R. (1951/1999). *Client-centered therapy: Its current practice, implications and theory*. Constable.
Rogers, C. R. (1957). The necessary and sufficient conditions of therapeutic personality change. *Journal of Consulting Psychology*, *21*(2), 95–103. https://doi.org/10.1037/h0045357
Rogers, C. R. (2004). *On becoming a person: A therapist's view of psychotherapy*. Constable & Robinson.
Ruch, W. F., Hofmann, J., Rusch, S., & Stolz, H. (2018). Training the sense of humor with the 7 humor habits program and satisfaction with life. *Humor*, *31*(2), 287–309. https://doi.org/10.1515/humor-2017-0099
Salameh, W. A. (1987). Humor in integrative short-term psychotherapy (ISTP). In W. Fry & W. Salameh (Eds.), *Handbook of humor and psychotherapy: Advances in the clinical use of humor* (pp. 195–240). Professional Resource Exchange.
Shapiro, D. E. (1995). Fledgling therapist disorder and fledgling therapist with Supervisoraphobia disorder: Proposed DSM-IV categories. *Journal of Mental Health Counseling*, *17* (4), 456.
Sultanoff, S. M. (1994/2002). Choosing to be amusing; assessing an individual's receptivity to therapeutic humor, *Journal of Nursing Jocularity*, *4*(4), 34–35.
Sultanoff, S. M. (2003). Integrating humor into psychotherapy. In C. Schaefer (Ed.), *Play therapy with adults* (pp. 107–143). John Wiley & Sons, Inc.
Tagalidou, N., Loderer, V., Distlberger, E., & Laireiter, A.-R. (2018). Feasibility of a humor training to promote humor and decrease stress in a subclinical sample: A

single-arm pilot study. *Frontiers in Psychology*, *9*, 577. https://doi.org/10.3389/fpsyg.2018.00577

Tallmer, M., & Richman, J. (1994). Jokes psychoanalysts tell. In H. S. Strean (Ed.), *The use of humor in psychotherapy* (pp. 179–188). Jason Aronson.

Tudor, K. (2024). Supervision. In G. Di Malta (Ed.), *The handbook of person-centred psychotherapy and counselling* (pp. 436–450). Bloomsbury Publishing.

Valentine, L., & Gabbard, G. O. (2014). Can the use of humor in psychotherapy be taught? *Academic Psychiatry*, *38*(1), 75–81. https://doi.org/10.1007/s40596-013-0018-2

Index

Pages in *italics* refer to figures.

For Product Safety Concerns and Information please contact our EU representative GPSR@taylorandfrancis.com Taylor & Francis Verlag GmbH, Kaufingerstraße 24, 80331 München, Germany